STUDY GUIDE

David VanHoose
University of Alabama

Brenda Abbott
Northern Alberta Institute of Technology

Sam Fefferman
Northern Alberta Institute of Technology

Ronald K. Kessler
British Columbia Institute of Technology

Terrence Sulyma
Northern Alberta Institute of Technology

ECONOMICS TODAY
The Macro View

Third Canadian Edition

Roger LeRoy Miller *Institute for University Studies, Arlington, Texas*
Brenda Abbott *Northern Alberta Institute of Technology*
Sam Fefferman *Northern Alberta Institute of Technology*
Ronald K. Kessler *British Columbia Institute of Technology*
Terrence Sulyma *Northern Alberta Institute of Technology*

PEARSON
Addison
Wesley

Toronto

Original U.S. edition published by Pearson Addison-Wesley, Inc., a division of Pearson Education, Needham Heights, Massachusetts. Copyright © 2001. This edition is authorized for sale in Canada only.

0-321-25353-1

Acquisitions Editor: Gary Bennett
Developmental Editor: Angela Kurmey
Production Editor: Jennifer Handel
Production Coordinator: Patricia Ciardullo

2 3 4 5 6 7 DPC 09 08 07 06

Printed and bound in Canada.

Contents

PREFACE

TO THE STUDENT

This Study Guide is designed to help you understand, review, and apply the theory, the issues, and the policies presented in the text *Economics Today: The Macro View*, Third Canadian Edition. In each Study Guide chapter, you are encouraged to:

- begin by getting an overview of where you are in the course and where you are going next.
- familiarize yourself with the economics jargon and concepts in the chapter before proceeding to more comprehensive problems.
- concentrate on applying the theory in the chapter to real-world applications after completing the comprehensive problems.

THE CONTENTS OF THE STUDY GUIDE

Both the sequencing and content of each Study Guide section provide you with thorough coverage of economic theory, policy, and applications covered in your text. **All of the questions in the Study Guide are organized by learning objective, so you can determine which of the learning objectives you have mastered and which will require further study.**

1. *Putting This Chapter Into Perspective*
   This section shows you where the particular chapter fits into the big picture.
2. *Learning Objectives*
   This list restates the learning objectives from the text. The objectives tell you what you will be able to do after you have completed the chapter.
3. *Chapter Outline*
   This section presents a sentence outline for the chapter. It provides you with a quick overview of the contents of each chapter.
4. *Key Terms and Concepts*
   This section provides a list of the most important terms and theoretical constructs used in the text chapter; these terms are crucial to your understanding and each is defined in the Glossary at the end of your text.
5. *Completion Questions*
   This set of short answer fill-in-the-blank questions is intended to test your knowledge of key terms and concepts and facts.
6. *True-False Questions*
   This section is another objective test to help you understand the chapter concepts in more depth. We explain what is wrong with each false statement in the answers section at the end of the Study Guide chapter.

7. *Multiple Choice Questions*

   The numerous multiple choice questions in each Study Guide chapter will help you identify areas that you may need to spend more time and effort on. Again, you will find that in the answers section of the Study Guide chapter, you are provided with a brief explanation of each multiple choice answer.

8. *Matching Questions*

   The matching questions are intended to review and sharpen your understanding of the concepts that you have already read about and worked with in the text and the related Study Guide chapter. Once you have mastered the questions in this section you should be ready to tackle the more comprehensive questions and applications that will follow.

9. *Working with Graphs*

   Because many students find working with graphs difficult, we have devoted an entire section in each of the chapters utilizing this very important tool of analysis. Many of the graphs presented in the Study Guide have numerical labels on the *x*- and *y*-axis, so as to make it easier for you to relate the graphic analysis to the economic concepts being explained and applied.

10. *Problems*

    This section focuses on comprehensive problems that typically consist of utilizing and applying more than one chapter concept. As you work with these problems, you will gain a greater appreciation and deeper understanding of the economic theory.

11. *Business Section*

    In this section, the economic theory in the text chapter is related or applied to a practical business problem. You will find that each business problem is classified according to the relevant functional area or field of business—marketing, accounting, finance, management, or small business. This section is consistent with the text's strong emphasis on applying economic theory to real-world applications.

12. *Answers*

    We have placed the answers at the end of each Study Guide chapter rather than at the end of the Study Guide. We believe that you will find this approach more convenient.

13. *White space*

    There is sufficient white space provided in the sections related to the Working with Graphs, Problems, and Business Section to enable you to display all of your answers to every question right in the Study Guide. This will enable you to effectively use the Study Guide for review purposes.

HOW TO USE THIS STUDY GUIDE

As you begin to examine a new chapter in your text, we suggest you consider the following strategy:

1. Before reading the new chapter in your text, read the sections in the related Study Guide entitled *Putting This Chapter Into Perspective*, *Learning Objectives*, and *Chapter Outline*.

2. Read the *Summary Discussion of Learning Objectives* located at the end of your text chapter.

3. At this point, we suggest that you start on the first page of the text chapter and read the entire chapter. As you are reading, take note of the definitions provided in the margin of the text. Highlight the *Concepts in Brief* sections in your text chapter as

you encounter them. Make sure that you read the brief real-world examples provided in the text, even if you do not fully understand how they relate to the theory in the chapter. Remember, these examples could be on your next exam.

4. After reading the text chapter once through, go back to the Study Guide. Take a quick look at the *Key Terms and Concepts*. Sharpen your pencil and start working on the Study Guide questions. Complete the questions in the order in which they are presented in the Study Guide. Remember to consult the *Glossary* at the end of the text if you are having problems with any terminology.

5. If you find that you are having difficulties in completing certain questions in the Study Guide, take note of the learning objective(s) related to these questions. Then proceed to review the content related to these learning objective in your text.

6. After you have checked your answer to the *Business Section* problems, we suggest that you return to the *For Critical Analysis* questions presented in the Example and Policy Example boxes and the Issues and Applications in your text and see if you can now answer them. If you are having difficulties, take a look at the suggested solutions displayed at the end of your text.

HOW TO PREPARE FOR QUIZZES, TESTS, AND EXAMS

In studying for quizzes, tests, and exams, review the Study Guide and text as follows:
1. Review your course outline and compare it to the Table of Contents in your text.
2. In your text:
   a. Review those chapters or sections of chapters covered in your course outline.
   b. Review the *Concepts in Brief* found at the end of each section in the chapter.
   c. Re-read the *Summary Discussion of Learning Objectives* at the end of the chapter.
   d. Try the *Problems* at the end of the chapter. The answers for all odd-numbered Problems are at the back of the text. The complete set of Problem answers (both odd- and even-numbered) appears in the *Instructor's Manual*.
3. In your Study Guide:
   a. Read the first three sections in your Study Guide—*Putting This Chapter Into Perspective*, *Learning Objectives*, and *Chapter Outline*.
   b. Review the key terms and concepts for each chapter assigned.
   c. Re-do the *Multiple Choice* sections of each assigned Study Guide chapter.
   d. Re-do the more comprehensive problems located in the *Working with Graphs* section, the *Problems* section, and the *Business Section*.

THE FLEXIBILITY AFFORDED BY THE LEARNING OBJECTIVES DESIGN

Since the new editions of the text and Study Guide are organized according to learning objectives and chapter sections, alternate instructional approaches and learning styles can now more easily be accommodated.

Many instructors may wish to omit certain sections of various chapters in the text. Since each question in the text and Study Guide is visibly related to a chapter learning objective and chapter section of the text, these instructors can now assign homework in the text and Study Guide based on only those learning objectives and chapter sections covered in the course.

In the classroom, after lecturing on a chapter section, many instructors like to have their students actively engaged in working on selected text and or Study Guide questions for part of the classroom session. The learning objective design effectively facilitates this instructional approach.

Many students may learn more effectively by actively working on questions in the text and Study Guide after reading each section of a chapter. Students taking this course at a distance might well fall into this category. The learning objectives design should appeal to you if you are one of these types of students.

CHAPTER 1

THE NATURE OF ECONOMICS

PUTTING THIS CHAPTER INTO PERSPECTIVE

The aim of Chapter 1 is to help you begin to get a feel for what economics and economic analysis is all about. The chapter describes the meaning and scope of economics, the economic way of thinking, and the methods of economics.

Economists are concerned with how people actually behave in the economic arena and not with how they themselves describe their actions, motivations, and beliefs. We contend that people act in ways that promote their own (sometimes broadly defined) self-interest, and that they respond predictably to economic incentives.

By combining this theory of human behavior with the concept of marginal analysis and the "other things constant" assumption, economists are able to (1) generate numerous insights and testable theories about behavior, (2) explain widely disparate social phenomena, (3) predict how people are likely to behave under numerous circumstances, and (4) assess how policies affect valued socio-economic goals.

LEARNING OBJECTIVES

After you have studied this chapter, you should be able to:

1.1 Explain the meaning of scarcity.

1.2 Define economics and distinguish between microeconomics and macroeconomics.

1.3 Describe how resource use decisions are affected by the rationality assumption, costs and benefits at the margin, and incentives.

1.4 Explain the three key processes involved in the scientific method.

1.5 Distinguish between positive and normative economics.

1.6   Describe the relationship between theories, policies, and socioeconomic goals.

CHAPTER OUTLINE

LO 1.1 - Explain the meaning of scarcity.
1. **Scarcity** refers to the condition that arises because wants always exceed what can be produced with the available limited resources.
   a. **Production** refers to any activity that results in the conversion of resources into goods and services. Limited resources include items such as **land**, **labour**, **physical capital**, **human capital**, and **entrepreneurship**.
   b. The incomes earned by land, labour, capital, and entrepreneurship are referred to as **rent**, **wages**, **interest**, and **profit**, respectively.
   c. Wants refer to the **goods** and **services** that we wish to consume as well as goals that we seek to achieve that require the use of limited resources.
   d. Scarcity is ever present in both rich and poor nations.

LO 1.2 - Define economics and distinguish between microeconomics and macroeconomics.
2. **Economics** is a social science that studies how people allocate limited resources to satisfy unlimited wants.
   a. Economics offers a framework of analysis that includes the economic way of thinking, the scientific approach, and policy analysis.
   b. These tools of analysis can prove useful for the day-to-day decisions made by individual consumers, workers, investors, managers, and owners of business firms, concerned citizens, and government policymakers.

3. Economics is broadly divided into microeconomics and macroeconomics.
   a. **Microeconomics** studies decisions undertaken by individuals (or households) and by firms that relate to a part of the economy.
   b. **Macroeconomics** studies the behaviour of the economy as a whole; it deals with **aggregate** behaviour such as unemployment, the price level, and national income.

LO 1.3 - Describe how resource-use decisions are affected by the rationality assumption, costs and benefits at the margin, and incentives.
4. **The economic way of thinking** assumes that individuals are motivated by self-interest and therefore respond to situations of scarcity in a rational manner.
   a. The **rationality assumption** is that an individual makes decisions based on maximizing his or her own self-interest.
   b. In maximizing self-interest, an individual compares **marginal benefits** with **marginal costs**. In order to appropriately identify the costs of any decision, the value of the next best alternative, the **opportunity cost**, should be considered. **Sunk costs** should be ignored. Individuals respond to **incentives**, which are inducements in the form of changed marginal benefits or marginal costs.

    c. Self-interest often means a desire for material well-being, but it can also be defined broadly enough to incorporate goals relating to love, friendship, prestige, power, and other human characteristics of human nature.

    d. By assuming that people act in a rational, self-interested way, economists can predict how individuals respond to incentives and can generate testable theories concerning human behaviour.

LO 1.4 - Explain the three key processes involved in the scientific method.

5. Economics is a social science that makes assumptions, forms theories or models, and tests these theories or models, with the facts.

    a. Economists, like all scientists, employ assumptions when developing theories or models. One important economic assumption is **ceteris paribus** or "all other things being equal".

    b. **Models** or **theories** are simplified representations of the real world. Such models help economists understand and predict economic phenomena in the real world. Models can be used to evaluate and formulate policies that can improve our individual or societal well-being.

    c. Like other social scientists, economists usually do not perform laboratory experiments; instead, they typically examine what already has occurred in order to test their theories. Models or theories are tested by the facts, which is called the **empirical** approach.

    d. Models or theories are evaluated on their ability to predict, and not on the realism of the assumptions employed.

6 Economists maintain that the unit of analysis is the individual; members of a group are assumed to pursue their own goals rather than those of a group.

LO 1.5 - Distinguish between positive and normative economics.

7. **Positive economics** is objective and scientific in nature, and deals with testable "if this, then that" hypotheses.

8. **Normative economics** is subjective and deals with value judgments, or with what "ought to be."

LO 1.6 - Describe the relationship between theories, policies, and socio-economic goals.

9. Economic theories (models) can be used to evaluate and formulate **policies** aimed at promoting **socio-economic goals**.

10. Commonly accepted socio-economic goals are: full employment, efficiency, economic growth, price stability, and equity

KEY TERMS AND CONCEPTS

Scarcity	Interest	Incentives
Production	Profit	Marginal benefit
Goods	Economics	Marginal cost
Services	Microeconomics	Ceteris paribus
Land	Macroeconomics	Models or theories
Labour	Aggregates	Empirical
Capital	Economic way of thinking	Positive economics
Entrepreneurship	Rationality assumption	Normative economics
Rent	Opportunity cost	Policies
Wages	Sunk cost	Socio-economic goals

COMPLETION QUESTIONS
Fill in the blank or circle the correct term.

(LO 1.1)
1. Scarcity refers to the condition that arises because human wants (exceed, are less than) what can be produced with (limited, unlimited) resources.

(LO 1.2)
2. Economics is a (natural, social) science.

3. Microeconomics deals with (individual units, the whole economy).

4. A nation's unemployment level is analyzed in (microeconomics, macroeconomics).

5. (Macroeconomics, Microeconomics) studies the causes and effects of inflation.

(LO 1.3)
6. In economics we assume that people (do, do not) intentionally make decisions that will leave them worse off.

7. The rationality assumption is that individuals (believe, act as if) they are rational.

8. It is rational to choose a course of action when the marginal benefit of the action (is less than, exceeds) the marginal cost of the action.

9. The highest valued alternative that must be sacrificed to satisfy a want is called (opportunity cost, sunk cost).

10. Economists maintain that incentives (are, are not) important to decision making.

11. Economists define self-interest (narrowly, broadly).

12.   Economists take the (individual, group) as the unit of analysis.

(LO 1.4)
13. Economic models are (simplified, realistic) representations of the real world.

14.   The ceteris paribus assumption enables economists to consider (one thing at a time, everything at once).

(LO 1.5)
15.   Economic statements that are testable by facts and are of an "if/then" nature are (positive, normative).

(LO 1.6)
16.   A superior economic policy promotes as many socio-economic goals as possible with (maximum, minimum) goal conflict.

TRUE-FALSE QUESTIONS

Circle **T** if the statement is true, **F** if it is false. Explain to yourself why a statement is false.

(LO 1.1)
T F   1.   The economic problem of scarcity is that available resources exceed human wants.

(LO 1.2)
T F   2.   Decisions regarding marriage, and the number of children to have, are outside the scope of economics as none of these decisions affect the use of one's resources.

T F   3.   Macroeconomics deals with aggregates, or totals, of economic variables.

T F   4.   When economists attempt to predict the number of workers a firm will employ, they are involved in macroeconomics.

(LO 1.3)
T F   5.   The economist's definition of self-interest includes only the pursuit of one's own material well-being.

T F   6.   In identifying the appropriate marginal costs of making a decision one should makes sure that all relevant sunk costs are included..

T F   7.   The rationality assumption is that individuals attempt, quite consciously, to make rational economic decisions, and will admit to it.

T   F   8.   Economists would argue that resources should continue to be allocated to activities that reduce criminal activity until all crime has been eliminated.

(LO 1.4)

T   F   9.   A model's usefulness depends crucially on the realism of the assumptions used in the model.

(LO 1.5)

T   F   10.   The statement "every working person should earn the same amount of income" is a positive statement.

T   F   11.   The statement "if every working person receives a tax decrease, Canada's inflation rate will increase" is a positive statement.

(LO 1.6)

T   F   12.   One socio-economic goal is full employment.

T   F   13.   It is widely agreed that the goal "equitable distribution of income" means that everyone should earn the same amount of annual income.

MULTIPLE CHOICE QUESTIONS
Circle the letter that corresponds to the best answer.

(LO 1.1)
1.   Scarcity refers to a condition
   a.   that only applies to poor individuals and poor nations..
   b.   where resources are unlimited.
   c.   where wants exceed resources.
   d.   wants are limited.

2.   An example of physical capital would be
   a.   certified training in electronics
   b.   shares of a corporation
   c.   skills that the owner brings to a business.
   d.   a new machine that increases the daily production of DVD's

3.   The payment of interest best relates to which factor of production:
   a.   land.
   b.   capital.
   c.   labour
   d.   entrepreneurship

(LO 1.2)
4.   Which of the following areas of study is concerned, primarily, with microeconomics?
   a.   the steel industry
   b.   inflation
   c.   the national unemployment rate
   d.   national income determination

5.   Macroeconomic analysis deals with
     a. the steel industry.
     b. how individuals respond to an increase in the price of gasoline.
     c. inflation.
     d. how a change in the price of energy affects a family.

(LO 1.3)
6.   Economists maintain that Mr. Smith will usually make decisions that promote the interests of
     a. his colleagues at work.
     b. himself.
     c. his class.
     d. his race.

7.   The concept of making decisions *at the margin* means that
     a. it is rational for one to choose an alternative as long it has some benefit.
     b. it is rational for one to choose the lowest cost alternative.
     c. it is rational to choose an alternative when its extra benefit exceeds its extra cost.
     d. it is rational to choose an alternative when its extra cost exceeds its extra benefit.

(LO 1.4)
8.   Ceteris paribus
     a. refers to changing many variables at the same time.
     b. is seldom practiced in laboratory research.
     c. refers to the practice of examining how one variable relates to another variable, holding all other factors constant.
     d. is another term for pursuing one's own self interest.

9.   An economic model is justifiably criticized if
     a. its assumptions are unrealistic.
     b. it cannot be tested in a controlled, laboratory experiment.
     c. it fails to predict.
     d. all of the above

(LO 1.5)
10. Which of the following is a normative statement?
     a. If price rises, people will buy less.
     b. If price rises, people will buy more.
     c. If price rises the poor will be less well off; therefore price should not be permitted to rise.
     d. If price rises people will buy less; therefore we would expect to observe that quantity demanded falls.

11. Which of the following is a positive statement?
    a. Full employment policies should be pursued.
    b. If minimum wage rates rise, then unemployment will rise.
    c. We should take from the rich and give to the poor.
    d. The government should help the homeless.

12. Normative economics statements
    a. are testable hypotheses.
    b. are value-free.
    c. are subjective, value judgments.
    d. can be scientifically established.

(LO 1.6)
13. Which of the following is **NOT** a commonly accepted socio-economic goal?
    a. equity
    b. equal distribution of income
    c. economic growth
    d. price stability

14. Suppose the government implements a policy that is aimed at increasing the number of skilled university and college graduates available to industry. This policy is most likely to promote the socio-economic goal of
    a. efficiency
    b. distribution of capital
    c. economic growth
    d. price stability

MATCHING

Choose the numbered item in Column (2) that best matches the term or concept in Column (1).

(1)	(2)

(LO 1.1)

a. scarcity	1. rational behaviour
b. profit	2. empirical
c. human capital	3. are the bases of policy

(LO 1.2)

| d. microeconomics | 4. nonscientific value-judgments |
| e. macroeconomics | 5. objective, scientific hypotheses |

(LO 1.3)

f. self interest	6. wants exceed resources
g. opportunity cost	7. model
h. marginal cost	8. highest valued alternative sacrificed

(LO 1.4)

i. simplification of reality	9. plan of action
j. testing theory with fact	10. payment to the entrepreneur

(LO 1.5)

k. positive economics	11. study of economic aggregates
l. normative economics	12. college education

(LO 1.6)

m. policy	13. study of individual behavior
n. socio-economic goals	14. extra cost
	15. inflation
	16. wages

PROBLEMS

(LO 1.3)

1. Suppose you have a friend currently working as a salesperson in a local computer store. She is thinking about going back to school full-time to finish her computer science degree. Your friend explains that she earns $15 000 (after taxes) per year in her current job, and that she estimates tuition will cost $1 600 per year. In addition, she estimates fees, supplies, books, and miscellaneous expenses associated with attending school will run $800 per year. She wants to attend a university that is located directly across the street from the store where she currently works. She claims that she pays $350 per month for rent and utilities and that she spends about $200 per month on food.

    Using what you have learned, calculate and explain to your friend the opportunity cost to her of another year back at school.

(LO 1.3)

2. Assume that Ms. Gentile values her time at $50 per hour because she has the opportunity to do consulting, and that Joe College values his time at $2 per hour. Assume that it costs $400 to fly from their hometown to Vancouver, and that the flight takes 6 hours. Assume that it costs $200 to take a bus, and that the bus trip takes 24 hours.

    a.   What is the cheaper way for Ms. Gentile to get to Vancouver? Why?

b.   Which transportation is cheaper for Joe College? Why?

BUSINESS SECTION

(LO 1.2)
Finance: Fundamental Stock Investment Analysis

How might you go about determining whether to buy or sell a specific company stock? Obviously if you could predict the stock price, you would buy the stock if the price is predicted to increase in the near future, and possibly sell if the price is expected to fall. According to what is often called *fundamental stock analysis*, the single most important factor affecting a stock price is the expected profitability of the company that originally issued the stock. According to fundamental stock analysis, a company's stock price will increase if investors expect that the annual profit of this firm will increase significantly in the near future.

According to the fundamental analysis approach, the expected profit of any corporation will be affected by both *macroeconomic* and *microeconomic* factors. Macroeconomic factors would include broad global and national events and trends. In formulating profit expectations, investors will also closely monitor microeconomic measures and trends at the specific industry and company level.

Business Application Problem

For each event and hypothetical company listed below, determine whether the event
     i.   is a macroeconomic or microeconomic event
     ii. will tend to increase or decrease the company's stock price. (Hint: predict how the event will affect the expected profit of the firm in question.)

a.   Event: Due to the declining Canadian dollar (exchange rate) Canadian companies which export products to the U.S. experience a major increase in annual sales. Company: Timber Corp, a Canadian lumber company that exports 80% of their products.

b.   Event: Special taxes are imposed on Canadian firms manufacturing cigarettes. Company: The Smoke Factory, a Canadian cigarette manufacturer.

c. Event: With global inflation escalating out of control, investors lose confidence in paper currency. As a result there is a worldwide trend towards the purchase of items that investors feel will retain their value over time.
Company: Bre-Y Mining Corp, a large multinational gold mining firm.

d. Event: As a result of new management, a department store is able to achieve the same annual sales as the previous year at a much lower level of operating costs.
Company: Wardwoods, a Canadian clothing department store.

e. Event: Due to an upward trend in Canadian interest rates, investors sell stocks in all the major Canadian industries in order to purchase Canadian bonds.
Company: Morgan Mutual Fund, a corporation that manages investor funds by buying blue chip stocks in a wide range of Canadian industries (on behalf of investors).

ANSWERS TO CHAPTER 1

COMPLETION QUESTIONS

1.   exceed; limited
2.   social
3.   individual units
4.   macroeconomics
5.   macroeconomics
6.   do not
7.   act as if
8.   exceeds
9.   opportunity cost
10. are
11. broadly
12. individual
13. simplified
14. one thing at a time
15. positive
16. minimum

TRUE AND FALSE QUESTIONS

1. F   The economic problem of scarcity is that human wants exceed available resources.
2. F   Marriage, and the decision to have children, is within the scope of economics as these decisions do affect how one allocates his or her limited resources.
3. T
4. F   Microeconomics focuses on the individual firm, consumer, or industry.

5.   F   Economists define self-interest more broadly to include power, desire to help others, friendship, love, and so on.
6.   F   Since sunk costs are irreversible costs incurred prior to making the decision, they should not be included in identifying marginal costs.
7.   F   That assumption is merely that people act as if they are rational, even if they do so unconsciously.
8.   F   Economists would argue that resources should continue to be allocated to criminal reducing activities only as long as the marginal benefit exceeds the marginal cost.
9.   F   All models employ simplified and somewhat unrealistic assumptions; what matters is how well they predict.
10.   F   This is a normative statement as it is a value judgement and the validity of this statement cannot be tested with facts.
11.   T
12.   T
13.   F   While it is difficult to get consensus on this goal, it is widely agreed that "equitable distribution of income" includes the desire to reduce the level of poverty in our society.

MULTIPLE CHOICE QUESTIONS

1.c;   Scarcity is the condition that arises because wants always exceed what can be produced with limited resources
2.d;   Since physical capital refers to manufactured items used to produce other goods, the machine would be classed as physical capital.
3.b;   The payment of interest best relates to capital, as one must wait a period of years to get the benefits
        needed to pay for this resource.
4.a;   Microeconomics focuses on the individual consumer, firm, or industry.
5.c;   Macroeconomics studies the behavior of the economy as a whole. Inflation measures the increase in the prices of all goods and services in the economy.
6.b;   Individuals are motivated by self-interest.
7.c;   Making decisions at the margin means choosing an alternative when the marginal (extra) benefit exceeds the marginal (extra) cost.
8.c;   Ceteris paribus is a common practice in all types of scientific research. It refers to the practice of examining how one variable relates to another variable, holding all other factors constant.
9.c;   A good model should yield usable predictions and implications for the real world.
10.c;   This statement contains the value judgement that the poor should never be made less well off. TIP: Normative economics involves value judgements.
11.b;   This statement is value free, and can be tested by factual evidence.
12.c.   Normative statements are based on what one prefers, likes, or desires.
13.b;   Equitable or "fair' distribution of income is a socio-economic goal. Many people would not consider an equal distribution of income to be equitable or fair, if some work harder than others.
14.c;   Economic growth, which means an economy with the ability to increase its rate of production in the future, due to a more skilled workforce.

MATCHING

a and 6;   b and 10;   c and 12;   d and 13;   e and 11;   f and 1;   g and 8;   h and 14;   i and 7;
j and 2;   k and 5;   l and 4; m and 9;   n and 3;

PROBLEMS

1. The opportunity cost of another year back at school for your friend is as follows:

Foregone after-tax salary	$15 000
Tuition costs	1 600
Expenses associated with school	800
Total opportunity costs	$17 400

2. a. Plane; flying costs her $400 plus 6 hours times $50 per hour, or $700, while taking a bus would cost her $200 plus 24 hours times $50 per hour, or $1400.
   b. Bus; taking the bus costs him a total of $248 while the total cost of flying is $412.

BUSINESS SECTION

a. i. Macroeconomic event, as the decline in the Canadian dollar is a broad national trend.
   ii. Increase the stock price, as Timber Corp's sales will increase which will result in an increased profit.
b. i. Microeconomic event as the tax focuses on a specific industry – cigarette manufacturing.
   ii. Decrease the price of the stock. A tax increase will raise the costs of production and reduce the annual profit.
c. i. Macroeconomic event, as the inflation is a broad global factor.
   ii. Increase the stock price. When inflation is out of control, investors often purchase gold, as it has historically been popular in times of economic crisis. As gold prices rise, the profits of gold mines increase.
d. i. Microeconomic event as this is a factor that affects the specific firm in question.
   ii. Increase the stock price. When sales stay the same but operating costs decrease, the annual profit will increase.
e. i. Macroeconomic event as interest rate trends tend to be a nationwide phenomenon.
   ii. Decrease the stock price. Since investors are selling stocks across all industries, this reduces stock prices, which, in turn, reduces the profit of Morgan Mutual Fund.

APPENDIX A

READING AND WORKING WITH GRAPHS

APPENDIX A PROBLEMS

1.   Graph the probable relationship between each of the following variables and state whether each relationship is either direct or inverse or independent (no relation likely exists).

   a.   Income and the amount of money spent on housing.

   b.   Annual rainfall in Vancouver and the annual value of ice-cream sales in Montreal.

   c.   Number of vegetarians per 10 000 people and meat sales per 10 000 people.

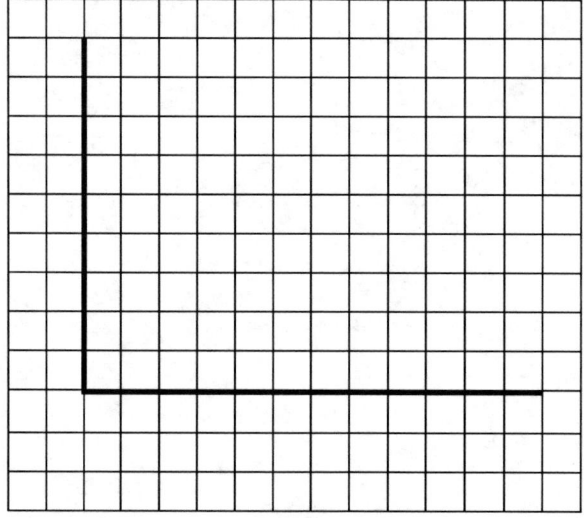

ANSWERS TO APPENDIX A

APPENDIX A PROBLEMS

1. a. The graph should be upward sloping from left to right indicating a direct relation.

    b. There should be no systematic relationship between these two variables, indicating the variables are independent.

    c. The graph should be downward sloping from left to right indicating an inverse relation.

CHAPTER 2

PRODUCTION POSSIBILITIES AND ECONOMIC SYSTEMS

PUTTING THIS CHAPTER INTO PERSPECTIVE

In Chapter 1 we examined the meaning and scope of the field of economics. Central to the definition of economics is the notion of scarcity - that our wants and goals exceed our limited resources. In the first part of Chapter 2 we present a model called the production possibilities curve and we use this model to sharpen your understanding of concepts related to scarcity - choice, tradeoffs, opportunity cost, efficiency, full employment and economic growth. The production possibilities curve is effectively used to highlight a very important choice that we all face - the trade-off between present and future goods.

As you progress through Chapter 2, you will examine the concepts of absolute and comparative advantage, which will help you understand how specialization and trade can enhance production possibilities. In the latter part of Chapter 2 you will study how different societies employ different economic systems in order to respond to the problem of scarcity. In this segment of the chapter you will focus on the features of the pure command, pure capitalist, and mixed economic systems.

LEARNING OBJECTIVES

After you have studied this chapter you should be able to:

2.1   Define the production possibilities curve and identify its assumptions.

2.2   Use the production possibilities curve to illustrate the concepts of scarcity, trade-offs, increasing opportunity cost, unemployment, productive efficiency, allocative efficiency, and economic growth.

2.3   Use the production possibilities curve to explain the trade-off between consumption goods and capital goods.

2.4   Distinguish between absolute advantage and comparative advantage and use these concepts to explain how specialization and trade can increase production and consumption.

2.5   Explain the differences between the pure capitalist, pure command, and mixed economic systems.

2.6   Describe the features of pure capitalism and explain how capitalism answers the three basic economic questions.

CHAPTER OUTLINE

LO 2.1 - Define the production possibilities curve and identify its assumptions.
1.   The **production possibilities curve** describes all possible combinations of two goods that can be produced assuming full and efficient employment of resources, a fixed time period, fixed quantity and quality of resources, and fixed **technology**.

LO 2.2 - Use the production possibilities curve to illustrate the concepts of scarcity, trade-offs, increasing opportunity cost, unemployment, productive efficiency, allocative efficiency, and economic growth.
2.   Because of scarcity, choice and opportunity costs arise.
   a.   Due to scarcity, people trade off options.
   b.   The production possibilities curve (PPC) is a graph of the trade-offs inherent in a decision.
      i.   When the opportunity cost of additional units of a good remains constant, the PPC curve is a straight line.
      ii.   When the **Law of Increasing Relative Costs** applies, the PPC curve is bowed outward.
      iii. Any point on a PPC assumes **productive efficiency** and full employment.
      iv.   Points inside a PPC reflect unemployment or productive inefficiency; points outside the PPC are unattainable by definition.
      v.   If a nation is producing that mix of goods (point on the PPC) most valued by its consumers, **allocative efficiency** is achieved.
      vi.   **Economic growth** shifts the production possibilities curve outward over time.

LO 2.3 - Use the production possibilities curve to explain the trade-off between consumption goods and capital goods.
3.   The PPC is effective in illustrating the choice between present goods and future goods.
   a.   There is a trade-off between present consumption and future consumption.
   b.   If a nation produces fewer **consumer goods** and more **capital goods** now, then it can consume more goods in the future than would otherwise be the case. This would result in a higher rate of economic growth or a greater outward shift in the nation's PPC.

LO 2.4 - Distinguish between absolute advantage and comparative advantage and use these concepts to explain how specialization and trade can increase production and consumption.

4. a. When individuals, firms, and regions, specialize according to **comparative advantage** (not **absolute advantage**), this results in an increase in productivity.
    b. **Division of labour** permits greater **specialization** and therefore increases output.

LO 2.5 - Explain the differences between the pure capitalist, pure command, and mixed economic systems.

5. a. In a **pure command system**, the government owns the resources, and the **three basic questions**—What, How, For Whom—are answered in a centralized manner by government.
    b. In **pure capitalism**, resources are privately owned, and the basic questions are answered in a decentralized manner by individual firms and households interacting in markets.
    c. In a **mixed economic system**, where there is both private and public ownership of resources, the basic questions are partly answered by government and partly by individual firms and households in markets.

LO 2.6 - Describe the features of pure capitalism and explain how capitalism answers the three basic economic questions.

6. In its theoretical form the pure capitalist economy has the following attributes:
    a. Private property rights are enforced by a judicial system.
    b. Self-interest governs decisions made by households and firms.
    c. The economy is to serve the consumer – "**consumer sovereignty**".
    d. A system of markets and prices guides the decisions of firms and resources.
    e. Competition between sellers and buyers helps to ensure consumer sovereignty.
    f. Limited government or "**laissez-faire**".

7. One way to remember the important attributes of pure capitalism is by thinking of the **Three P's**: Private property, Profits, and Prices.

8. Under capitalistic nations the price, or market, system answers the three economic questions.
    a. Consumer demand and resource availability determine what goods and services will be produced. In other words, the forces of demand and supply determine "What, and how much to produce"; market price must be sufficiently high to make a good profitable for producers to produce.
    b. Profit maximization via the price system assures that the "How" question is answered so that the least-cost combination of resources will be used to produce outputs.
    c. Under such a system "For Whom" is answered by the distribution of money income; those with high money incomes get more goods than those with low money incomes.

i. The quantity, quality, and type of the various human and non-human resources that a person owns determines his or her money income.

ii. A specific good or service is allocated to the highest bidders; hence the market
rations each output to specific individuals.

d. Under capitalism voluntary exchanges in markets take place; as such, resources (inputs) are allocated to businesses, and goods and services (outputs) are allocated to households.

KEY TERMS AND CONCEPTS

Production possibilities curve (PPC)

Technology

Productive efficiency

Allocative efficiency

Economic growth

Law of increasing relative costs

Capital goods

Consumption goods

Absolute advantage

Comparative advantage

Specialization

Division of labour

Economic system

Pure command economy

Pure capitalist economy

Mixed economy

Basic economic questions

Laissez-faire

Consumer sovereignty

Three P's

COMPLETION QUESTIONS

Fill in the blank or circle the correct term.

(LO 2.1)

1. The production possibilities curve describes all possible combinations of two goods that can be produced based on the following four assumptions:

    _____,_____,_____,
    _____.

(LO 2.2)

2. The production possibilities curve illustrates the notion of a trade-off through its (positive slope, negative slope).

3. If ,when producing additional units of a product, the opportunity cost increases, the production possibilities curve will be a (bowed-out curve, straight line); if the opportunity cost stays constant, the production possibilities curve will be a (bowed-out curve, straight line).

4. Economic growth will cause the production possibilities curve to shift (inward, outward).

5. The law of increasing relative cost is relevant to situations where resources (are, are not) perfectly adaptable for alternate uses.

6. If an economy is productively inefficient, its actual output combination will lie (inside, outside) the production possibilities curve.

7. (Productive efficiency, Allocative efficiency) is concerned with producing the mix of goods and services most valued by consumers.

(LO 2.3)

8. (Consumer goods, Capital goods) contribute to economic growth.

9. If a nation currently uses more of its resources to produce capital goods, this will enhance (current consumption, future consumption)

(LO 2.4)

10. Productivity is enhanced when individuals, regions, and nations specialize in those activities for which they have a(n) (comparative, absolute) advantage.

11. When an autoworker specializes in the production of bumpers and another autoworker specializes in car doors, this is an example of the _____

.

(LO 2.5)

12. Resource allocation involves answering the three basic questions of _____, _____, and _____ goods and services will be produced.

13. Under a command economy, economic decisions were made by (a central authority, many individuals); the closer we go to a pure capitalist economy, the (less, more) political centralization there is.

14. One of the important features of a command economy is that the non-labour means of production are owned by the _____.

15. Central planning is important under a _____(capitalist, command) economy.

16. The forces that determine relative rewards from production in a command economy are set by the (market, government).

17. Real world economies are _____ economies, because they have elements of both _____ and _____ economies.

(LO 2.6)

18.   People respond to incentives, therefore property rights (are, are not) important.

19.   In its purest form, capitalism has the following attributes: _____,
_____, _____ and _____, _____

20.   Under _____ (capitalism, communism) individuals have vast,
government-protected private property rights.

21.   Under (a command economy, a price system) resources will be more likely
allocated such that the least-cost combination will be chosen by producers.

22.   Under capitalism specific goods and services are allocated to the (highest bidders,
most worthy individuals).

TRUE-FALSE QUESTIONS
Circle **T** if the statement is true, **F** if it is false. Explain to yourself why a statement is false.

(LO 2.1)

T   F   1.   The production possibilities curve describes the minimum production combinations possible for a given fixed period of time.

T   F   2.   A given production possibilities curve assumes that the quantity of resources and technology are fixed.

(LO 2.2)

T   F   3.   The marginal benefit derived from moving away from the allocatively efficient production combination will always exceed the marginal cost of such a move

T   F   4.   Any point on the production possibilities curve is a productively efficient point, assuming full employment.

T   F   5.   Whenever one moves from a point inside the production possibilities curve to a point on the curve, an opportunity cost is incurred.

T   F   6.   If a production possibilities curve is linear, the cost of producing additional units of a good rises.

T   F   7.   At any given moment in time, it is impossible for an economy to be inside its production possibilities curve.

(LO 2.3)

T   F   8.   A nation that seeks to increase its investment in capital goods typically must sacrifice current consumption.

(LO 2.4)

T   F   9.   People have little incentive to specialize in jobs for which they have a comparative advantage.

T   F   10.   If an individual has an absolute advantage in the production of all goods, this individual will not gain from specialization and trade.

(LO 2.5)

T   F   11.   In a command economic system, producers follow the commands of many individuals, through the market.

T   F   12.   Under pure capitalism, all resources are publicly owned.

T   F   13.   In the real world, economies tend to be mixed systems.

(LO 2.6)

T   F   14.   In theory, capitalism is supposed to serve the firms.

T   F   15.   Laissez-faire is a feature of the command economic system.

T   F   16.   Pure capitalism answers the How question in a productively efficient manner.

MULTIPLE CHOICE QUESTIONS
Circle the letter that corresponds with the best answer.

(LO 2.1)

1.   Which of the following is not an assumption of the production possibilities curve
     a.   fixed time-period
     b.   fixed technology.
     c.   fixed resources
     d.   unemployment.

(LO 2.2)
2.   For any given year, a production possibilities "boundary" exists due to
     a.   better technology
     b.   economic growth
     c.   limited resources
     d.   growing labour force

3.   Which of the following will result in a shift outward in the entire production possibilities curve?
     a.   productive efficiency
     b.   a smaller labour force
     c.   economic growth
     d.   full employment

4.   Which statement concerning a production possibilities curve is NOT true?
     a.   A trade-off exists along such a curve.
     b.   It is usually linear.
     c.   Points inside it indicate productive inefficiency.
     d.   A point outside it is currently impossible to attain.

5.   The production possibilities curve is bowed outward because
     a.   the relative cost of producing a good rises as more of it is produced.
     b.   of the law of decreasing relative costs.
     c.   all resources are equally suited to the production of any good.
     d.   all of the above.

(LO 2.3)
6.   When a nation expands its capital stock, it is usually true that
     a.   it must forego output of some consumer goods in the present.
     b.   the human capital stock must decline.
     c.   fewer consumer goods will be available in the future.
     d.   no opportunity cost exists for doing so.

(LO 2.4)

7. When nations and individuals specialize
   a. overall living standards rise.
   b. trade and exchange increases.
   c. people become more vulnerable to changes in tastes and technology.
   d. all of the above

8. Ms. Boulware is the best lawyer and the best secretary in town.
   a. She has a comparative advantage in both jobs.
   b. She has an absolute advantage in both jobs.
   c. She has a comparative advantage in being a secretary.
   d. all of the above

9. Kate and Jake work together in a business that assembles exercise bikes and mini-gyms. It takes Kate one hour to assemble each product. It takes Jake one hour to assemble the bikes and two hours to assemble the mini-gyms. Which of the following is correct:
   a. Kate should specialize in assembling both products.
   b. Kate should specialize in assembling bikes.
   c. Jake should specialize in assembling mini-gyms
   d. Jake should specialize in assembling bikes.

(LO 2.5)

10. Which of the following is **NOT** a key attribute of any actual command system?
    a. The government owns the major productive resources.
    b. A high degree of individual incentives motivates production.
    c. Relative rewards for production are set by the state.
    d. Production is guided by central planning.

11. Canada would best be described as a
    a. Pure capitalist system
    b. Pure command system
    c. Mixed capitalist system
    d. Mixed command system

(LO 2.6)

12. Which of the following is NOT a feature of pure capitalism
    a. Monopoly companies supply all the products.
    b. Laissez-faire
    c. Consumer sovereignty
    d. Private property

13. In pure capitalism, the WHAT question is ultimately based on
    a. government plans
    b. lowest cost products
    c. what firm want to produce, regardless of consumer demand
    d. consumer demand and resource availability.

MATCHING

Choose the numbered item in Column (2) that best matches the term or concept in Column (1).

(1)	(2)

(LO 2.1)
a. production possibilities   1.   most valued mix of goods is produced
(LO 2.2)
b. economic growth   2.   specialization
c. constant opportunity cost   3.   maximum production combinations
d. allocative efficiency   4.   ability to produce at a lower unit cost
e. productive inefficiency   5.   specializing in one's comparative advantage
(LO 2.3)
f. capital   6.   PPC shifts outward
(LO 2.4)
g   absolute advantage   7.   straight line PPC
h. productivity increase   8.   pure capitalism
i. comparative advantage   9.   centralized planning
(LO 2.5)
j. command system   10.   increased future consumption
(LO 2.6)
k. laissez-faire   11.   inside the PPC
                                      12.   bowed out PPC

WORKING WITH GRAPHS

(LO 2.1 and LO 2.2)

1.   Given the following information, graph the production possibilities curve in the space provided and then use the graph to answer the questions that follow.

Combination (points)	Autos (100 000 per year)	Wheat (100 000 tonnes per year)
A	16	0
B	14	4
C	12	7
D	9	10
E	5	12
F	0	13

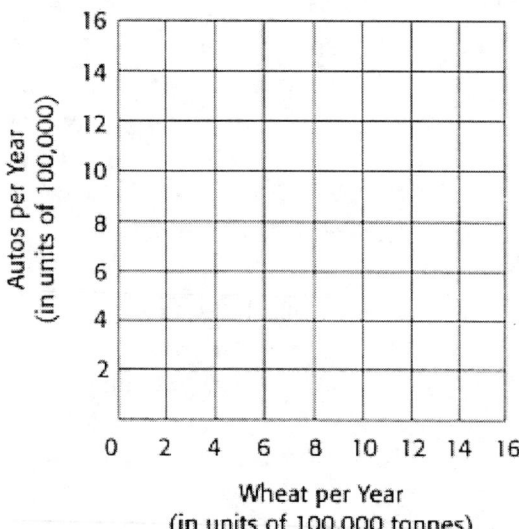

Wheat per Year
(in units of 100,000 tonnes)

a. If the economy is currently operating at point C, what is the opportunity cost of moving to point D? to point B?

b. Suppose that the economy is currently producing 1 200 000 autos and 200 000 tonnes of wheat per year. Label this point in your graph with the letter G. At point G, the economy would be suffering from what? At point G we can see that it is possible to produce more wheat without giving up any auto production, or produce more autos without giving up any wheat production, or produce more of both. Label this region in your graph. This region appears to contradict the definition of a production possibilities curve. What is the explanation for this result?

c.   Suppose a new fertilizer compound is developed that will allow the economy to produce an additional 150 000 tons of wheat per year if no autos are produced. Sketch in a likely representation of the effect of this discovery, assuming all else remains constant.

d. What sort of impact (overall) will this discovery have on the opportunity cost of more wheat production at an arbitrary point on the new production possibilities curve, as compared to a point representing the same level of output of wheat on the original curve?

(LO 2.2)
2.   Consider the graphs below, then answer the questions that follow.

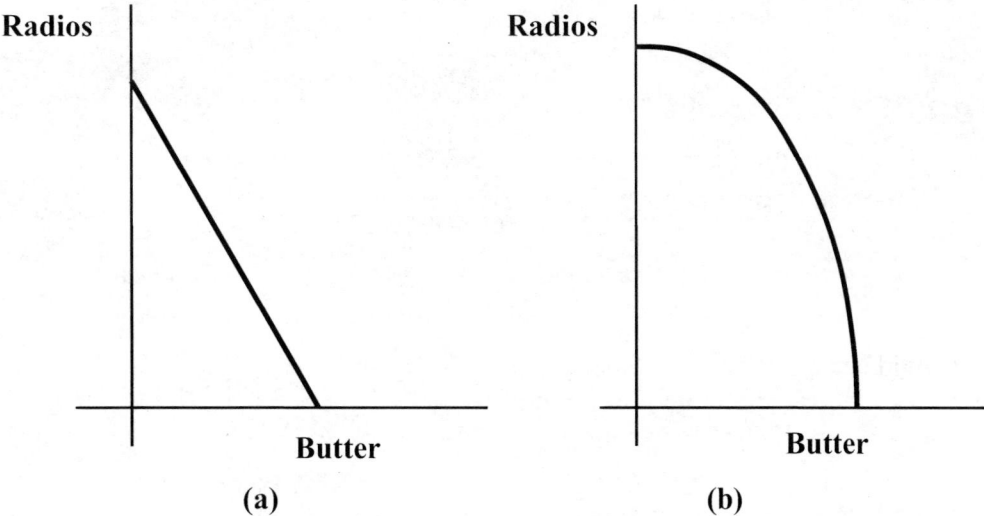

(a)   (b)

a.   Which graph, (a) or (b), shows constant relative costs of producing additional units of butter? Why?

b.   Which graph, (a) or (b), shows increasing relative costs of producing additional units of butter? Why?

c.   Which graph seems more realistic, (a) or (b)? Why?

(LO 2.3)

3.   As an elected government official, you are particularly concerned with how your nation's limited resources are allocated in the production of various capital and consumer goods. The graph below describes alternate production possibilities for the next budget year (year 2006) for your country.

Production Possibility Curve for the Year 2006

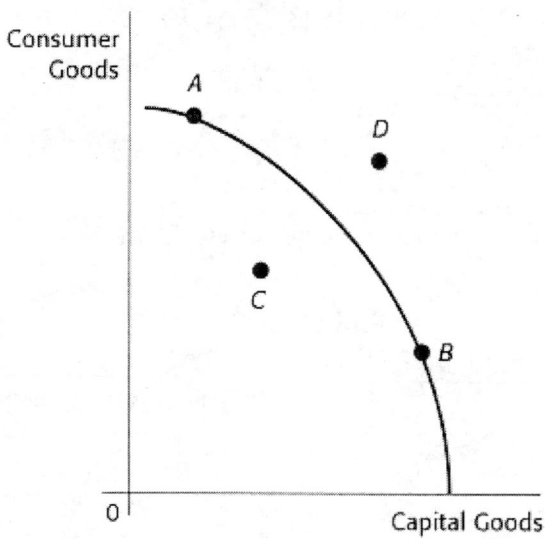

a.   Provide examples of consumer goods.

b.   Provide examples of capital goods.

c.   Which of the production combinations labeled above would be considered a productively inefficient point?

d.   Which of the production combinations labeled above is unattainable in the year 2006? What makes this point unattainable?

e.   Which production combination – A or B – will result in a higher rate of economic growth in future years?

f.   Which production combination would you feel more comfortable borrowing funds for (i.e. running a deficit)—combination A or B? Briefly explain.

g.   In general, what is the opportunity cost of choosing a production combination that will result in a very high rate of economic growth? Explain.

PROBLEMS

(LO 2.1 and LO 2.2)

1.   Assume that, given its resource base, an economy is able to produce output combinations A, B, C, and D. Society values combination A at $10 000, combination B at $20 000, combination C at $30 000, and combination D at $15 000.

a.   What is the opportunity cost of producing combination A?

b.   What is the opportunity cost of producing combination B?

c.   What is the opportunity cost of producing combination C?

d.   What is the opportunity cost of producing combination D.

e.   If the community wanted to maximize the value of its output, given its resource base, which combination should it produce?

f.   If the community were to achieve allocative efficiency, which combination would it choose?

(LO 2.3)

2. If a *nation* wants to increase its future consumption it must forego some present consumption because it must allocate some resources to the production of capital goods. Suppose *you* want to increase your future consumption, given a fixed lifetime income, what can you do?

(LO 2.4)

3. The Hughes family consists of Mr. Hughes, Mrs. Hughes, and their son, Scotty, who is too young to work outside of the home. Assume that Mr. Hughes can earn $30 per hour (after taxes) any time he chooses, Mrs. Hughes can earn $5 per hour, and the family values homemaker activities at $6 per hour.

    a. Because the family requires income to purchase goods and services, who will probably work in the marketplace?

    b. Who will probably do the housework?

    c. If the family must pay $3 per hour to have its lawn mowed, who will be assigned that work?

    d. If Scotty can now earn $4 per hour on a job, who now might mow the grass?

    e. If wage rates in the marketplace for Mrs. Hughes rise to $7 per hour, what is the family likely to do?

(LO 2.5 and LO 2.6)

4. The following questions illustrate how the three basic economic questions- *what, how,* and *for whom* – are all interrelated in a capitalist system.

    a. Explain how *for whom* is affected if *what* changes, for example if tastes change in favour of figure skating and away from professional football.

b. Explain how *for whom* is affected if *how* changes because unions increase wage rates relative to other factors of production.

c. Explain how a change in *for whom* (taxing some and giving to others) might change *what* to produce.

BUSINESS SECTION

LO 2.3
Finance: Is Deficit Financing Always Undesirable?

Deficit financing refers to the practice of having to incur a new debt when purchasing a good. Understanding the difference between *consumer* and *capital goods* may shed some light on whether or not deficit financing is appropriate. In general, economists are more likely to suggest financing capital goods on a deficit basis than consumption goods. Since most of the benefits of a capital good accrue in future periods, it is rational to borrow funds and then gradually pay back the loan in the future when the benefits of the investment good accrue. This holds true in the case of both private and public sector goods as the following problem will illustrate.

Business Application Problem

For each pair of goods listed below, indicate which good is better suited to deficit financing.

a. Spending $20 000 on a "fully loaded" sports car vs. spending $20 000 obtaining a Bachelor Of Commerce degree

b. Constructing a civic convention centre vs. constructing community leisure pools with water slides.

c. Constructing an exercise gym on the work site, which is to be freely available to your employees vs. paying for free trips to Mexico on behalf of your employees.

d. An insurance salesman purchases an annual seasons pass to a posh golf course vs. a college instructor purchases an annual season's pass to a posh golf course.

e. Constructing an expensive, beautifully designed city hall vs. subsidizing the city's major league sports team.

ANSWERS TO CHAPTER 2

COMPLETION QUESTIONS

1. full and efficient employment, fixed time-period, fixed quantity and quality of resources, fixed technology.
2. negative slope
3. bowed-out curve, straight line.
4. outward
5. are not
6. inside
7. Allocative efficiency
8. Capital goods
9. future consumption
10. comparative
11. division of labour
12. what, how, for whom
13. a central authority; less
14. state
15. command
16. government
17. mixed, command and capitalist
18. are
19. private ownership of resources, self-interest, consumer sovereignty, markets and prices, competition, limited government.
20. capitalism
21. a price-system
22. highest bidders

TRUE-FALSE QUESTIONS

1. F   The production possibilities curve describes the *maximum* production combinations possible
2. T
3. F   The marginal cost will always exceed the marginal benefit when moving away from an allocatively efficient point.
4. T
5. F   It is possible to avoid incurring an opportunity cost when moving from inside to on the production possibilities curve. The increased production comes from putting unemployed resources back to work or is derived from gains in efficiency.
6. F   A linear PPC implies a constant cost of additional production.
7. F   Productive inefficiency or unemployment often causes an economy to be inside its PPC.
8. T
9. F   People can earn more income in jobs for which they have a comparative advantage.
10. F   The gains from trade are based on comparative advantage and not absolute advantage.
11. F   Commands are set by a centralized government.
12. F   All resources are privately owned.
13. T
14. F   Capitalism is supposed to serve consumers, which is called consumer sovereignty.
15. F   Laissez-faire is a feature of the capitalist economic system, and refers to limited government.
16. T

MULTIPLE CHOICE QUESTIONS

1.d;   Full and efficient employment is assumed on the curve.

2.c;   Limited resources imposes a boundary on what combinations can be produced.

3.c;   Economic growth increases a nation's potential to produce different production combinations which causes the PPC to shift outward.

4.b;   The law of increasing relative costs causes the curve to be bowed outward.

5.a;   This is the law of increasing relative costs.

6.a;   If additional limited resources are allocated to capital goods, less resources are available for consumer goods.

7.d;   If specialization based on comparative advantage increases, trade and exchange must also increase, resulting in a higher standard of living.

8.b;   She produces both services at a lower cost.

         TIP: Absolute advantage is the ability to produce a good or service at an absolutely lower cost, while comparative advantage is the ability to produce at a lower opportunity cost compared to others.

9.d;   Kate's opportunity cost of assembling 1 bike is 1 mini-gym, which is higher that Jake's opportunity cost of .5 mini-gyms. Jake has the comparative advantage in the exercise bikes.

10.b;   There is a low degree of individual incentive to be productive as rewards are fixed government salaries.

11.c;   Canada is a mixed capitalist system as most goods and services are provided by the private sector but the government does provide major services such as education and health care.

12. a;   The pure capitalist model assumes lots of competition in every market, in order to achieve consumer sovereignty.

13. d;   A capitalist system will tend to produce those goods which are in high consumer demand, assuming that the appropriate resources are available. This will enhance the profits of firms.

MATCHING

a and 3;   b and 6;   c and 7;   d and 1;   e and 11;   f and 10;   g and 4;   h and 5;   i and 2;
j and 9;   k and 8;

WORKING WITH GRAPHS

1. See the following graph.

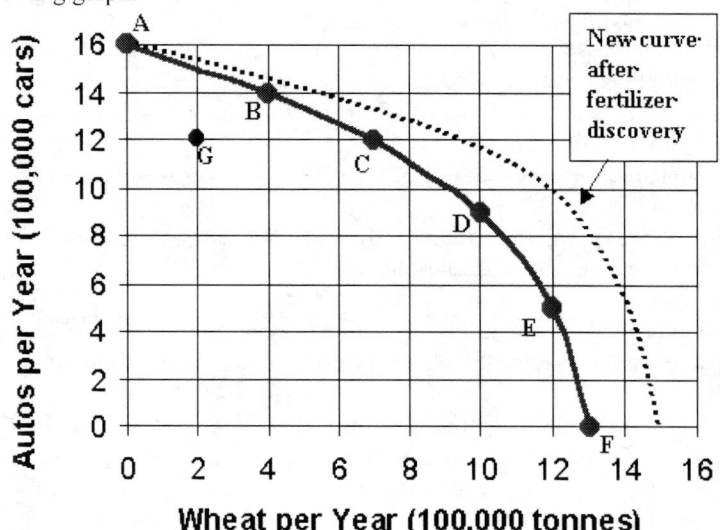

a. The move from C to D "costs" 300 000 autos—that is, the economy must give up 300 000 autos (1 200 000 – 900 000) to make such a move. The move from C to B "costs" 300 000 tonnes of wheat. Notice that in both cases there are gains (C to D involves 300 000 more tonnes of wheat and C to B means 200 000 more autos are produced), but we measure opportunity costs in terms of movements along a production possibilities curve and what has to be given up to make the choice reflected in the move.

b. See the preceding graph. Remember, the production possibilities curve shows all possible combinations of two goods that an economy can produce by the efficient use of all available resources in a specified period of time. Since point G is not on the production possibilities curve, the statement contained in this portion of the question does not contradict the definition of the curve. Point G is inside the curve, which implies available resources are not being used efficiently.

c. See the preceding graph.

d. It will lower the opportunity cost of additional wheat production.

2. a. Graph (a) shows constant relative costs because the PPC is linear.

b. Graph (b) shows increasing costs because the PPC is bowed outward.

c. Graph (b) is more realistic because it is likely that the production of radios and butter requires specialized resources.

3. a. vacations, automobiles for personal enjoyment, computer games, city swimming pools, dining at restaurants, visiting the local pub, watching videos etc.

b. new machinery, new equipment, new plant facilities, credit education, city convention centers, computer hardware and software used for business purposes ,etc.

c. **C**.

d. **D**; due to the fixed level of resources and technology related to the year 2006.

e. **B**.

f. **B**. If one wisely borrows for capital goods, the resulting economic growth should more than pay for the principal and interest related to the borrowed funds.

g. Lower consumption in the current year as illustrated when comparing combination **A** with **B**.

PROBLEMS

1.   a. $30 000   c. $20 000   e. C
       b. $30 000   d. $30 000   f. C

2. If you want to increase your future consumption (for retirement, say) then you will have to save more out of your current income. The principal and interest that accrue will permit you to purchase more goods in the future than you otherwise would have been able to. Note that by doing so you must forego some present consumption in order to increase your future consumption. In that sense, what is true for the nation is also true for an individual.

3.   a.   Mr. Hughes
     b.   Mrs. Hughes or Scotty
     c.   Scotty
     d.   The family (or perhaps Scotty) will hire someone to mow the lawn.
     e.   Mrs. Hughes may enter the labour force and the family may hire someone to do housework.

4.   a.   The incomes of football players will fall; incomes of figure skaters will rise. Thus a change in tastes (what) redistributes income from one group to another, and so for whom changes.

     b.   If wage rates rise relative to the price of capital and land, then producers will increase their demand for non-labour resources; non-labour resources will be substituted for labour. Income will be redistributed from some newly laid-off labourers to people who own property or are skillful at designing and producing capital. Thus a change in how leads to changes in for whom.

     c.   To the extent that people with low incomes have tastes different than people with high incomes, then "taxing the rich to give to the poor" will affect what is produced .

BUSINESS SECTION

     a.   A Bachelor of Commerce Degree is a capital good from an individual's view, to the extent that it increases the individual's future earning power.

     b.   A civic convention center would be considered to be a capital item from a city's viewpoint. One of the primary uses of this type of government resource is to generate revenues for the city in future years by bringing in visitors or convention delegates who will spend money on the city's hotels, restaurants, shops, and entertainment spots. Also, new business can be generated for firms in the cities who showcase their products and services through events like trade shows.

     c.   The exercise gym can be viewed as a capital item from the employer's view, to the extent it contributes towards a healthier, more productive employee who is rarely absent from work.

     d.   The seasons pass would more likely be a capital good for the insurance salesman to the extent that he meets potential clients on the golf course.

     e.   From a city's view, it would seem that a sports team would more likely enhance future revenues as opposed to a city hall. The sports team would bring in players and fans from outside the city. As a result, more money would be spent on the city's hotels, restaurants, shops, and entertainment spots.

APPENDIX B

THE PRODUCTION POSSIBILITIES CURVE AND COMPARATIVE ADVANTAGE

APPENDIX B PROBLEMS

1. Answer each of the following based on the before specialization and trade production possibilities for the nations of Cheer and Bleak for the two products crackers and cheese, as shown in the accompanying graphs. Before specialization and trade each nation is producing and consuming production combination C.

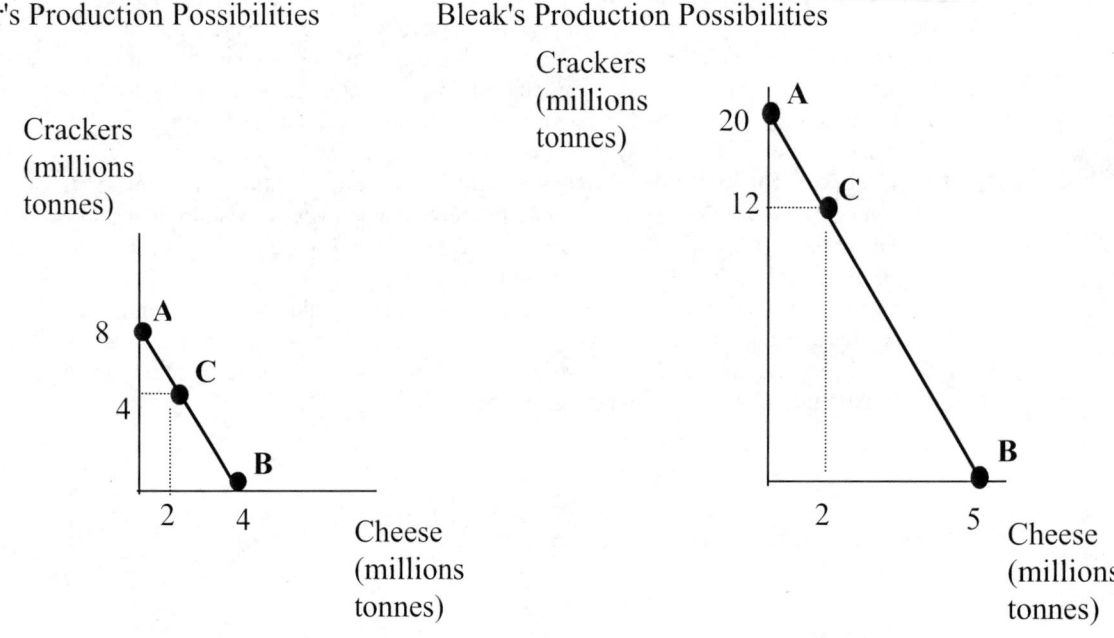

a. Which nation has the absolute advantage in the production of each product?

b.   Compute the opportunity cost of producing 1 cheese for each nation.

c.   Which nation has the comparative advantage in the production of each product?

d.   Before specialization each nation is producing combination C on their respective production possibilities curve. Assuming that each nation decides to specialize in their area of comparative advantage, compute the gains in total combined production for each product.

e.   In order for both nations to share the gains from specialization, the terms of trade for 1 cheese should be somewhere between ___ and ___ crackers.

ANSWERS TO APPENDIX B

APPENDIX B PROBLEMS

1.   a.   Bleak has the absolute advantage in both products.
     b.   Cheer's OC of one cheese is 2 crackers; Bleach's OC of one cheese is 4 crackers.
     c.   Cheer has the comparative advantage in cheese; Bleak has the comparative advantage in crackers.
     d.   Before specialization the combined production of cheese and crackers was 4 and 16, respectively. After specialization the combined production of cheese and crackers is 4 and 20, respectively. After specialization total combined production increases by 4 crackers (in millions of tonnes).
     e.   The terms of trade for 1 cheese should be somewhere between 2 and 4 crackers.

CHAPTER 3

DEMAND AND SUPPLY

PUTTING THIS CHAPTER INTO PERSPECTIVE

This chapter is one of the most important chapters in the text. To students who take the time to study it, the returns are exceptionally high. Chapter 3 analyzes the economist's most indispensable tools: demand and supply. Specifically, in this chapter you will study (a) demand and supply, (b) how demand and supply determine equilibrium (or market-clearing) price, (c) how periods of surpluses or shortages result if price is not at the equilibrium level, and (d) how the equilibrium level can change in response to changes in non-own price factors.

It is important that you master the material in this chapter, because you will be applying and reapplying these same tools and principles to many different situations. When presented with a problem, the economist will first try to express the problem in terms of the concepts of demand and supply and then proceed to economic analysis proper. It is with this thought in mind that an anonymous writer once noted: "You can make even a parrot into a learned economist—all it must learn are the two words *supply* and *demand*."

Mastering Chapter 3, however, will require some time. Many pitfalls to understanding economics can be avoided if you learn and understand the key definitions in this chapter. You must understand *exactly* what demand and supply mean; *exactly* what quantity demanded and quantity supplied mean; *exactly* what a change in demand and a change in supply mean; *exactly* what a surplus and a shortage mean. A universal confusion exists for students and others about the distinction between a change in demand (or supply) and a change in quantity demanded (or quantity supplied). Similarly, unless you know exactly what a shortage or a surplus is, you will be continually misinterpreting economic events.

LEARNING OBJECTIVES

After you have studied this chapter you should be able to:

3.1   Explain the law of demand.

3.2   Distinguish between a change in quantity demanded and a change in demand.

3.3 Explain the law of supply.

3.4 Distinguish between a change in quantity supplied and a change in supply.

3.5 Explain how the forces of demand and supply interact to determine equilibrium price and quantity.

3.6 Describe how changes in demand and supply can change equilibrium price and quantity.

CHAPTER OUTLINE

LO 3.1 - Explain the law of demand.
1. The **law of demand** states that at higher prices a lower quantity will be demanded than at lower prices, other things being equal.
    a. For simplicity, things other than the price of the good itself are held constant.
    b. Buyers switch their demand based on changes in **relative prices**, not **money prices**.

2. The demand schedule for a good is a set of pairs of numbers showing various possible prices and the quantity demanded at each price, for some time period.
    a. **Demand** must be conceived of as being measured in constant-quality units.
    b. A **demand curve** is a graphic representation of the demand schedule and it is negatively sloped, reflecting the law of demand.
    c. A **market demand** curve for a particular good or service is derived by summing all the individual demand curves for that product at each price.

LO 3.2 - Distinguish between a change in quantity demanded and a change in demand.
3. The determinants of demand include all factors (other than the good's own price) that influence the amount purchased.
    a. When deriving a demand curve, other determinants of demand are held constant. When such non-price determinants do change, the original demand curve shifts to the left (decrease in demand) or to the right (increase in demand).
    b. The major determinants of demand are consumers' income, tastes and preferences, changes in their expectations about future relative prices, the price of **substitutes** and **complements** for the good in question, population, and age composition of the population.
    c. A **normal good** is one in which consumer income is directly related to the demand for the good. An **inferior good** is one in which consumer income is inversely related to the demand for the good.
    d. If the price of Good B is directly related to the demand for Good A, then A and B are substitutes. If the price of Good B is inversely related to the demand for Good A, then A and B are complements.

e. A change in demand is a shift in the demand curve, whereas a change in quantity demanded is a movement along a given demand curve.

LO 3.3 - Explain the law of supply.

4. **Supply** is the relationship between price and the quantity supplied, other things being equal.
    a. The **law of supply** states that a direct or positive relationship between price and quantity supplied exists, other things being equal.
        i.   As the relative price of a good rises, producers have an incentive to produce more of it.
        ii. As a firm produces greater quantities in the short run, a firm often requires a higher relative price before it will increase output.
    b. A supply schedule is a set of numbers showing prices and the quantity supplied at those various prices.
    c. A **supply curve** is the graphic representation of the supply schedule; it is positively sloped.
    d. By summing individual supply curves for a particular good or service, at each price, we derive that good or service's market supply curve.

LO 3.4 - Distinguish between a change in quantity supplied and a change in supply.

5. The determinants of **supply** include all factors (other than the good's own price) that influence the amount that firms are willing to supply.
    a. When deriving a **supply curve**, other determinants of supply are held constant. When such non-price determinants do change, the original supply curve shifts to the left (decrease in supply) or to the right (increase in supply).
    b. The major determinants of supply are the prices of resources (inputs) used to produce the product, technology, taxes and subsidies, price expectations of producers, and the number of firms in an industry.
    c. A change in price, holding the determinants of supply constant, causes a movement along—but not a shift in—the supply curve.

LO 3.5 - Explain how the forces of demand and supply interact to determine equilibrium price and quantity.

6. By graphing demand and supply on the same coordinate system, **equilibrium** can be found at the intersection of the two curves.
    a. **Equilibrium** is a situation in which the plans of buyers and of sellers exactly coincide, so that there is neither excess quantity supplied or excess quantity demanded; at the **equilibrium price**, quantity supplied equals quantity demanded.
    b. At a price below the equilibrium price, quantity demanded exceeds quantity supplied, and excess demand, or a **shortage**, exists.
    c. At a price above the equilibrium price, quantity supplied exceeds quantity demanded, and an excess supply, or a **surplus**, exists.
    d. Seller competition forces price down, and eliminates a surplus.
    e. Buyer competition forces price up, and eliminates a shortage.

LO 3.6 - Describe how changes in demand and supply can change equilibrium price and quantity.

7. Changes in **demand** and/or **supply** lead to changes in the **equilibrium price** and the equilibrium quantity.

   a. If the demand curve shifts to the right (left), given supply, then the equilibrium price rises (falls) and the equilibrium quantity rises (falls).

   b. If the supply curve shifts to the right (left), given demand, then the equilibrium price falls (rises) and the equilibrium quantity rises (falls).

   c. When both supply and demand change, it is not always possible to predict the effects on the equilibrium price and the equilibrium quantity.

KEY TERMS AND CONCEPTS

Relative price	Market demand	Supply
Money Price	Normal goods	Supply curve
Law of demand	Inferior goods	Market clearing, or equilibrium price
Demand	Complements	Equilibrium
Demand curve	Substitutes	Surplus
Market	Law of supply	Shortage

COMPLETION QUESTIONS

Fill in the blank or circle the correct term.

(LO 3.1)

1. The law of demand is that, other things being equal, more is bought at a (lower, higher) price and less is bought at a _____ price.

2. A _____ relates various possible prices to the quantities demanded at each price.

3. There is a(n) (direct, inverse) relationship between price and quantity demanded, and demand curves will be (positively, negatively) sloped.

4. By convention, economists plot (price, quantity) on the vertical axis and (price, quantity) on the horizontal axis.

(LO 3.2)

5. A change in quantity demanded is a (movement along, shift in) the demand curve; and a change in demand is a _____ the demand curve.

6. When the other determinants of demand change, the entire demand curve shifts; the five major non-own-price determinants of demand are _____,

   _____, _____, _____,

   and _____.

7. Videocassettes and videocassette players are (substitutes, complements); if the price of videocassette players rises, then the demand for videocassettes will _____.

8. When the price of peaches rises, the demand for pears rises; peaches and pears are (substitutes, complements).

9. A rise in demand causes the demand curve to shift to the (left, right); an increase in quantity demanded occurs when there is a movement (up, down) the demand curve.

10. Without a used CD market, the quantity demanded for new CDs at a given price would be (smaller, larger).

(LO 3.3)

11. The law of supply relates prices to quantities supplied; in general, as price rises, quantity supplied (rises, falls). Therefore a(n) (direct, inverse) relationship exists, and the supply curve is (positively, negatively) sloped.

12. A _____ relates various prices to the quantities supplied at each price.

13. The supply curve is positively sloped because as price rises, producers have an incentive to produce (less, more).

(LO 3.4)

14. When the non-price determinants of supply change, the entire supply curve will shift; five major non-price determinants of supply are _____, _____, _____, _____, and _____.

(LO 3.5)

15. At the intersection of the supply and demand curves, the quantity supplied equals the quantity demanded, and at that price a(n) _____ exists; at a price above that intersection, quantity supplied exceeds quantity demanded and a(n) _____ exists; at a price below that intersection, quantity demanded exceeds quantity supplied, and a(n) _____ exists.

16. *Analogy*: An excess quantity supplied is to a surplus as a(n) _____ is to a shortage.

(LO 3.6)

17. If the demand for pizza rises, given the supply, then the equilibrium price of pizza will (rise, fall) and the equilibrium quantity will (rise, fall).

18. If demand shifts to the left, given supply, then the equilibrium price will (rise, fall) and the equilibrium quantity will (rise, fall).

19.   If supply shifts to the right, given demand, then the equilibrium price will (rise, fall) and the equilibrium quantity will (rise, fall).

20.   If both demand and supply shift to the right then the equilibrium price (will rise, will fall, is indeterminate) and the equilibrium quantity (will rise, will fall, is indeterminate).

21.   If, at the same time, there is an increase in demand and a decrease in supply, then the equilibrium price (will rise, will fall, is indeterminate), and the equilibrium quantity (will rise, will fall, is indeterminate).

TRUE-FALSE QUESTIONS

Circle the **T** if the statement is true, the **F** if it is false. Explain to yourself why a statement is false.

(LO 3.1)

T F   1.   Buyers are concerned with absolute, not relative prices.

T F   2.   A demand schedule relates quantity demanded to quantity supplied, other things being constant.

T F   3.   A graphical representation of a demand curve is called a demand schedule.

(LO 3.2)

T F   4.   A change in the quantity demanded of cigarettes results from a change in the price of cigarettes.

T F   5.   The existence of a used CD market increases the demand for new CDs.

T F   6.   If the price of tennis racquets rises, the demand for tennis balls will tend to rise also.

T F   7.   If the price of butter rises, the demand for margarine will rise.

(LO 3.3)

T F   8.   As producers increase output in the short run, the cost of additional units of output tends to rise.

(LO 3.4)

T F   9.   An increase in price leads to a leftward shift in demand and a rightward shift in supply.

(LO 3.5)

T F 10.   If price is below the equilibrium price, a shortage exists.

(LO 3.6)

T F 11. If supply shifts to the left, given demand, then the equilibrium price and the equilibrium quantity will rise.

T F 12. If demand shifts to the left, given supply, then the equilibrium price and the equilibrium quantity will fall.

T F 13. If both supply and demand shift to the right, then equilibrium price and equilibrium quantity are indeterminate

T F 14. If the supply of good A increases relative to its demand, then good A is now more scarce, and its relative price will rise.

T F 15. If the published price is constant, but it takes consumers longer to wait in lines, there is a shortage.

MULTIPLE CHOICE QUESTIONS

Circle the letter that corresponds to the best answer.

(LO 3.1)

1. A demand schedule
    a. relates price to quantity supplied.
    b. when graphed, is a demand curve.
    c. cannot change.
    d. shows a direct relationship between price and quantity demanded.

2. If the price of milk rises, other things being constant,
    a. there is a decrease in demand.
    b. buyers will substitute milk for other beverages.
    c. there is a decrease in quantity demanded.
    d. the demand for cola drinks will fall.

(LO 3.2)

3. Which of the following will not occur if the price of hamburger meat falls, other things being constant?
    a. The demand for hamburger buns will increase.
    b. People will substitute hamburgers for hot dogs.
    c. The demand for hot dogs will rise.
    d. The quantity of hamburgers demanded will increase.

4. If the price of Good A rises and the demand for Good B rises, then A and B are
    a. substitutes.
    b. complements.
    c. not related goods.
    d. not scarce goods.

5. If income falls and the demand for steak falls, then steak is a(n)
    a. substitute good.
    b. complement good.
    c. normal good.
    d. inferior good.

6. Which of the following probably will **NOT** lead to a fall in the demand for hamburgers?
    a. a decrease in income
    b. an expectation that the price of hamburgers will rise in the future
    c. a decrease in the price of hot dogs
    d. a change in tastes away from hamburgers

7. When a demand curve for Good A is derived,
    a. the price of A changes.
    b. the price Good B, a substitute, changes.
    c. money income changes.
    d. consumer tastes change.

(LO 3.3)
8. If the price of gasoline increases
    a. the quantity supplied of gasoline will decrease.
    b. the quantity supplied of gasoline will stay constant.
    c. the quantity supplied of gasoline will increase.
    d. the supply curve for gasoline will shift to the right.

(LO 3.4)
9. Which of the following will lead to an increase in supply?
    a. an increase in the price of the good in question
    b. a technological improvement in the production of the good in question
    c. an increase in the price of labour used to produce the good in question
    d. All of the above

(LO 3.5)
10. Several years ago some cities in North America passed a law that limited showers to 4 minutes, with a possible 30-day jail sentence for violators. Which of the following statements is probably true for those cities?
    a. A surplus of water existed.
    b. The price of water was too high.
    c. A shortage of water would exist regardless of how high its price got.
    d. The price of water was below the equilibrium price.

Consider the graph below when answering questions 11 and 12.

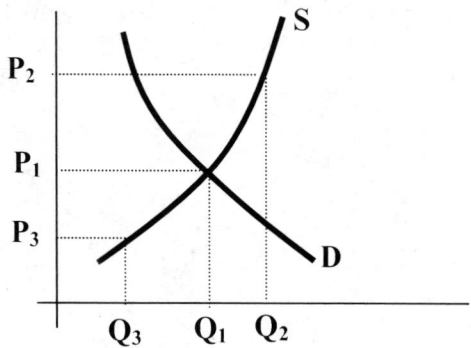

11. Given the figure above,
     a. the equilibrium price is P_1, the equilibrium quantity is P_2.
     b. the equilibrium quantity is P_1.
     c. the equilibrium price is P_3, the equilibrium quantity is Q_1.
     d. the equilibrium quantity is Q_1, the equilibrium price is P_1.

12. Which of the following is **not** true?
     a. A shortage exists at P_2.
     b. The equilibrium price is P_1.
     c. An excess quantity demanded exists at P_3.
     d. The market-clearing price is P_1.

13. If a surplus exists at some price, then
     a. sellers have an incentive to raise the price.
     b. buyers have an incentive to offer a higher price.
     c. sellers cannot sell all they wish to at that price.
     d. seller inventories are falling.

14. If a shortage exists at some price, then
     a. sellers can sell all they desire to sell at that price.
     b. sellers have an incentive to raise the price.
     c. buyers cannot get all they want at that price.
     d. All of the above.

(LO 3.6)
15. If the demand for hamburgers rises, with a given supply, then
     a. the supply of hamburgers will rise because price rises.
     b. the equilibrium price of hamburgers will fall and the equilibrium quantity will rise.
     c. the equilibrium quantity and the equilibrium price of hamburgers will rise.
     d. the quantity supplied of hamburgers will decrease.

16. If demand shifts to the right (given supply), then equilibrium
    a. price will rise.
    b. price is indeterminate.
    c. price and equilibrium quantity are indeterminate.
    d. price will fall.

17. If supply shifts to the right (given demand), then equilibrium
    a. quantity will increase.
    b. price will rise.
    c. price and equilibrium quantity will fall.
    d. price and equilibrium quantity rises.

18. If both supply and demand shift to the left, then equilibrium
    a. price is indeterminate and equilibrium quantity rises.
    b. price is indeterminate and equilibrium quantity falls.
    c. price falls and equilibrium quantity falls.
    d. price falls and equilibrium quantity is indeterminate.

19. If the demand for Good A falls relative to its supply, then
    a. Good A is now relatively more scarce.
    b. Good A is now relatively less scarce.
    c. the relative price of good A will rise.
    d. the actual price of good A will rise, even if A is not price flexible.

20. If the demand for Good B rises relative to it supply, then
    a. Good B is now relatively more scarce.
    b. the relative price of good B will rise.
    c. the actual price of good B will rise, even if good B is price inflexible.
    d. All of the above

21. If the demand for Good A rises relative to its supply, and markets are price-flexible, then
    a. no shortage of A can exist in the long run.
    b. no shortage of A can exist in the short run.
    c. the published price of A remains constant, but its actual price falls.
    d. the published price of A remains constant, but its actual price rises.

22. If the demand for Good A rises relative to its supply, and markets are price-inflexible, then
    a. a shortage can exist in the short run.
    b. a shortage can exist in the long run.
    c. the published price of A might remain constant, but its actual price rises.
    d. All of the above

23.   If the demand for economists falls relative to their supply, then
    a.   more college students will major in economics.
    b.   some economists will change professions.
    c.   a shortage of economists will result, in the long run.
    d.   All of the above

MATCHING

Choose the numbered item in Column (2) that best matches the term or concept in Column (1).

| (1) | (2) |

(LO 3.1)
a.   demand schedule
                                         1.   law of supply

(LO 3.2)
b.   bread and butter
      2.   relation between price, quantity demanded
c.   eyeglasses and contact lenses
      3.   population increases
d.   demand shifts to the left
      4.   raw-material prices rise

(LO 3.3)
e.   supply curve
      5.   income falls and normal good

(LO 3.4)
f.   supply shifts to the left
      6.   market-clearing price

(LO 3.5)
g.   equilibrium price
      7.   surplus
h.   excess quantity demanded
      8.   complements
i.   excess quantity supplied
      9.   substitutes

(LO 3.6)
j.   equilibrium price rises
     10.   shortage
     11.   increase in supply

WORKING WITH GRAPHS

(LO 3.2)
1.   Consider the two graphs below, in panels **(a)** and **(b)**.

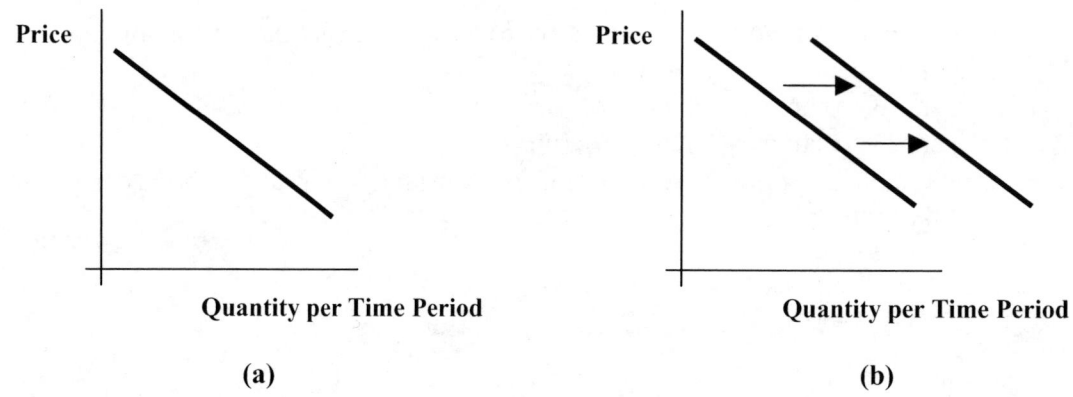

      (a)   (b)

Which panel shows an increase in quantity demanded? Which shows an increase in demand?

(LO 3.4)

2.   Distinguish between a decrease in supply and a decrease in quantity supplied, graphically, using the space below. Use two panels.

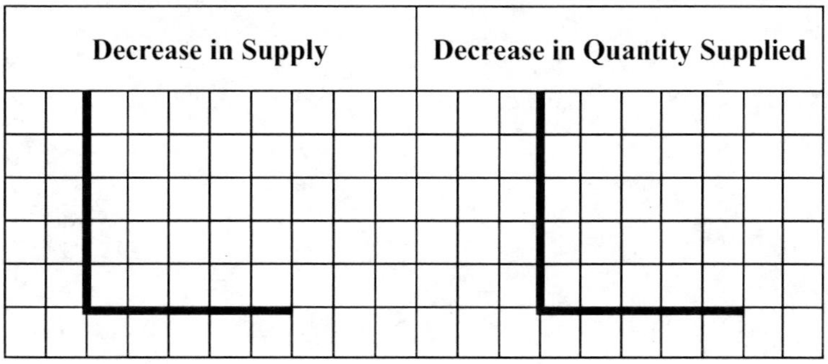

Decrease in Supply	Decrease in Quantity Supplied

(LO 3.1)

3.   Use the demand schedule below to plot the demand curve on the following coordinate grid. Be sure to label each axis correctly.

Price per Bottle of Shampoo	Quantity of Bottles Demanded per Week (thousands)
$6	8
$5	10
$4	12
$3	14
$2	16
$1	18

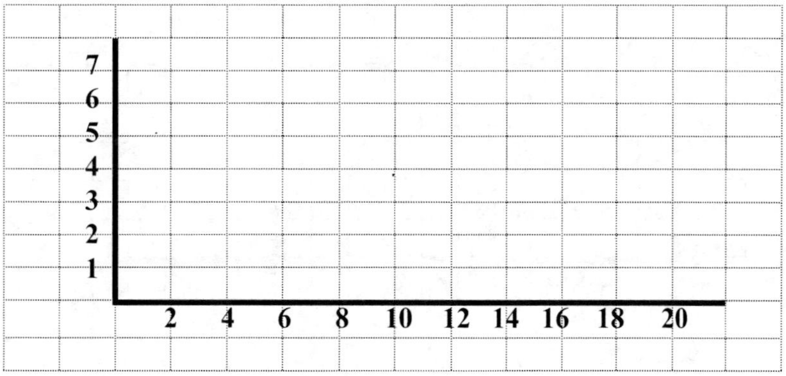

(LO 3.3)

4. Use the supply schedule below to plot the supply curve on the coordinate grid in problem 3.

Price per Bottle of Shampoo	Quantity of Bottles Supplied per Week (thousands)
$6	18
$5	15
$4	12
$3	9
$2	6
$1	3

(LO 3.5)

5. Using the graphs from problems 3 and 4, indicate on the graph the equilibrium price and the equilibrium quantity for bottles of shampoo. What is the equilibrium price? the equilibrium quantity?

6. Continuing with the previous example, assume that the government fixes the price at $3 per bottle of shampoo. What is the quantity demanded at that price? The quantity supplied? Does a surplus or a shortage exist at that price?

7. Consider the graphs below in panel **(a)**. Then show, in panel **(b)**, the new equilibrium price (label it P_1) and the new equilibrium quantity (label it Q_1) that results due to a change in tastes in favor of the good in question.

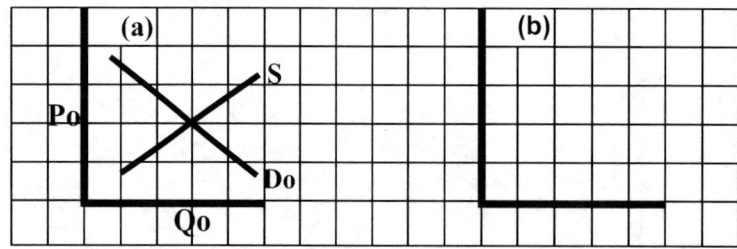

PROBLEMS

(LO 3.2)

1. List the non-price determinants of demand that will lead to a decrease in demand. Be specific.

(LO 3.4)

2. List the non-price (other) determinants of supply that will lead to an increase in supply. Be specific.

(LO 3.6)

3. Concerning apples, indicate whether each event leads to (i) a rightward shift in demand, (ii) a leftward shift in demand, (iii) an increase in quantity demanded, (iv) a decrease in quantity demanded, (v) a rightward shift in supply, (vi) a leftward shift in supply, (vii) an increase in quantity supplied, (viii) a decrease in quantity supplied.

    (Note: some events may lead to more than one of the above.)

    _____ a) An early frost in Ontario destroys some apple orchards.
    _____ b) Apple pickers organize a union which raises wage rates.
    _____ c) The price of apples rises.
    _____ d) The price of apples falls.
    _____ e) The Federal government lowers the price of apples below equilibrium and freezes the price at the lower level.
    _____ f) Apple growers leave the industry.
    _____ g) Pears (but not apples) are demonstrated to cause cancer in lab rats.
    _____ h) The government subsidizes apple growers at 3 cents per apple.
    _____ i) News is released that the government forecast is for a poor apple crop next year.
    _____ j) The price of pears rises (assume now that apple growers can also grow pears).

(LO 3.6)

4. For each of the statements (a) through (j) in the previous question, decide whether the market clearing *(equilibrium)* price for apples will rise, fall, or be unaffected.

    a) _____   f) _____
    b) _____   g) _____
    c) _____   h) _____
    d) _____   i) _____
    e) _____   j) _____

BUSINESS SECTION

(LO 3.2)
Marketing: Market Segmentation - The Aging Population

A typical first year text in economics tends to focus on a market at the product (or resource) level. However, in order to gain a better understanding of consumer demand, the marketing staff of a company will often segment (subdivide) a product market in order to identify a potentially profitable target market or market niche. In short, a market segment (target market) consists of a group of consumers who respond in a similar way to a given set of marketing efforts.

A very useful basis of market segmentation in the 1990s has been the age related demographic trends inherent in the Canadian population. David Foot, in his book "Boom, Bust & Echo", illustrates that during the current period (1991–2001) the age group between 15 and 34 years of age will experience zero to negative growth. The baby boom generation aged between 35 and 54 is now considered to be the consumers with the highest level of buying power. Within this group those between 45 and 54 are experiencing the fastest growth rates. As well, the population 65 years and over, the "grey population" is also experiencing significant positive growth rates.
Source: David Foot, *Boom, Bust & Echo*, , page 84 (Macfarlane Walter & Ross, 1996).

Business Application Problem

Contrast the effect that the aging population will have upon the demand for each of the following sets of items.

    a. Tennis vs. golf

    b. Diet Coke vs. Pepsi

    c. Urban condominiums vs. suburban homes

    d. Minivans vs. recreational vehicles

    e. Red meat vs. chicken

ANSWERS TO CHAPTER 3

COMPLETION QUESTIONS

1. lower; higher
2. demand curve or schedule
3. inverse; negatively
4. price; quantity
5. movement along; shift in
6. income, tastes and preferences, prices of related goods, expectations about future relative prices, population
7. complements; fall
8. substitutes
9. right; down
10. smaller
11. rises; direct; positively
12. supply curve or schedule
13. more
14. prices of inputs, technology, taxes, subsidies, price expectations, number of firms in industry
15. equilibrium; surplus; shortage
16. excess quantity demanded
17. rise; rise
18. fall, fall
19. fall, rise
20. indeterminate, will rise
21. rise, indeterminate

TRUE AND FALSE QUESTIONS

1. F   Buyers respond to changes in relative prices.
2. F   A demand schedule relates quantity demanded to price.
3. F   A graphical representation of a demand schedule is a demand curve.
4. T
5. F   As a substitute it decreases the demand for new CDs.
6. F   The demand for tennis balls will tend to fall, because they are complements.
7. T
8. T
9. F   An increase in price leads to a decrease in quantity demanded and an increase in quantity supplied – movement along the curves occurs.
10. T
11. F   The equilibrium quantity falls.
12. T
13. F   Equilibrium quantity rises.
14. F   Good A is now less scarce, and its relative price will fall.
15. T

MULTIPLE CHOICE QUESTIONS

1. b;   Graphing the quantity demanded against the product's own price displays a negatively sloped demand curve.
2. c;   If the price of milk rises, there will be a decrease in quantity demanded, not a decrease in demand, and a movement along the demand curve will occur.
   TIP: If the price of milk rises, this will result in a movement along the milk's demand curve, not a shift in the milk's demand curve.

3.c;   Since hamburgers and hot dogs are substitutes, the demand for hot dogs will fall, not increase.

4.a;   If A and B are substitutes, then when the price of A rises, consumers will buy less of A and more of B. As a result, this will cause the demand for B to increase or the demand curve for B to shift rightward.

5.c;   A normal good is one in which there is a direct relation between income and demand.

6.b;   If consumers expect the price of hamburgers to rise in the future, they are likely to increase their demand for hamburgers in the current period.

7.a;   When a demand curve is derived, all other non-own price factors are assumed to remain to stay the same.

8.c;   According to the law of supply, there is a direct relation between the price of gasoline and the quantity supplied of gasoline.

9.b;   A technological improvement in the production of a good will make the good more profitable to sell at each possible price. Graphically this implies a rightward shift in the supply curve or what we term an increase in supply.

TIP: An increase in quantity supplied is caused by a change in the product's own price; an increase in supply is caused by a change in non-own price factors.

10.d;   The price of water was below equilibrium, which resulted in a shortage situation. Instead of letting the price rise to its equilibrium level, the government reacted to the shortage by passing a law limiting showers to 4 minute episodes.

11.d;   Equilibrium occurs at the point at which the supply and demand curves meet.

12.a;   Since P2 is a price above the equilibrium price, there will be as surplus, not a shortage.

13.c;   If a surplus exists at some price, this means that the quantity demanded by consumers is less than the quantity supplied by sellers.

TIP: If a surplus occurs, sellers have an incentive to lower the price to eliminate the surplus.

14.d;   If a shortage exists at some price, then buyers cannot get all they want at that price. As a result, sellers have an incentive to raise the price as the sellers will be able to sell all that they desire to sell at the new price.

15.c;   If the demand for hamburgers rises, there will be a rightward shift in the demand curve for hamburgers. If the supply curve remains unchanged the equilibrium price and quantity for hamburgers will both increase. As price increases, the quantity supplied will rise but there will not be a rise in supply.

16.a;   If demand shifts right, this reflects an increase in demand. An increase in demand will eventually cause the equilibrium price to rise.

TIP: Sketch an original demand and supply curve. Then, draw a new demand curve to the right of the original demand curve. At the new intersection between demand and supply what has happened to price (on the vertical axis)?

17.a;   If supply shifts rightward, this reflects an increase in supply. This increase in supply will temporarily cause a surplus which, in turn, will cause the new equilibrium price to be lower. At the lower price consumers will be encouraged to purchase more and therefore the higher level of output will be maintained.

TIP: Sketch an original demand and supply curve. Then, draw a new supply curve to the right of the original supply curve. At the new intersection between demand and supply what has happened to quantity (on the horizontal axis)?

18.b;   TIP: One way to solve this is to analyze one shift at a time. A shift left in demand (decrease in demand) will cause the equilibrium price to fall and equilibrium quantity to fall. A shift left in supply (decrease in supply) will cause the equilibrium price to rise and equilibrium quantity to fall. From the results in the previous two sentences we can see that we can only predict that the quantity will fall.

19.b;   Since good A is now relatively less scarce, the equilibrium price will fall.

TIP:You can analyze this change by using a graph to sketch a decrease in demand (shift left in demand) while holding the supply curve constant. You will see that the new equilibrium price will be lower. The lower price implies that good A is now relatively less scarce.

20.d;   The equilibrium price will increase, as Good B is relatively more scarce.

TIP: You can analyze this change by using a graph to sketch an increase in demand (shift right in demand) while holding the supply curve constant.

21.a; If the demand for Good A rises there will be a shortage in the short run causing the price of Good A to rise. As the price rises, this will lead to an increase in quantity supplied which will eliminate the shortage in the long run.

22.d; If the price does not increase, in the short run, then the quantity supplied will not increase in the long run. The shortage will therefore remain in the long run.

23.b; TIP: You can analyze this change by simply assuming a decrease in demand with supply remaining constant. At the original wage (price) there will now be a surplus of economists. This will cause the equilibrium wage (price) to decline. As the wages of economists decline, the surplus will be eliminated by having some economists switch into other professions.

MATCHING

a and 2;   b and 8;   c and 9;   d and 5;   e and 1;   f and 4;   g and 6;   h and 10;   i and 7;   j and 3;

WORKING WITH GRAPHS

1. Panel (a); Panel (b)

2.

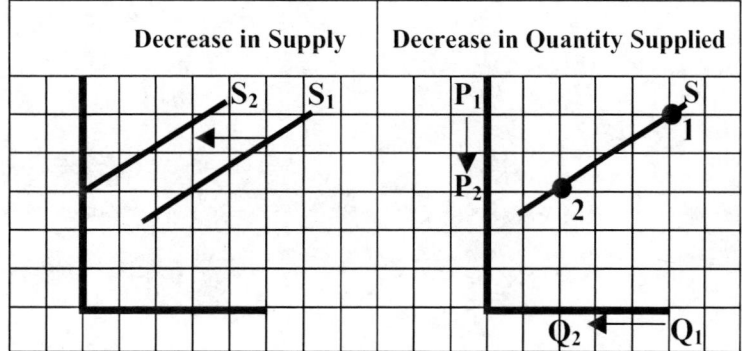

3. See graph below in 4.

4. See graph below.

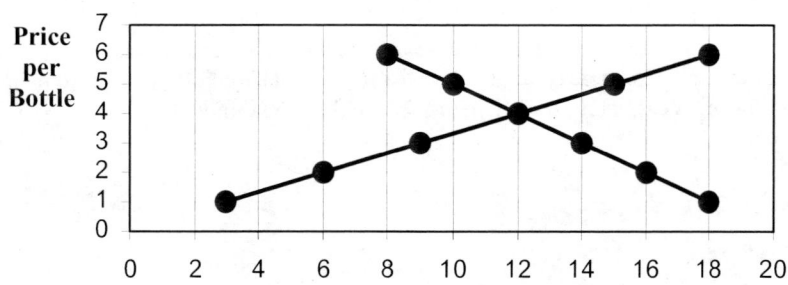

5. $4; 12 thousand bottles (see graph above)

6. 14 thousand bottles; 9 thousand bottles; shortage of 5 thousand bottles.

7.

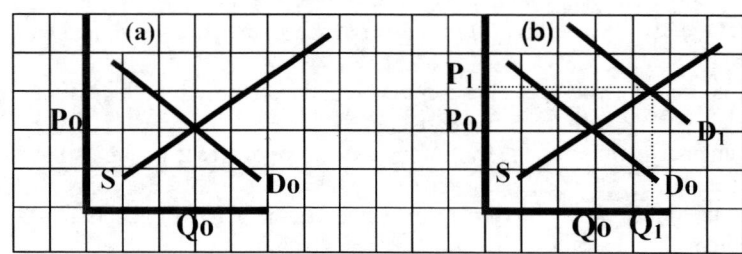

PROBLEMS

1.   Income falls for a normal good; change in tastes occurs away from the good; price of a substitute falls or price of a complement rises; expectations exist that the good's future relative price will fall; decrease in population occurs.

2.   Reduction in the price of inputs; decrease in a sales tax on the good or increase in the (per unit) subsidy of the good; expectation that the future relative price will fall; increase in the number of firms in the industry.

3.   a.   vi and iv   f.   vi and iv
      b.   vi and iv   g.   i and vii
      c.   iv and vii   h.   v and iii
      d.   iii and viii   i.   i
      e.   iii and viii   j.   i and vi

4.   a.   rise   f.   rise
      b.   rise   g.   rise
      c.   be unaffected   h.   fall
      d.   be unaffected   i.   rise
      e.   be unaffected   j.   rise

BUSINESS SECTION

   a.   Decrease in demand for tennis, increase in demand for golf (less strenuous).
   b.   Increase in demand for Diet Coke (healthier), decrease in demand for Pepsi (younger generation image).
   c.   Increase in demand for urban condominiums, decrease in demand for suburban homes.
   d.   Decrease in demand for minivans, increase in demand for recreational vehicles (for retirement).
   e.   Decrease in demand for red meat, increase in demand for chicken (healthier).

CHAPTER 4

INTRODUCTION TO MACROECONOMICS

PUTTING THIS CHAPTER INTO PERSPECTIVE

In your lifetime you will hear the words recession, depression, inflation, and unemployment hundreds of times. Chapter 4 is important because it introduces you to macroeconomics, which is the study of these big issues in the economic world. In fact, a proper understanding of the ideas and terms of macroeconomics is important to anyone who works in the business world, and for everyone who wants to understand and influence economic policies as a citizen.

This chapter is a survey of what you will be studying in the rest of the course, so you shouldn't expect to understand everything. Later chapters will give much more detail and depth to the issues discussed in this chapter. While you are studying this chapter (and after you finish your study of economics) keep in mind that in practice these oft-spoken words—economic growth, recession, depression, unemployment, inflation, fiscal policy, monetary policy and international trade—are difficult to conceptualise, to define, and to measure.

When thinking about these ideas, it's important for us to place these concepts in perspective. Over long periods, output in the Canadian economy has grown at an average annual rate of about 4%. As annual output rises, so do employment and living standards. Unfortunately national output does not grow smoothly; although the long-run trend is approximately 4% per year, in any given period *actual* growth is likely to be above or below that rate (called business fluctuations). When actual economic growth is falling (economic growth is negative) we are in a recession. Higher unemployment usually accompanies recession and slow (or negative) growth rates. When the actual national output growth rate is high, then the economy is in an expansion (or boom) phase. Unfortunately, during expansion phases inflation often is a side effect. To complicate things even further, deviations from the trend growth are irregular in timing, magnitude, and duration.

These business fluctuations can have a variety of sources, some of which are controllable (like war or government policies), and some which are not (such as natural disasters). For Canadians, one of the most important sources of both growth and business fluctuations comes from international trade and our close relationship with the United States.

Because we must spend much of our time modelling and simplifying the real world in economics, there is a lot of room for discussion about how the models ought to be built, which assumptions are correct, and what ought to be done. On top of all that, it is also clear that the behaviour of people changes over time. We don't necessarily react the same way to a depression as our parents or grandparents did. Looking back to our previous history may not always inform us about what to do today!

However, it does not need to be overwhelming. We will spend time looking at the basic issues of our economy, and how to apply them to your everyday life and so we hope to make this as enjoyable as possible.

LEARNING OBJECTIVES

After you have studied this chapter you should be able to:

4.1   Explain why the study of macroeconomics is important.

4.2   Describe economic growth and business fluctuations and explain their effects.

4.3   Calculate the rate of unemployment and discuss the three kinds of unemployment.

4.4   Explain how inflation is measured and describe the effects of inflation and deflation.

4.5   Explain why trade is an important issue for Canadians.

4.6   Name the basic economic policies available to government.

CHAPTER OUTLINE

LO 4.1 - Explain why the study of macroeconomics is important.
1.   **Macroeconomics** is the study of the "big picture" economic issues.
   a.   Economics depends on the measurement of relevant variables.
   b.   Models are used to understand and predict economic events.

LO 4.2 - Describe economic growth and business fluctuations and explain their effects.
2.   **Economic growth** is the increase in the value of goods and services produced in an economy, usually measured by **Gross Domestic Product (GDP)**, which is defined as the value of goods and services produced in a year.
   a.   Canada has experienced high and sustained rates of economic growth since Confederation.
   b.   Economic growth usually increases the standard of living for a country, allowing people to have more goods and services, and increases life expectancy and education.

3. The ups and downs in economic activity are called **business fluctuations**.
    a. Business fluctuations are also called (together) a **business cycle**. The phases of the business cycle are **peak, contraction**, **trough** and **expansion**.
    b. **Inflation** (an increase in the average price level) tends to be higher during an expansion phase, and unemployment rates are lower.
    c. During a contraction phase **unemployment** rates are higher and the inflation rate is typically lower. A severe contraction is called **a depression**.
    d. A contraction in GDP means a loss of billions of dollars of GDP. It also means personal hardship for those who are unemployed.

LO 4.3 - Calculate the rate of unemployment and discuss the three kinds of unemployment.

4. When unemployment exists, the economy is inefficient and produces less goods and services than it otherwise could, and results in personal hardship for the individuals affected.
    a. Unemployment is a **stock** variable, while other variables are **flow** variables (measured over a period of time).
    b. When calculating the unemployment rate, the population is first broken down into the **working age population** which is the number of people 15 years of age and older.
    c. People move between 3 different groups within the working age population. These groups are the **employed**, the **unemployed**, and those "**not in the Labour force**."
    d. The **unemployment rate** is the percentage of the measured **labour force** (defined as the number of employed and unemployed) that is unemployed.
    e. The unemployment rate varies directly with the average duration of unemployment, other things being constant.
    f. Because of the **discouraged worker** phenomenon, the official unemployment rate understates true unemployment.
    g. **Labour force participation rates** show how the composition of the **labour force** changes over time.

5. Unemployment has been categorized into three types: frictional, cyclical, and structural.
    a. **Frictional unemployment** exists when people are between steady jobs.
    b. **Structural unemployment** results when resources are reallocated so that individuals with specific skills cannot find jobs for long periods. **Seasonal unemployment** results from differences in the demand for labour over the seasons of the year and is a form of structural unemployment.
    c. **Cyclical unemployment** is due to **recessions** and **depressions.**

6. Employment for all workers at all times is impossible to attain because of frictional unemployment.

    a. **Full employment** is said to prevail when only frictional and structural unemployment exists.

    b. The **natural rate of unemployment** is the sum of structural and frictional unemployment.

LO 4.4 - Explain how inflation is measured and describe the effects of inflation and deflation.

7. **Inflation** is an upward movement in the average of all prices, and is **flow** measure. An extremely rapid rise in prices is called **hyperinflation**. When average prices fall, this is called **deflation**.

8. The value of money is reflected in its **purchasing power** which is the amount of goods and services it can buy. Measures of inflation include the **consumer price index (CPI)**, the **producer price index (PPI)**, and the **GDP deflator**.

    a. **Nominal values** refer to values of something at the current value or in today's dollars. **Real values** are those that have been corrected for changes in prices.

    b. Inflation is measured by computing a price index, which measures costs of a basket of goods and services in any given year as compared to the cost of a basket of goods and services in a base year.

    c. The **consumer price index** measures the cost of an unchanging representative basket of *consumer* goods through time.

    d. **Producer price indices** measure the cost of an unchanging basket of goods sold in primary markets by producers of *commodities* in all stages of processing.

    e. The **GDP deflator** measures the value of *all goods and services* produced by an economy; the "basket" changes over time. It is measured as the implicit price level change that occurs when nominal GDP is divided by real GDP.

9. The effects of inflation are measured by how your **real income** is affected. Real incomes are reduced when incomes rise more slowly than inflation.

    a. If inflation is fully **anticipated**, ill effects are slight as people adjust their income for the effects of inflation. Most of the problems of inflation are accounted for by **unanticipated inflation**

    b. Cost-of-living adjustments (COLAs) are clauses in wage contracts, which automatically adjust wages when prices increase.

    c. The **nominal interest rate** is (approximately) equal to the sum of the **real interest rate** and the **anticipated inflation rate**.

    d If inflation is higher than unanticipated, creditors are worse off because the real value of their monetary assets falls; debtors are better off because the real value of their monetary debts falls.

10. Besides the effects of unanticipated inflation, there are other costs to inflation.

    a. The resources used to protect against inflation and to pay for the **repricing (menu cost)** are a cost of inflation.

    b. The tax system is based on nominal income, so inflation may effectively increase tax rates, particularly on interest income.

    c. Uncertainty that inflation creates may also divert resources from other uses.

LO 4.5 - Explain why trade is an important issue for Canadians.

12. Most industrialized nations engage in extensive trading and investment relationships. Such economies are called **open economies**.
    a. Trade accounts for 40 percent of Canada's GDP of which about 85% is with the United States.
    b. When exports exceed imports, this is called a **trade surplus**.
    c. The **exchange rate** is the amount of money that can be purchased with one unit of foreign currency.

LO 4.6 - Name the basic economic policies available to government.

13. Governments engage in a variety of policies to encourage growth and to stabilize economic fluctuations.
    a. Most western countries are **mixed economies**, where the mix of goods and services produced is determined partially by the market, and partially by government spending.
    b. Governments also engage in stabilization policies. The two main ones are **fiscal policy** (government spending and taxation) and **monetary policy** (determination of short-term interest rates and the growth of the money supply).
    c. **Trade policies** are also important in determining economic output. These include tariffs, quotas and exchange rate policies.

KEY TERMS AND CONCEPTS

Unemployment	Discouraged workers	Anticipated inflation
GDP deflator	Inflation	Unanticipated inflation
Labour force	Deflation	Nominal rate of interest
Stock	Purchasing power	Real rate of interest
Flow	Recession	Cost-of-living
Frictional unemployment	Depression	adjustment
Seasonal unemployment	Hyperinflation	Real income
Structural unemployment	Price index	Repricing, or menu,
Cyclical unemployment	Business fluctuations	cost of inflation
Full employment	Base year	Contraction
Natural rate of	Labour force	Expansion
unemployment	participation rate	
Producer price index	Consumer price index	Mixed Economy
Macroeconomics	Economic Growth	Monetary policy
Open Economy	Fiscal policy	
Trade policy	Tariff	Exchange rate

COMPLETION QUESTIONS
Fill in the blank or circle the correct term.

(LO 4.1)

1. Economists study economics by looking backwards and _____ economic variables. Economists look forward by creating _____.

2. Macroeconomics is the study of _____ issues, such as _____, _____, and _____.

(LO 4.2)

3. When measuring economic growth the fundamental economic measure is _____.

4. Sustained economic growth usually enhances the _____ of the population.

5. The ups and downs in overall economic activity are called _____, and sometimes called the _____.

6. The phases of the business cycle are called _____, _____, _____, and _____.

7. An expansion phase may be accompanied by _____. A contractionary phase is usually accompanied by _____.

(LO 4.3)

8. The unemployment rate is calculated by dividing the number of unemployed by the sum of the (a) employed plus the (b) (unemployed, workers not in the labour force).

9. A _____ is measured per unit of time, while _____ is measured at a given moment in time.

10. Homemakers are officially considered as (unemployed, employed, not in the labour force).

11. The natural rate of unemployment is the sum of _____ unemployment and _____ unemployment.

12. Discouraged workers currently are not looking, but have looked, for a job, and they are counted officially as (employed, unemployed, not in the labour force); because of this official classification, some people believe that the measured unemployment rate (overstates, understates) true unemployment.

13. The percentage of working-age individuals who are in the labour force is called the _____.

14. Unemployment has been categorized into three basic types: _____, _____, and _____.

15. Because transactions costs exist within job markets, some frictional unemployment is (avoidable, unavoidable).

16. _____ unemployment varies with the business cycle.

17. There is consensus among economists that the current natural unemployment rate for the Canadian economy is consistent with about _____ percent actual unemployment.

(LO 4.4)

18. When inflation is higher than increases in nominal income, we say that _____ has fallen.

19. Inflation is measured in Canada using the _____.

20. The CPI and PPIs measure the cost of a(n) (unchanging, changing) basket of products through time, whereas the GDP deflator measures a(n) (changing, unchanging) basket of products.

21.   To the extent that price indexes do not adjust for quality improvements, they (overstate, understate) the true rate of inflation.

22.   Many of the problems associated with inflation have occurred because the inflation rate was _____.

23.   When the inflation rate is extremely high it is referred to as _____; when the average price level falls this phenomenon is referred to as _____.

24.   The nominal interest rate equals the real interest rate (plus, minus) the anticipated inflation rate.

25.   When inflation is unexpectedly high, (debtors, creditors) benefit at the expense of (debtors, creditors).

26.   When unanticipated deflation occurs, debtors are economically (worse, better) off.

27.   A dollar's _____ is the amount of goods and services that it can buy.

(LO 4.5)
28.   International trade is governed in Canada by two major agreements: _____ and _____.

29.   A(n) _____ economy is one that trades with other countries. A(n) _____ economy is one that isolates itself from other countries.

30.   The country Canada trades most with is _____.

31.   When a country imports less than it exports, this is called a trade _____.

(LO 4.6)
32.   By altering short-term interest rates the government is exercising _____ policy.

33.   A _____ exchange rate is a government policy, which lets supply and demand determine the value of a currency.

34.   When an economy has both markets and some government intervention it is called a _____.

35.   When the government exercises its spending and taxation powers it is called _____ policy.

TRUE-FALSE QUESTIONS

Circle the **T** if the statement is true, the **F** if it is false. Explain to yourself why a statement is false.

(LO 4.1)

T   F   1.   Models are used only in economics.

T   F   2.   Models are used only to study the past. They are useless in looking at the future.

(LO 4.2)

T   F   3.   The unemployment rate rises in the contraction phase of a business cycle.

T   F   4.   Business fluctuations tend to be relatively constant in timing, magnitude, and duration, at least in Canada.

T   F   5.   Economic growth has little effect on our lives and standard of living.

T   F   6.   Business fluctuations occur with a regular pattern, so they can be easily anticipated.

T   F   7.   Business cycle phases are called (in order) contraction, trough, expansion and peak.

T   F   8.   Canada has experienced a long-term trend of rising output, without any significant business fluctuations.

T   F   9.   The expansion phase is usually accompanied by rising unemployment.

T   F   10.   A recession usually is accompanied by inflation.

T   F   11.   Canada produces about twice as much as it did in 1870.

(LO 4.3)

T   F   12.   Income is a flow, inflation is a flow, and the number unemployed is a stock.

T   F   13.   Homemakers and students are officially counted as part of the labour force.

T   F   14.   If the average duration of unemployment rises, other things being constant, the unemployment rate will fall.

T   F   15.   People not working who have looked for a job six months ago but are not looking now are counted as discouraged workers, and therefore are officially unemployed.

T   F   16.   Because of transaction costs in the labour market, there will always be some frictional unemployment.

T   F   17.   The opportunity costs due to unemployment, in terms of foregone national output, are usually trivial.

T   F   18.   Frictional unemployment can be reduced to zero.

T   F   19.   Cyclical unemployment is related to the seasons of the year.

T   F   20.   The natural rate of unemployment is the sum of frictional unemployment and structural unemployment.

T   F   21.   Full employment is reached when cyclical unemployment is zero.

T   F   22.   Structural unemployment varies with the business cycle.

(LO 4.4)

T   F   23.   As inflation occurs, the purchasing power of a unit of money falls.

T   F   24.   Anticipated inflation causes fewer economic problems than unanticipated inflation.

T   F   25.   During periods of correctly anticipated inflation, debtors gain at the expense of creditors.

T   F   26.   Real interest rates are those that the banks charge for borrowing.

T   F   27.   The CPI measures the cost of an unchanging basket of goods and services.

(LO 4.5)

T   F   28.   An open economy is one where foreigners can trade and invest easily.

T   F   29.   A trade surplus occurs when a country exports more than it imports.

T   F   30.   An exchange rate is the price you pay for one unit of foreign currency.

(LO 4.6)

T   F   31.   Significant government intervention policies include fiscal, monetary, trade and exchange rate policies.

T   F   32.   A tariff is a tax charged on imported goods.

MULTIPLE CHOICE QUESTIONS

Circle the letter that corresponds to the best answer.

(LO 4.1)

1. Which of the following is NOT a reason why models are used in macroeconomics?
   a. We want to look at the relationship between variables.
   b. They are based on past behaviour.
   c. Models are used to take corrective action before problems happen.
   d. Models are easy to make.

(LO 4.2)

2. Canada's economic growth is usually measured by
   a. the rate of unemployment.
   b. the increase in trade.
   c. the increase in real GDP.
   d. the rate of inflation.

3. Real GDP is defined as
   a. the value of all physical goods produced in an economy in a year.
   b. the value of all goods and services, less net exports, produced in an economy in a year.
   c. the value of all goods and services produced if the economy were operating at full employment.
   d. the value of all goods and services produced in an economy in a year.

4. Canada's output has increase approximately how many times since Confederation?
   a. 2 times.
   b. 10 times.
   c. 150 times.
   d. 1000 times.

5. If we look back at several business fluctuations we could conclude that they are
   a. non-periodic recurrent fluctuations in overall economic activities.
   b. of similar duration.
   c. of similar magnitude.
   d. All of the above.

6. The business cycle is usually described with the following phases (in order)
   a. expansion, peak, contraction, trough.
   b. expansion, peak, trough, contraction.
   c. expansion, trough, contraction, peak.
   d. expansion, duration, trough, expansion.

7.   When we relate business fluctuations to inflation and increasing unemployment, we note that
    a.   inflation is associated with a trough, and unemployment with a peak.
    b.   unemployment is associated with a trough and inflation with an expansion.
    c.   there is no relationship between unemployment, inflation and the business cycle.
    d.   unemployment is associated with recession and inflation with a peak.

(LO 4.3)
8.   The Canadian labour force includes
    a.   the unemployed.
    b.   "stay at home" parents.
    c.   children.
    d.   none of the above

9.   Which of the following statements is a stock concept?
    a.   The number of unemployed.
    b.   National income.
    c.   The number of job losers.
    d.   The number of job finders.

10.   Which of the following is a flow concept?
    a.   Monthly income.
    b.   Inflation rate.
    c.   Annual consumption.
    d.   All of the above.

11.   Which of the following persons is officially unemployed?
    a.   a housewife.
    b.   a student.
    c.   a resident in an institution.
    d.   a non-working individual who has looked for a job within the past week.

12.   If homemakers were counted in the labour force and considered employed, then
    a.   the female participation rate would rise.
    b.   the overall official unemployment rate would fall.
    c.   overall official employment would rise.
    d.   All of the above

13.   If the average duration of unemployment rises, other things being constant,
    a.   the participation rate will rise.
    b.   the unemployment rate will rise.
    c.   total employment must fall.
    d.   total unemployment must fall.

14.   Which of the following persons is not like the others?
   a.   discouraged worker
   b.   seeking work within the past four weeks
   c.   laid off from a job within the past 26 weeks and awaiting recall
   d.   waiting to start a new job within the next four weeks

15.   Discouraged workers are officially
   a.   unemployed.
   b.   employed.
   c.   not in the labour force.
   d.   in the labour force.

16.   Which of the following statements is false?
   a.   It is possible for the total number of employed and the total number of unemployed to rise in the same period.
   b.   It is possible for the total number of employed to rise and the unemployment rate to rise in the same period.
   c.   If the average duration of unemployment falls, other things being constant, the unemployment rate will fall.
   d.   The definitions of employment, unemployment, and labour force are not subject to disagreement among economists.

17.   Which of the following is least like the others?
   a.   frictional unemployment.
   b.   seasonal unemployment.
   c.   discouraged worker unemployment.
   d.   cyclical unemployment.

18.   "Full" employment is considered to occur if
   a.   every man, woman, and child is working.
   b.   everyone age 15 and over is working.
   c.   only frictional and structural unemployment exist in the economy
   d.   the unemployment rate is 12%.

19.   The teenage unemployment rate is usually high because
   a.   many are new entrants in the labour force.
   b.   teenagers have a shorter duration of unemployment than adults.
   c.   teenagers stay on a given job longer than adults.
   d.   All of the above

20.   When did Canada's unemployment rate reach a peak of close to twenty percent?
   a.   1921
   b.   1933
   c.   1945
   d.   1974.

21. Which of the following types of unemployment is created by a mismatch of employer's needs and employee skills?
     a. frictional unemployment.
     b. structural unemployment.
     c. cyclical unemployment.
     d. All of the above.

22. The natural rate of unemployment is the sum of
     a. structural and cyclical unemployment.
     b. structural and frictional unemployment.
     c. frictional and cyclical unemployment.
     d. structural, frictional and cyclical unemployment.

(LO 4.4)
23. Price indices
     a. are a way to link unemployment to the price level.
     b. measure the rate of inflation for a specified group of products.
     c. measures the value of GDP.
     d. measures the rate of change of income.

24. The consumer price index
     a. measures the cost of an unchanging basket of goods and services.
     b. does not take into account relative price changes, and therefore is biased.
     c. does not completely account for quality changes, and therefore is biased.
     d. All of the above.

25. If the inflation rate is correctly anticipated,
     a. net creditors will be hurt.
     b. inflation may not be a major problem.
     c. net debtors will be hurt.
     d. people will hold more cash than they want to hold.

26. Unanticipated deflation
     a. hurts net debtors.
     b. causes no economic problems.
     c. hurts people who hold cash.
     d. hurts fixed income groups.

27. Which of the following statements is true?
    a. If there is zero anticipated inflation, the nominal interest rate equals the real interest rate.
    b. The real interest rate equals the nominal interest rate plus the anticipated inflation rate.
    c. The real interest rate equals the nominal interest rate divided by the anticipated inflation rate.
    d. Borrowers will not permit lenders to raise the nominal interest rate if all expect that the inflation rate will rise.

28. Which of the following groups is most hurt by unanticipated inflation?
    a. workers with cost of living adjustment clauses in their labour contracts
    b. Social Security recipients whose benefits are indexed to inflation
    c. workers who sign new work agreements every day
    d. wealthy people who hold much cash in their wall safes

(LO 4.5)
29. The majority of Canadian trade is with
    a. the United Kingdom
    b. the United States
    c. Japan
    d. the European Community.

(LO 4.6)
30. Canada's economy can be best described as a
    a. command economy.
    b. pure capitalist economy.
    c. mixed economy.
    d. integrated economy.

31. The use of government spending and tax policies to influence the economy is described as
    a. fiscal policy.
    b. monetary policy.
    c. exchange rate policy.
    d. trade policy.

32. The control by government over short-term interest rates and the amount of money in circulation is described as
    a. fiscal policy.
    b. monetary policy.
    c. exchange rate policy.
    d. trade policy.

33. The regulation and taxation of the flow of goods and services over the borders is best described as
    a. fiscal policy.
    b. monetary policy.
    c. exchange rate policy.
    d. trade policy.

34. The intervention of the government into the market for Canadian currency is called
    a. fiscal policy.
    b. monetary policy.
    c. exchange rate policy.
    d. trade policy.

MATCHING

Choose the item in Column (2) that best matches an item in Column (1).

(1)   (2)

(LO 4.2)
a. economic growth   1. government spending and
b. business fluctuation   taxes
c. recession   2. tax on imports
(LO 4.3)   3. increasing real GDP
d. labour force   4. falling purchasing power of money
e. structural unemployment   5. mis-match of skills and jobs
f. working-age population   6. nominal rate of interest
(LO 4.4)   7. cyclical unemployment
g. price index   8. expansion
h. inflation   9. people 15 years of age and older
i. tariff   10.GDP deflator
j. fiscal policy   11. actively seeking work
                                12. unemployed plus employed

PROBLEMS

(LO 4.2)
1. Suppose that you looked back at the data for the past 14 years and saw the following data (see next page):

Year	Unemployment Rate	Inflation Rate	GDP Growth
1	8.8	4.1	4.25%
2	7.8	4.4	4.97%
3	7.5	4.0	2.62%
4	8.1	5.0	0.19%
5	10.3	4.8	-2.09%
6	11.2	3.6	0.87%
7	11.4	1.5	2.34%
8	10.4	1.8	4.80%
9	9.4	0.2	2.81%
10	9.6	2.2	1.62%
11	9.1	1.6	4.22%
12	8.3	1.6	4.10%
13	7.6	0.9	5.53%
14	6.8	1.7	5.26%

a. In which years was the economy in a recession?
b. In which years was the economy in a trough?
c. In which years was the economy in an expansion phase?
d. In which years was the economy in a peak?
e. What was the overall growth in the economy during this period? (Ignore the effect of compounding).
f. Suppose you found a $20 bill that had been tucked into a book for this entire period. How much purchasing power would you have lost? (Ignore the effect of compounding inflation).

2. We learned in this chapter that there were costs associated with unemployment. Do you think that they are more severe costs associated with frictional or structural unemployment?

(LO 4.3)

3. Assume that the labour force data for September 2001 is as follows (in millions)

Adult population (at least 15 years)	19.3190
Labour force	13.1168
Employed	11.9754

a. Calculate the number of people (15 years old and over) not in the labour force.

b. Calculate the number of unemployed individuals.

c.   Calculate the unemployment rate.

d.   Calculate the participation rate.

4.   Suppose that an economic slump occurs and that (a) many minorities stop looking for jobs because they know that the probability of finding a job is low, and (b) many people who are laid off start doing such work at home as growing food, painting, repairing their houses and autos, and so on. Which of these events implies that the official unemployment rate overstates unemployment, and which implies the opposite?

5.   From the list below, classify each of the unemployed individuals as representing one of (F) frictional, (S) structural, or (C) cyclical unemployment.

_____ a)   James Engine is an auto worker from Oshawa who has been laid off because of the recent sharp decline in GDP, which has resulted in a severe decrease in auto sales.

_____ b)   Digs McDuff, from northeast B.C., finds he can no longer get work in the coal mines because of new automated mining techniques.

_____ c)   Priscilla Primm is unable to locate work after finishing her high school education and entering the labour force.

_____ d)   Leroy Walker, a letter carrier, finds himself unemployed because of the increased trend to send mail using electronic means such as email and the internet.

_____ e)   Oscar Hammerhead, a skilled carpenter, has found himself out of work because of the housing slump brought on by high interest rates and the recession.

_____ f)   Alice Weatherby quits her job as a salesperson out of frustration stemming from her lack of promotion. She begins to look for a management position in a similar work setting.

_____ g)   Patricia Matren re-enters the labour force after having a child. Being a computer programmer she expects to find work within the next few weeks.

_____ h)   Flaps Peterson, an airline pilot, suddenly finds himself laid off because of the dramatic decline in the demand for air transportation caused by the recent recession.

(LO 4.4)

6.   Suppose we define our relevant "market basket" of goods as containing the following:

10 apples   4 pounds of bananas   7 oranges   2 pineapples

Suppose we also have the following price information for the years 2001 and 2007:

Fruit	2001	2007
Apples	.10 each	.18 each
Oranges	.15 each	.23 each
Bananas	.25 per lb.	.20 per lb.
Pineapples	.50 each	.65 each

What is the 2007 FPI (fruit price index) using 2001 as the base year? What does this index tell us?

7.   In Canada, the Consumer Price Index increased from a level of 75.5 to 83.7 during the period 1981 – 1982. During this same period, suppose Jorgan Maples, a Canadian, received a nominal wage increase of 7%:

a.   Calculate the 1982 Canadian inflation rate.

b.   Calculate Jorgan's percentage change in real income for the 1981 – 1982 period.

8.   Consider the following table for an economy that produces only four goods:

Goods & Services	1997 Price	1997 Quantity	2006 Price	2006 Quantity
Pizza	$ 4	10	$ 8	12
Cola	12	20	36	15
T-shirts	6	5	10	15
Business equipment	25	10	30	12

Assuming a 1997 base year:

a. What is nominal GDP for 1997? For 2006?

b. What is real GDP for 1997? For 2006?

c. What is the implicit GDP price deflator for 1997? For 2006?

d. What is the CPI for 1997? For 2006?

e. Based on the CPI, what is the rate of inflation during the period 1997 – 2006?

BUSINESS SECTION

(LO 4.4)
Finance: The Rule of 70

When a measure grows at an annual percentage rate (compound rate) over a period of years, the time required for the measure to double in size is approximated by the *Rule of 70 as follows:*

$$\text{Doubling Time in Years} = \frac{70}{\text{Annual Percentage Growth Rate}}$$

In periods of rapid inflation consumers, wage earners, pensioners, and investors, often use the Rule of 70 to quickly appreciate the impact that unanticipated inflation can have on ones real purchasing power.

Sample Problem

As an example, in the summer of 1998, Indonesia's inflation rate was 40% per year.
(Source: Emerging Asia Chart Room. Dr. Yardeni's Economic Network. 4 September 1998. Online. Internet. 24 September 1998. Available http://www.yardeni.com/public/asiacpc.pdf)

If this inflation rate continues, how long, in years, will it take for prices to double in the Indonesian economy?

Answer:

Doubling Time = 70/40 = 1.75 years. Therefore every two years the bundle of goods one is used to buying will double in price! In other words, without anticipating this inflation, ones real purchasing power would be cut in half every two years.

Application Problem 1

1. a. Canada experienced high annual inflation rates over a ten year period beginning in 1973. Given that the CPI in 1972 was 36 and the CPI in 1973 was 39.9, calculate the 1973 inflation rate in Canada. Keep your work to two decimals.

   b. Assuming that the 1973 inflation rate, calculated in part a., persisted for the next 10 years, how long did it typically take for the cost of living to double?

   c. A life insurance salesperson sells a $100 000 life insurance policy to a Canadian client in 1973. By 1980, how much life insurance should this salesperson have sold to this client in order to ensure that the client's family maintains the same level of protection in real terms. Assume the 1973 inflation rate above.

   d. At age 60 a Canadian fireman retires in 1973 with a "comfortable fixed pension" amounting to $2000 per month to be received every month until he dies. By 1980, what is this monthly pension worth in real income terms, when compared to 1973?

   e. In 1973, upon the death of her husband, a widow receives a life insurance annuity amounting to $1500 to be paid every month as long as she is alive. By 1980, what is this annuity worth, in real terms, when compared to 1973?

f.   In 1973, a single mother raises her family on the interest she receives on 30-year term bonds inherited from her parents. On a monthly basis this interest works out to be $1400. In 1980, what is the monthly interest worth, in real terms, compared to 1973?

g.   In the early 1980's in Canada interest rates peaked, and the inflation rate started to decline to about 4% a year in 1985. Suppose, when interest rates peaked in 1982, an investor managed to lock all her financial assets into long term government bonds promising to pay a compound annual rate of interest of 13% per year for the next 25 years (strip bonds). Assuming this compound rate of return, how often will the investor double her money?

h.   Between 1989 and 1998 the top performing Canadian equity mutual funds were earning an annual compound rate of about 20% per year. How frequently were investors in these mutual funds doubling the value of their investment?

i.   At age 60, a hard working college professor has accumulated a savings account worth $100 000. If this professor wants to double this amount in 5 years time, what target compound annual rate of return should she attempt to achieve?

ANSWERS TO CHAPTER 4

COMPLETION QUESTIONS

1. measuring; models
2. "big-picture"; inflation, unemployment, economic output
3. real Gross Domestic Product (GDP)
4. standard of living
5. business fluctuations; business cycle
6. peak, contraction, trough, expansion
7. inflation, unemployment
8. unemployed
9. flow; stock
10. not in the labour force
11. frictional, structural
12. not in the labour force; understates
13. labour force participation rate
14. frictional; cyclical; structural
15. unavoidable
16. Cyclical
17. 7.5% – 9.4%
18. real income
19. Consumer Price Index (CPI)
20. unchanging; changing
21. overstate
22. unanticipated
23. hyperinflation, deflation
24. plus
25. debtors; creditors
26. worse
27. purchasing power
28. North American Free Trade Agreement (NAFTA) and World Trade Organization (WTO)
29. open; closed
30. United States
31. surplus
32. monetary
33. flexible
34. mixed economy
35. fiscal

TRUE-FALSE QUESTIONS

1. F   They are used in every field of study.
2. T   Models are especially used to help make decisions in the future.
3. T
4. F   All are highly variable.
5. F   Costs could be in the tens of billions of dollars.
6. F   They are difficult to anticipate.
7. T
8. F   While we have experienced a long trend of rising out, we have had serious business fluctuations, most notably in the 1930s and in the 1980s.
9. F   Usually, unemployment falls.
10. F   The unemployment rate will rise.
11. F   Canada produces about 150 times as much.

12.   T
13.   F   Assuming they have no part-time employment, they are officially counted as "not in the labour force."
14.   F   The unemployment rate will rise.   .
15.   F   Discouraged workers are "not in the labour force."
16.   T
17.   F   It is usually very great.
18.   F   Some transactions costs are always present.
19.   F   It is related to the business cycle.
20.   T
21.   T
22.   F   Cyclical unemployment varies with the business cycle.
23.   T
24.   T
25.   F   Neither group gains or benefits at the expense of the other because the nominal interest rate will reflect the anticipated inflation rate.
26.   F   Bank interest rates are always nominal rates.
27.   T
28.   T
29.   T
30.   T
31.   T
32.   T

MULTIPLE CHOICE QUESTIONS

1.d;   Models are not easy to make but are used anyway in economics.
2.c;   Real GDP is the measure of economic growth most widely used.
3.d;   Real GDP is the value of ALL goods and services ACTUALLY produced.
4.c;
5.a;   Business fluctuations reflect recurrent fluctuations in business activity such as real GDP, unemployment, and inflation. History has shown that each fluctuation is not of similar magnitude or duration
6.a;
7.d;
8.a;   The Canadian labour force includes individuals aged 15 years or older who either have jobs or are looking and available for jobs; the number of employed plus the number of unemployed.
9.a;   The number of unemployed is measured at a given point in time and is not a measure defined over a period of time. In general, a stock concept refers to the quantity of something, measured at a given point in time—for example, an inventory of goods or a bank account balance.
10.d;   Monthly income, the inflation rate, and annual consumption are each flow concepts as they are quantities measured over a period of time.
       TIP: The inflation rate, as announced in the media, is typically an annual rate.
11.d;   The only option that includes a non-working individual actively seeking work is option d.
       TIP: An individual is considered unemployed if available for work and in any one of the three categories: not working but making specific efforts to find a job within the past four weeks, or laid off from a job within the previous 26 weeks and waiting for recall, or waiting to begin a new job within the next four weeks.
12.d;   If homemakers were counted as being in the labour force this would increase the participation rate. If they were also considered employed this would both increase official employment and decrease the official unemployment rate.
13.b;   If the average duration of unemployment rises then, as the months progress, there will be more people unemployed in a given month.

14.a;   The discouraged worker is the only option, of the four listed, that is not counted as officially unemployed by Statistics Canada.

15.c;   Statistics Canada does not include discouraged workers as being in the labour force as they have not been actively seeking work within the past four weeks.

16.d;   The option d is false as there is disagreement among matters such as the classification of individuals such as the discouraged job seeker or part time worker

17.c;   Discouraged worker unemployment, unlike the other options, is not an official category or type of unemployment. This is because discouraged workers are not even counted in the labour force.

18.c;   The definition of "Full" employment allows for some frictional unemployment. This type of unemployment is considered unavoidable in a dynamic economy where freedom of choice is considered to be an important social value.

19.a;   The teenage unemployment rate is usually high because they typically are new entrants to the labour force. Lacking experience, it will usually take them longer to find a job. As well, when layoffs take place they are often the first to be laid off due to their low seniority status.

20.b;   The year 1933 was the worst year of the Great Depression.

21.b;

22.b;

23.b;   Price indexes measure the average cost of a bundle of goods relative to a base period cost. The change in cost over time is how inflation is measured.

24.d;   The CPI tracks the change in the cost of the same basket of consumer goods. In reality, as the price of some of the items in the CPI basket increases, consumers will switch to cheaper alternatives. This type of consumer behaviour implies that the change in the CPI overstates the true degree of inflation

25.b;   If inflation is anticipated, this would eliminate the unexpected, undesirable redistribution effects of inflation. As an example, lenders would demand higher interest rates and workers would have COLA clauses to protect themselves against inflation.

26.a;   Deflation will hurt debtors. This is because when the debtors pay back the principal amount borrowed it will be "more expensive" to pay back in real purchasing power terms.

27.a;   If a zero inflation rate is anticipated, creditors and savers would maintain their real income with the nominal and real rates being identical. Put differently, if positive inflation is anticipated, the nominal rate would have to exceed the real rate in order to maintain purchasing power. **TIP**: % change in real income = % change in nominal income – inflation rate

28.d;   Wealthy people who hold their cash in wall safes are not gaining any interest growth in their wealth. Therefore they are being "hurt" as the purchasing power of their cash or their real wealth is decreasing.

29.b;

30.b;   We have elements of both government and private production.

31.a;

32.b;

33.d;

34.c;

MATCHING

a and 3;   b and 8;   c and 7;   d and 12;   e and 5;   f and 9;   g and 10;   h and 4;
i and 2;   j and 1;

PROBLEMS

1. a. Years 5-6 (unemployment is rising, GDP is falling)
    b. Years 7-8 (unemployment is constant, GDP is only slowly increasing)
    c. Years 1-3, 9-14 (GDP is rising, inflation is steady, unemployment falling)
    d. Year 4. Inflation was rising to 5%
    e. If you take the simple sum of the growth rates, real GDP increased about 42%.
    f. If you take the simple sum of the inflation rate, prices rose about 39.5%. Thus, purchasing power fell by about 40%, or a loss of $8.

2. In general, we would expect that structural unemployment would be much more severe problem. The inability to find work in the long run imposes much greater costs on the individuals and on society at large. These people need to be either retrained or moved to a different place, both expensive. With frictional unemployment, we can expect these workers to find work after a short period of time, and can be beneficial to productivity by helping better match workers and jobs.

3. a. 6.2022 million
    b. 13.1168-11.9754 = 1.1414 million
    c. 100 x (1.1414/13.1168) = 8.7%
    d. 100 x (13.1168/19.3190) = 67.9%

4. If minorities become discouraged from looking for jobs, they will not be counted as officially unemployed, and therefore the actual employment rate will understate "true" unemployment. If people perform do-it-yourself activities, they are "really" working, but they won't be counted in the labour force if they quit looking for a job; or they will be counted as unemployed if they continue their job search. Either way, such do-it-yourself activities cause the official unemployment rate to overstate the "true" unemployment rate.

5. a. C;   b. S;   c. F;   d. S;   e. C;   f. F;   g. F;   h. C

6.

Fruit	Q-01		P-07	Total	Q-01	P-01	Total
Apples	10		$.18	$1.80	10	$.10	$1.00
Oranges	7		.23	1.61	7	.15	1.05
Bananas	4		.20	.80	4	.25	1.00
Pineapples	2		.65	1.30	2	.50	1.00
				$5.51			$4.05

Therefore, the FPI = 100*($5.51 / $4.05) = 136. This means that on average, fruit is 1.36 times more expensive in 2001 than in 1997. In other words, fruit prices have risen 36 percent from 1997 to 2001.

Notice that fruit prices have risen at a different rate across different types of fruit. Bananas have actually become cheaper in the above problem. Remember, a price index measures average overall tendencies by calculating the ratio of costs of the same "market basket" of goods at two or more points in time.

7. a. 100 x (83.7 - 75.5)/75.5 = 10.86%   b. 7% - 10.86% = -3.86%

8. a. Nominal GDP for 1997 = ($4) (10) + ($12) (20) + ($6) (5) + ($25) (10) = $560. Nominal GDP for 2006 = ($8) (12) + ($36) (15) + ($10) (15) + ($30) (12) = $1,146.
    b. Real GDP for 1997 = $560. Real GDP for 2006 = ($4) (12) + ($12) (15) + ($6) (15) + ($25) (12) = $618.
    c. Implicit GDP deflator for 1997 = (nominal GDP1997/real GDP1997) x 100 = ($560/$560) x 100 = 100.0. Implicit GDP deflator for 2006 = (nominal GDP2006/real GDP2006) x 100 = ($1146/$618) x 100 = 185.4.
    d. CPI for 1997 = 100, because it is the base year.
        CPI for 2006 = (P2006Q1997/P1997Q1997) x 100 = ($850/$310) x 100 = 274.
            P2006Q1997 = ($8) (10) + ($36) (20) + ($10) (5) = $850.
            P1997Q1997 = ($4) (10) + ($12) (20) + ($6) (5) = $310.
    e. 100 x (274 – 100)/100 = 174%

BUSINESS SECTION

1. a.   1973 Inflation rate = ((39.9 – 36) / 36) * 100 = 10.83%
    b.   70/10.83 = 6.5 years.
    c.   Since the cost of living has doubled the salesperson should have sold at least $200 000 worth of insurance.
    d.   Since prices have doubled, the pension is only worth about $1000 per month, in real terms.
    e.   The real value of the monthly annuity is about $1 500/2 = $750 per month.
    f.   The real monthly interest is about $700.
    g.   70/13 = 5.4 years.
    h.   70/20 = 3.5 years.
    i.   (70/x) = 5, so x = 14% per year rate of return.

CHAPTER 5

MEASURING THE ECONOMY'S PERFORMANCE

PUTTING THIS CHAPTER INTO PERSPECTIVE

Chapter 5 presents an introduction to national income accounting – the main procedure used to measure the economy's performance between two points in time. More specifically, this chapter shows exactly how gross domestic product, net domestic product, national income, personal income, disposable personal income, and personal saving are calculated.

Because a certain amount of arbitrariness is involved in defining these terms, the interpretation of what changes in these variables mean, with regard to the economic well-being of the community, is a tricky business. Further, because interpretation of changes in the statistics that are supposed to represent these concepts is difficult, it is also difficult to conduct economic policy. Stated differently, if our economic data do not transmit reliable and accurate information, then we should exercise great care when we develop economic policy to stabilize the economy. We return to this last, exceedingly important point in later chapters.

There are three main goals in Chapter 5. First, the chapter introduces you to the concepts and definitions of national income accounting. In order to understand the macroeconomic theories analyzed in the next four chapters, you must be familiar with the meaning of the key terms in this chapter. Furthermore, before policymakers can perform the governmental economic function of enhancing the nation's economy or stabilizing the economy, they must be able to (a) understand how the macroeconomy works, and (b) measure the key economic variables with accuracy. After all, economic policy is not likely to be successful unless we know how the economy is actually performing and how to change it in desired directions. Such knowledge requires more than a nodding acquaintance with the material in this chapter.

The second objective of this chapter is to indicate that the value of national output is identical to the value of national income. It is important for you to understand that total expenditures for output determine the value of national output and, in turn, that total expenditures become income to those people who have produced national output.

Third, Chapter 5 stresses that national income accounting is a very imprecise measure of national output and that it is an even less precise measure of comparing economic welfare (well-being) for the residents of other nations. In later chapters we analyze the problems involved in conducting policy to affect variables that can be only crudely measured.

It may be necessary for you to memorize some of the material in this chapter—in particular, how each of those income/output measures mentioned in the first paragraph of this preview are defined. Perhaps the task can be made easier if you try to understand what each term actually tries to measure; each one really does attempt to measure something different.

LEARNING OBJECTIVES

After reading this chapter, you should be able to:

5.1   Describe the circular flow of income and output.

5.2   Define gross domestic product (GDP).

5.3   Explain the two main methods of computing GDP: the expenditure and income approaches.

5.4   Explain how various subcomponents of GDP are calculated.

5.5   Compute variants of GDP and explain their uses.

5.6   Understand the limitations of using GDP as a measure of national welfare.

CHAPTER OUTLINE

LO 5.1 - Describe the circular flow of income and output.
1. **National income accounting** is a measurement system used to estimate national income and its components.
2. The economy can be modelled as a **circular flow** of income and spending. A reverse flow of goods and services moves in the opposite direction.
   a. In a simple model, all income is immediately spent by households on business output, and all revenue received for factors of production is paid to households.
   b. Since every transaction is both spending by households and revenue for businesses, all spending should equal all income in the simple model.
   c. In a more sophisticated version of the circular flow, financial markets, and two other sectors – governments and foreigners, allow for a more realistic model of the economy. The possibility of savings and net exports means that not all income is necessarily re-spent in the domestic economy, but must be "recycled" through these markets.

LO 5.2 - Define Gross Domestic Product (GDP).

3. **Gross domestic product** (**GDP**), is the total market value of all the final goods and services produced in the economy during the year.

    a. In order to avoid double counting, only **final goods and services** are counted in GDP determination.

    b. Because non-productive transactions do not contribute to output or to economic welfare, they are excluded from GDP determination.

        i.   Such financial transactions as (a) purchases and sales of securities and (b) private and public transfers are non-productive activities; they are therefore excluded from GDP determination.

        ii. The transfer of used goods is considered a non-productive activity because by definition used goods are produced (and counted) in a previous period.

        iii. Other transactions excluded from GDP determination are homemaker activities, underground activities, most illegal activities, volunteer activities, and do-it-yourself activities; in principle most of these activities should be counted in GDP determination, but they are difficult to measure.

LO 5.3 - Explain the expenditure and income approaches to computing GDP.

4. There are two basic approaches to measuring GDP: the expenditure approach and the income approach.

5. The **expenditure approach** measures GDP by summing the value of household consumption expenditures, government expenditures, gross private domestic investment, and net exports.

    a. Household **consumption** expenditures (C) fall into three categories: durable, nondurable, and **services**.

    b. **Government** expenditures (G) equal the cost of goods and services purchased by governments, because such goods are usually provided at a zero price to users.

    c. **Gross private domestic investment** (I) equals the sum of **fixed investment**, inventory investment, and consumer expenditures on new residential structures.

    d. **Net exports** (X-M) equal the value of exports minus the value of imports.

6. The **income approach** measures GDP by adding up the income received by all factors of production, including wages, interest, rent, and profits. Non-income expense items also must be included.

    a. Indirect business taxes less subsidies plus depreciation, equal total **non-income expense** items.

    b. **Indirect business taxes** include the value of excise, sales, and property taxes.

    c. Depreciation is also referred to as **capital consumption allowance**.

LO 5.4 - Explain how various subcomponents of GDP are calculated.

7. **Net domestic product** (**NDP**) equals gross domestic product minus depreciation. **Net investment** represents the changes in capital stock over time and is equal to gross investment less depreciation.

8. Other components of national income accounting are national income at factor cost (NI), personal income (PI), disposable personal income (DPI), and personal saving (S).

    a. **National income at factor cost** (NI) equals NDP minus indirect business taxes less subsidies; using the income approach, NI equals the sum of all factor payments to resource owners.

    b. **Personal income** (PI) equals NI minus undistributed corporate retained earnings, minus other earnings not paid to persons, plus public transfer payments. Using the income approach, PI equals the amount of income that households actually receive before they pay their personal income taxes.

    c. **Disposable personal income** (DPI) equals PI minus personal income taxes and non-tax payments; DPI equals the income that households have to spend for consumption and saving.

    d. **Personal saving** (S) is what is left over from disposable personal income after consumption.

LO 5.5 - Compute variants of GDP and explain their uses.

9. Because we are really interested in variations in the real output of the economy, and in order to eliminate the effects of inflation and deflation, nominal GDP is divided by a GDP price deflator in order to obtain **real GDP**.

10. Real GDP divided by population yields **per capita real GDP**; this latter statistic provides a better measure of a nation's living standard.

LO 5.6 - Understand the limitations of using GDP as a measure of national welfare.

11. The official GDP measure underestimates national output and economic welfare because it does not take into account quality improvements, do-it-yourself activities, volunteer activities, homemaker's services, increased leisure, some illegal activities, and underground economy activities.

    a. In general, an underground economy will be more important the higher the marginal tax rates on income, and the higher the legally mandated benefits that employers must pay to workers.

    b. The official GDP does not distinguish the composition or the distribution of output in the economy. Also, because there is no deduction for environmental degradation, GDP is overstated.

12. Because GDP is difficult to measure, international GDP comparisons are very difficult. A recent improvement is the **purchasing power parity** concept, which takes into account the costs of goods and services that are not traded internationally— and therefore are not reflected in foreign exchange rates.

KEY TERMS AND CONCEPTS

National income
  accounting
Factor Markets
Foreign Markets
Expenditure approach
Value Added
Gross private domestic
  investment
Gross domestic product
  (GDP)
Net domestic product (NDP)
Capital consumption
  allowance
Current dollars
Nominal values
Purchasing power parity

Circular Flow
Total income
Financial Markets
Total Expenditure
Income approach
Services
Fixed investment
Producer durables
Gross domestic
  income (GDI)
Personal saving (S)
Depreciation

Constant dollars
Real values

Total Output
Final goods and services
Product Markets
Intermediate Goods
Net Investment
Durable consumer goods
Non-durable consumer goods
Inventory investment
National income (NI)
Personal income (PI)
Disposable personal income
  (DPI)
Non-income expense items
Indirect business taxes less
  subsidies
Foreign exchange rate

COMPLETION QUESTIONS
Fill in the blank or circle the correct term.

(LO 5.1)
1.   The circular flow model shows four groups in the economy:_____,
     _____, _____, and _____.

2.   Every purchase of goods and services represents _____ for the seller and
     _____ for the buyer.

3.   In the enhanced circular flow, leakages leave the economy and "recycle" through
     the _____ and _____markets; taxes are recycled by the
     _____ sectors.

(LO 5.2)
4   GDP represents the total market value of all (final, final and intermediate) goods
     and services produced during a year.

5.   In order to avoid double counting, _____ goods are not counted; only
     final goods are included in national income accounting.

6.   Non-productive activities, such as financial transactions, (are, are not) counted in
     GDP determination; if you sell your 4-year-old car to your friend, this activity (is,
     is not) counted in GDP determination.

7. When a person receives a welfare payment, the value (is, is not) counted as a productive activity; counting transfers as a productive activity would be an example of _____ counting.

(LO 5.3)

8. The two basic methods of GDP determination are the _____ approach and the _____ approach. The expenditure approach to national income includes the sum of the values of _____, _____, _____, and _____. The income approach estimates national income by summing _____, _____, _____, _____, _____, and _____.

9. Because many government goods and services are provided to users free of charge, such items are valued at their _____ of production.

10. Consumer durable goods are arbitrarily defined as items that last more than _____ year(s).

11. Net exports is equal to total exports (plus, minus) total imports.

(LO 5.4)

12. Net investment equals gross private domestic investment minus _____.

13. Gross domestic product minus depreciation equals _____; non-income expense items include indirect business taxes less subsidies and _____; national income equals NDP minus _____; personal income minus personal income taxes and non-tax payments equals _____.

(LO 5.5)

14. Inflation causes us to (understate, overstate) the value of output and economic welfare, while deflation causes us to (understate, overstate) such values. For that reason, economists attempt to correct for price level changes by attempting to convert the less accurate (nominal, real) values into the more accurate (nominal, real) values.

15. When nominal GDP is divided by the _____, real GDP is determined; when real GDP is divided by population, _____ is determined.

(LO 5.6)

16. Do-it-yourself activities, volunteer activities, homemakers' activities, increased leisure, improved quality and (legal) underground economy activities (are, are not) productive activities; such activities (are, are not) counted in the official GDP

figures; for that reason the GDP figures (overestimate, underestimate) national output and economic welfare.

17. GDP accounting has been criticized. GDP understates productive activities and economic welfare because it (includes, excludes) household production, do-it-yourself activities, and otherwise legal activities in the _____ economy. Because various things such as pollution (are, are not) subtracted from GDP, GDP overstates economic welfare.

18. The purchasing power parity approach to making international comparisons of living standards (does, does not) consider relative costs of goods that are not traded internationally.

TRUE-FALSE QUESTIONS
Circle the **T** if the statement is true, the **F** if it is false. Explain to yourself why a statement is false.

(LO 5.1)

T   F   1.   In the circular flow model, money flows in the same direction as goods and services.

T   F   2.   The four main sectors of the economy are households, businesses, governments and foreigners.

(LO 5.2)

T   F   3.   Gross domestic product is a stock concept.

T   F   4.   Both final and intermediate goods are counted when measuring GDP.

T   F   5.   Homemakers' activities are non-productive transactions.

T   F   6   When Mr. Smith purchases a share of stock, investment rises; therefore GDP rises.

T   F   7.   Public transfers are counted in GDP, but private transfers are not.

T   F   8   A nation's underground economy becomes larger as marginal tax rates rise on income.

T   F   9.   Whether or not a good is durable is an arbitrary decision.

(LO 5.3)

T   F   10.   In the expenditure approach, the value G equals the sum of all the receipts governments realize from the sale of their services, plus taxes.

T F 11. When one purchases a new shirt, consumption takes place in the official GDP accounts.

T F 12. If net exports rise, other things being constant, then GDP rises.

T F 13. Personal income taxes are a form of indirect tax.

(LO 5.4)

T F 14. The sum of household consumption plus saving equals disposable personal income.

T F 15. GDP minus depreciation equals net private domestic investment.

(LO 5.5)

T F 16. Inflation causes us to overstate national income and output.

T F 17. Nominal GDP is always different from real GDP.

T F 18. Per capita GDP is calculated by taking the population of the country and dividing by nominal GDP.

(LO 5.6)

T F 19. Levels of education and life expectancy are useful in determining the overall welfare of a nation.

T F 20. Purchasing power parity is used to calculate the cost of living in different countries.

MULTIPLE CHOICE QUESTIONS

Circle the letter that corresponds to the best answer.

(LO 5.1)

1. In the circular flow of income, which of the following markets is *not* included?
    a. the financial markets
    b. the goods and services market
    c. the labour market
    d. the factor resource market.

(LO 5.2)

2. Gross domestic product includes
    a. only intermediate goods and services.
    b. only final goods and services.
    c. both intermediate and final goods.
    d. neither intermediate nor final goods.

3.   In order to avoid overstating national output and income,
      a.   intermediate goods are ignored.
      b.   used good transactions between non-businesses are ignored.
      c.   public and private transfers are ignored.
      d.   All of the above

4.   Which of the following activities is not considered in GDP determination and therefore causes economic welfare to be overestimated?
      a.   do-it-yourself activities
      b.   pollution damage
      c.   homemaker activities
      d.   private and public transfers

5.   Which of the following might increase the size of a nation's underground economy?
      a.   Higher marginal tax rates on income
      b.   Higher unemployment benefits
      c.   Higher welfare benefits
      d.   All of the above

6.   Which of the following is a non-productive transaction?
      a.   Mr. Gentile gives his niece $50 for her birthday.
      b.   Mrs. Patullo cooks for her family.
      c.   Mrs. Arianas is a waitress in the "underground" economy.
      d.   All of the above

7.   Which of the following is a transfer payment?
      a.   Mr. Farano pays his son for painting the house.
      b.   Mr. Scheifele gets paid for tending bar but does not declare his income.
      c.   Mrs. Niemeck gets paid by the government for teaching.
      d.   Mrs. Carson receives an old age security payment.

8.   Which of the following activities is ignored in the official national-income accounts?
      a.   Mr. Pulsinelli gives his son $500 for Christmas.
      b.   Mrs. Pulsinelli sells her used car to the Harrymans.
      c.   Beth Pulsinelli paints her own house.
      d.   All of the above

(LO 5.3)
9.   When a Canadian purchases a bottle of French wine,
      a.   consumption falls.
      b.   investment rises by the purchase price.
      c.   consumption rises by the purchase price.
      d.   net exports fall.

10. If total exports exceed total imports, other things being constant, then
    a. total expenditures fall.
    b. net exports are positive.
    c. GDP falls.
    d. investment rises.

11. Which is not a component of indirect business taxes?
    a. sales taxes
    b. excise taxes
    c. corporate income taxes
    d. property taxes incurred by business persons

12. Which of the following is a non-income expense item?
    a. depreciation
    b. excise and sales taxes
    c. property taxes incurred by businesspersons
    d. All are non-income expense items.

(LO 5.4)
13. Net investment equals
    a. GDP minus capital consumption allowances.
    b. gross private domestic investment plus depreciation.
    c. gross private domestic investment minus depreciation.
    d. planned saving minus net saving.

14. GDP minus depreciation equals
    a. net investment.
    b. capital consumption allowances.
    c. NDP.
    d. NI.

15. National income…
    a. minus depreciation equals NDP.
    b. plus depreciation plus indirect business taxes equals GDP.
    c. minus inflation equals real GDP.
    d. plus transfer payments equals PI.

16. Which of the following is not included in national income?
    a. corporate taxes
    b. Employment Insurance and Canada Pension Plan
    c. government transfer payments
    d. undistributed corporate profits

(LO 5.5)
17.   Concerning real vs. nominal values,
    a.   people respond to changes in real values.
    b.   economists attempt to convert real into nominal values.
    c.   current values are real values.
    d.   nominal values have been adjusted for changes in the price level.

18.   If this year's real GDP is 1.1 trillion dollars, and nominal GDP is also 1.1 trillion dollars then
    a.   there has been no inflation between the base year and the current year.
    b.   the current year is also the base year.
    c.   both a. and b. are possible.
    d.   real and nominal GDP must always be different because of inflation.

(LO 5.6)
19.   Which of the following best represents a nation's standard of living?
    a.   nominal GDP
    b.   real GDP
    c.   per capita real GDP
    d.   per capita nominal GDP

MATCHING
Choose the item in Column (2) that best matches an item in Column (1).

   (1)   (2)

(LO 5.2)

(1)		(2)
a. intermediate good	1.	depreciation
b. final good	2.	NDP

(LO 5.3)

c. expenditure approach	3.	C+I+G+(X-M)
d. capital consumption allowance	4.	wages+rents+profits+interest payments
e. income approach		
f. non-income expense item	5.	flour used by a baker
g. producer durable	6.	bread used by a family

(LO 5.4)

h. GDP minus depreciation	7.	price-level adjusted GDP

(LO 5.5)

i. constant dollars	8.	capital good
	9.	indirect business taxes

PROBLEMS

(LO 5.2)
1. What happens to the official measure of GDP if:
   a. a woman marries her butler?

   b. an addict marries his cocaine supplier?

   c. homemakers perform the same jobs but switch houses and charge each other for their services?

(LO 5.5)
2. Consider the following table and then
   a. Calculate real GDP for each of the years indicated.

Year	Nominal GDP	GDP Deflator	Real GDP (1986 dollars)
1995	2957.8	195.60	_____
1996	3069.3	207.38	_____
1997	3304.8	215.34	_____
1998	3661.3	223.38	_____

   b. Interpret what a GDP deflator of 223.38 for the year 1998 means.

   c. Determine whether or not inflation occurred over the 1995-1998 period.

(LO 5.4)
3. Suppose you are given the following information about some hypothetical economy and its national income accounts. Use this information to answer the questions that follow. (Amounts are in billions of dollars)

Indirect business taxes less subsidies	$ 148
Corporate profits before taxes	101
Corporate retained earnings	24
Farm and non-farm unincorporated business income	73
Interest and investment income	98
Exports	18
Imports	10
Net domestic product	1436
Government expenditures on goods & services	323
Government transfer payments	230
Employment insurance and C.P.P contributions	120
Consumption expenditures	1055
Gross investment	220
Disposable personal income	1123

Calculate the following:

a.   GDP.

b.   depreciation (capital consumption allowances).

c.   national income at factor cost (NI).

d.   personal income (PI).

e.   personal income taxes.

f.   net exports.

g.   personal saving (S).

(LO 5.3)

4.   Suppose you own a small skateboard factory that has sales, expenses, and profits as shown below.

Total sales	$25 000

Expenses

Wages and salaries	9000
Interest on loans	800
Rent	4200
Raw materials	7000

Profits	$ 4000

What is the value added to GDP of the productive activities of your firm?

(LO 5.6)

5.   What happens to economic welfare in the three examples in problem 1?

BUSINESS SECTION

(LO 5.3)
Accounting: Calculating GST Payable in Canada

In Canada, at the federal level, the most important indirect tax is the 7% Goods and Services Tax (GST) which is collected by Canadian businesses. While accountants and small business owners typically calculate the GST payable by businesses to the government, the economic theory in Chapter 8 helps one understand the rationale behind these tax computations. More specifically, as the examples below will illustrate, the GST payable by each business is based on *the value added* by the business.

Those of you who have had some business experience may have wondered how it is possible for the manufacturer, the wholesaler, and the retailer to each add 7% to their selling prices while the federal government receives only 7% of the price of the *final good*. The reason all of this is possible is that each business is allowed to deduct the GST paid on inputs, goods and services purchased from other businesses. This deduction is called the GST Input Tax Credit. In economics terms, this means that the GST is based on the value added by each business enterprise as follows:

Economists method: GST Payable = 7% x Value Added

Application Problem 1

GST Paid by Businesses Involved in the Manufacture and Distribution of a 16-hp *Lawn Tractor*

Lawn Tractor	Accountant's Method				Economist's Method	
	Selling Price	GST Collected	GST Input Tax Credit	Tax Payable	Value Added	Tax Payable
Materials Sold to Manufacturer	$ 500	7% x 500= $35	7% x 0 = $0	35 – 0= $35	?	?
Lawn Tractor Sold to Wholesaler	$1 100	7% x 1100= $77	7% x 500= $35	77 – 35= $42	?	?
Lawn Tractor Sold to Retailer	$1 600	?	?	?	?	?
Lawn Tractor Sold to Consumer	$2 000	?	?	?	?	?
				Total Tax Payable = ?		Total Tax Payable = ?

1. a. Fill in the blank spaces in the table in the section entitled Accountant's Method.

    b. Calculate the Total Tax Payable using the Accountant's Method.

    c. Fill in the blank spaces in the table in the section entitled Economist's Method.

    d. Calculate the Total Tax Payable using the Economist's Method.

2. Assuming that the GST is based on total value added in the Canadian economy (with some exemptions); will the GST tax the same economic activity twice?

3. Historically, the GST replaced a federal sales tax, which was imposed on goods (not services) at the manufacturer's level. Would the 7% GST yield more or less tax revenue than a 7% tax on goods levied at the manufacturers level?

ANSWERS TO CHAPTER 5

COMPLETION QUESTIONS

1.   households, businesses, foreigners and governments.
2.   revenue; expenditure
3.   financial; foreign; government
4.   final
5.   intermediate
6.   are not; is not
7.   is not; double
8.   expenditure; income; consumption, gross investment, government expenditures on goods and services, net exports; wages, corporate profits before taxes, interest and investment income, farm and non-farm unincorporated business income, inventory valuation adjustments and non-income expense items.
9.   cost
10. three
11. minus
12. depreciation (or sometimes called capital consumption allowance)
13. NDP; depreciation; indirect business taxes; disposable personal income
14. overstate; understate; nominal; real
15. GDP deflator; per capita real GDP
16. are; are not; underestimate
17. excludes; underground; are not
18. does

TRUE-FALSE QUESTIONS

1.   F   Money flows in the opposite direction to goods and services.
2.   T
3.   F   GDP is measured per unit of time; hence, it is a flow concept.
4.   F   Only the value of final goods are counted, to avoid double counting.
5.   F   They are productive; if someone outside the family did them, you would probably have to pay for such services.
6.   F   Common stock purchases are simply financial transactions.
         TIP: Don't confuse investment in economics with "financial investment" which is really savings
7.   F   Neither is counted, as neither represents payments for goods and services produced.
8.   T   Evidence suggests that people will try to evade taxes when rates are higher.
9.   T
10. F   G equals the value (at cost) of government purchases of goods and services.
11. T
12. T
13. F   They are direct taxes.
14. T
15. F   It equals NDP.
16. T
17. F   Nominal GDP is always the same in the base year, or if the price level doesn't change from the base year.
18. F   The formula is reversed.
19. T
20. F   Purchasing power parity is used to compare GDP across different countries where the cost of living is different.

MULTIPLE CHOICE QUESTIONS

1.c;   The labour market is part of the factor resource market.

2.b;   Gross domestic product includes only final goods and services so as to avoid double counting economic activity.

     TIP: GDP attempts to measure the dollar value of all new productive activity that occurs during the current year for a nation, without double counting the same productive activity.

3.d;   Since GDP attempts to measure just the new economic activity occurring during the current year, used goods and transfers are ignored. If final and intermediate goods were both included, economic activity would be double counted.

4.b;   Pollution damage causes GDP to overestimate economic welfare. To get a more accurate measure of economic welfare, the pollution damage should be subtracted from GDP.

5.d;   Higher marginal tax rates will result in more people under-reporting their income (productive activity). As well, if people are collecting generous unemployment or welfare benefits they are more apt to refrain from reporting extra income earned for fear of losing these benefits.

6.a;   A cash gift is a pure money transfer with no new productive activity occurring.

7.d;   Transfer payments includes payments not related to new productive activity. An old age security payment is the only option not related to new productive activity.

8.d;   A cash transfer as well as a used car is deliberately not included in GDP to avoid double counting of current year economic activity. The act of painting ones own home should be counted in GDP but is not captured as it is a non- market activity.

9.d;   When a Canadian purchases a French wine, this increases imports, which in turn will reduce net exports according to the tip shown below.

     TIP: Net exports = Exports – Imports

10.b;   Based on the tip shown above, if exports exceed imports, then net exports (exports – imports) is positive.

11.c;   Sales taxes, excise taxes and property taxes incurred by businesses are all indirect taxes as they are likely to be shifted onto the consumer through increases in the prices of the goods and services affected by these non-income based taxes. Corporate income taxes are based on income so they are called direct taxes.

     TIP: Indirect taxes are non-income taxes paid by consumers when they purchase goods and services. Direct taxes are based on income.

12.d;   All the options listed are non-income expense items. An income expense item would be an expense related to payment of a resource such as a wage or rent or interest or profit expense.

13.c;   Net investment equals gross private domestic investment minus depreciation. This measures the net addition to the nation's capital stock that occurred during the current year.

14.c;   By definition, Net Domestic Product (NDP) equals GDP minus depreciation.

15.b;   National income equals total income earned by the resources or factors of production. Put differently, national income reflects all the income-related expenses. If we add depreciation and indirect taxes to national income, we will derive the total value of the final product—GDP.

16.c;   Since national income focuses on income *earned* (not received), government transfer payments such as UIC and welfare payments are not included in national income.

17.a;   It is assumed that people know the difference between real and nominal values and respond accordingly.

18.c;   Since we don't know the base year, it is possible that either a. or b. is true.

19.c;   Of the options listed, per capita real GDP best represents a nation's standard of living as it adjusts for both inflation and the population size.

     TIP: Per Capita Real GDP is not a perfectly accurate measure of economic welfare due to considerations such as the existence of the underground economy, differences in leisure time, pollution damage and variations in product quality.

MATCHING

a and 5;   b and 6;   c and 3;   d and 1;   e and 4;   f and 9;   g and 8;   h and 2;   i and 7

PROBLEMS

1.   a.   falls;   b. unaffected, because illegal activities not counted anyway;   c. rises

2.   a.

Year	Real GDP (1986 dollars)
1995	1512.2
1996	1480.0
1997	1534.7
1998	1639.0

      b.   The overall price level in 1998 was about 2.23 times higher than it was in 1986 (the base year).

      c.   Inflation occurred in every year over that period because the GDP deflator went up every year.

3.   a.   To get GDP: C + I + G + (X-M) = 1055 + 220 + 323 + 8 = 1606

      b.   To get depreciation: GDP - NDP = 1606 – 1436 = 170

      c.   To get national income: NDP - indirect taxes = 1436 - 148 = 1288

      d.   To get PI: national income - corporate retained earnings + transfer payments =
                    1288 - 24 + 230 = 1494

      e.   To get personal income taxes: PI - DPI = 1494 - 1123 = 371
              To get net exports: X = exports - imports = 18 - 10 = 8
              To get personal saving DPI – C = 1123 – 1055 = 68

4.   Value added is measured by the difference in the cost of the raw materials used to produce a product and the final value of that product. Thus
              value added = total sales - cost of raw materials or
              value added = $25 000 - $7 000 = $18 000

Wages, interest, and rent and profits represent the added value from labour and capital at this stage in production (which would also add to $18 000).

5.   a. remains constant;   b. difficult to tell; it depends on one's value judgement;
      c. remains constant

BUSINESS SECTION

1.   a.

GST Collected:	$112,	$140
GST Input Tax Credit	$ 77,	$112
Tax Payable:	$ 35,	$ 28

      b.   Total Tax Payable = $35 +$42 +$35 +$28 = $140

      c.   Value Added: $500, $600, $500, $400

      d.   Tax Payable $ 35, $ 42, $ 35, $ 28

      Total Tax Payable = $35 +$42 +$35 +$28 = $140, the same as the accounting method.

2.   As the text explains, the notion of value added avoids double counting economic activity.

3.   The GST would likely yield more revenue. A 7% GST would theoretically tax all economic activity – both goods and services at all stages of production and distribution.

CHAPTER 6

ECONOMIC GROWTH AND DEVELOPMENT

PUTTING THIS CHAPTER INTO PERSPECTIVE

This chapter is concerned with economic growth: its definition, impact on living standards, and its determinants. In order to have growth, saving must occur. Growth is also affected by other factors. New growth theorists emphasize the impact of technology, research and innovation on growth. In these theories technology improvements are a function of the size of the reward. A variety of government policies have a substantial impact on growth. Besides some benefits, economic growth has costs, particularly on the environment. Economic development for developing countries has somewhat different problems than those found in industrialized nations.

LEARNING OBJECTIVES

After you have studied this chapter you should be able to:

6.1   Define economic growth and explain some of the limitations of that definition.

6.2   Explain why productivity increases are crucial for maintaining economic growth.

6.3   Describe the fundamental determinants of economic growth.

6.4   Understand the basis of new growth theory.

6.5   Outline some of the costs and benefits of economic growth.

6.6   Discuss the fundamental factors that contribute to international economic development.

CHAPTER OUTLINE

LO 6.1 - Define Economic growth and explain some of the limitations of that definition.

1. **Economic growth** is defined as the rate of increase in per-capita real GDP.
   a. Graphically, economic growth can be viewed as a rightward shift in a country's production possibilities curve.
   b. The definition of economic growth does not; measure the distribution of output and income, reflect increases in leisure time, or reflect the type of products that are purchased.

LO 6.2 - Explain why productivity increases are crucial for maintaining economic growth.

2. Increases in real GDP are closely linked to the productivity of all underlying inputs in production, capital, labour, and technology.
   a. An increase in the amount of resources available, or productivity of any of these input resources, contributes to overall growth.

LO 6.3 - Describe the fundamental determinants of economic growth.

3. **Saving**, or non-consumption of income, is an important determinant of economic growth.
   a. When people save, they free-up resources from the production of consumer goods.
   b. If such freed resources are then allocated to the production of capital or investment goods, economic growth will occur.
   c. Thus, if people consume less today, they can consume more in the future.
   d. Other determinants of economic growth include: commitment to the protection and use of private property, a market economy, political stability, population growth and immigration.

LO 6.4 - Understand the basis of new-growth theory.

4. **New-growth theorists** maintain that if technological advances are rewarded, they will be forthcoming.
   a. **Patents** provide property rights to intellectual achievements and inventions; thus patents encourage economic growth.
   b. As long as it is profitable for people to find new ideas, they will be forthcoming, and economic growth will continue.
   c. If people have incentives to increase their human capital through education and training, economic growth will be enhanced.

LO 6.5 - Outline some of the costs and benefits of economic growth.
5. Government actions make a substantial difference in encouraging growth.
    a. Governments can support free markets and private property, encourage political stability, and control immigration.
    b. Governments investing in human capital and in infrastructure, and encouraging savings, are all actions that encourage economic growth.

6. While economic growth has many benefits, there are also costs associated with economic growth.
    a. The environment is limited in its ability to sustain high levels of consumption. Economic growth as it currently happens often results in environmental degradation.
    b. **Sustainable development** is a principle that suggests economic growth should occur with much less impact upon the environment.
    c. The benefits of economic growth include a higher standard of living, a reduction in population growth, and new technologies that help deal with environmental problems

LO 6.6 - Discuss the fundamental factors that contribute to international economic development.
7. **Development economics** is the study of why some countries grow and develop while others do not, and of policies that might help the developing economies get richer.
    a. Roughly 2/3 of the world's population lives at or below a subsistence level.
    b. Most of the world's population growth over the next 50 years will occur in developing nations.
    c. Economic growth generally leads to lower population growth.

8. Economies move through stages of development. First is the agricultural stage, when most of the population is involved in agriculture. Then comes the manufacturing stage, when much of the population becomes involved in the industrial sector of the economy. And finally there is a shift toward services.
    a. The lack of natural resources does not necessarily hinder development, nor does its presence guarantee that development will occur.

9. Four factors seem to be critical in helping economic development: an educated population, a system of property rights, letting "creative destruction" run its course, and limiting protectionism.

KEY TERMS AND CONCEPTS

Economic growth
Labour productivity
Development economies

New-growth theory
Sustainable development
Saving

Innovation
Patent
Private property

COMPLETION QUESTIONS

Fill in the blank or circle the correct term.

(LO 6.1)

1.   Economic growth is the rate of increase in _per capital GDP_

2.   Graphically, economic growth shows a _rightward_ shift in a nation's production possibilities curve.

(LO 6.2)

3.   Numerically, economic growth is equal to the _____ of the growth rate of capital and the growth rate of labour, plus _____.

(LO 6.3)

4.   Other things constant, if people wish to consume more in the future they must _save_ more now.

5.   Resources freed by saving must be allocated to _____ goods to help economic growth.

(LO 6.4)

6.   New growth theorists predict that technology, research, and innovation (need not, must be) rewarded.

7.   Inventions usually require _____ to be useful.

8.   When people or governments invest in education and training, economists refer to this as increases in human _____.

(LO 6.5)

9.   Sustainable development encourages economic growth to occur with much less impact on _____.

10.   The   main   benefits   of   economic   growth   are   _____, _____, and _____.

(LO 6.6)

11.   Economic growth leads to (lower, higher) population growth.

12.   The stages of economic development are: _____, _____ and _____ economies.

13.   Economic development is enhanced by _____, _____, _____, and _____.

TRUE-FALSE QUESTIONS

Circle the **T** if the statement is true, the **F** if it is false. Explain to yourself why a statement is false.

(LO 6.1)

T (F)   1.   Increases in nominal GDP is the basic measure of economic growth.

(T) F   2.   An increase in labour productivity would result in an outward shift of the nation's PPC curve.

(LO 6.2)

T (F)   3.   Economic growth is unrelated to changes in technology.

(LO 6.3)

(T) F   4.   If people save more a nation's growth rate probably will rise.

(T) F   5.   When a nation invests in education, human capital increases and economic growth is enhanced.

T (F)   6.   Government policies have little impact on economic growth.

(LO 6.4)

(T) F   7.   Inventions contribute to economic growth.

T (F)   8.   Inventions, research, and technology occur automatically, according to the new growth theorists.

T (F)   9.   Economic growth must eventually approach zero, because resources are finite.

(LO 6.5)

T (F)   10.   Economic growth has no costs associated with it.

(LO 6.6)

T F   11.   Economic growth can benefit low-income people.

T F   12.   Large changes in a nation's growth rate are required before significant changes in living standards can occur.

T F   13.   If a nation better protects property rights, its economic growth rate will rise, other things constant.

MULTIPLE CHOICE QUESTIONS

Circle the letter that corresponds to the best answer.

(LO 6.1)

1.   Economic growth is defined as
     a.   increases in nominal GDP
     b.   increases in real GDP.
     c.   increases in real GDP per capita.
     d.   None of the above.

2.   When economic growth occurs, the production possibilities curve
     a.   shifts leftward.
     b.   shifts rightward.
     c.   is unaffected.
     d.   rotates about the vertical axis.

3.   Economic growth
     a.   shifts the production possibilities curve leftward.
     b.   assures full employment.
     c.   may be uneven over time.
     d.   creates unemployment.

(LO 6.2)

4.   The overall rate of economic growth can be measured by the
     a.   rate of growth of capital productivity
     b.   rate of growth of capital and labour productivity.
     c.   rate of growth of capital resources, labour resources and capital and labour productivity.
     d.   rate of growth in capital and labour resources.

(LO 6.3)

5.   Which of the following contributes to economic growth?
     a.   Technological progress.
     b.   Well-defined property rights.
     c.   Human capital investment.
     d.   All of the above

6.   Before capital accumulation can take place,
   a.   saving must decline.
   b.   household saving must be converted into business investments.
   c.   a large resource base is necessary.
   d.   households must forego future consumption for more present consumption.

7.   Which of the following does **NOT** contribute to economic growth?
   a.   Protected property rights
   b.   Investments in education
   c.   Nationalization of foreign investments
   d.   Increasing the ratio of investment to real GDP

8.   Which of the following government policies will not encourage economic growth?
   a.   enacting anti-monopoly policies.
   b.   investing in infrastructure.
   c.   raising taxes on savings.
   d.   subsidizing education.

(LO 6.4)
9.   Which of the following is **NOT** true?
   a.   Saving, if converted into investment, will contribute to economic growth.
   b.   Economic growth can help people of all income levels.
   c.   Economic growth assures full employment.
   d.   Immigration increases a nation's growth rate, other things constant.

10.   Which of the following will likely increase productivity?
   a.   Increase in population.
   b.   Investment in research and development.
   c.   Higher corporate taxes.
   d.   Elimination of patent protection.

(LO 6.5)
11.   Which of the following is a benefit of economic growth?
   a.   guaranteed full employment.
   b.   low inflation rate.
   c.   higher average standard of living.
   d.   more equal distribution of income.

(LO 6.6)
12.   What is the correct order for the stages of economic development?
   a.   agricultural, service, industrial, post-modern.
   b.   agricultural, industrial, service, post-modern.
   c.   agricultural, service, industrial.
   d.   agricultural, industrial, service.

MATCHING

Choose the item in Column (2) that best matches an item in Column (1).

	(1)		(2)
	(LO 6.1)		
4	a. economic growth	1.	patents ✓
	(LO 6.3)		
6.	b. saving	2.	new-growth theory ✓
9	c. contracts enforced	3.	low impact on the environment
	by government		
	(LO 6.4)	4.	rate of change of per-capita real GDP ✓
1	d. inventions	5.	education ✓
5	e. human capital	6.	non-consumption of income ✓
	(LO 6.5)	7.	consumer goods
3	f. sustainable development	8.	industrial stage
	(LO 6.6)		
8	g. economic development	9.	well-defined property rights

PROBLEMS

(LO 6.2)

1. Consider the hypothetical economy depicted in the following table, then answer the following questions. (Hint: each of the following questions is based on a change from one year to the next. For example, the situation in question "a" exists when going from year 1 to year 2.) Note that quantity of labour represents number of workers per year, and productivity of labour represents the real value of the output of each worker over the year.

Year	Quantity of Labour (millions)	Productivity of Labour (thousands of $)	Real GDP (billions of $)	Population (millions)	Per Capita Real GDP (thousands of $)
1	1	$10.0	$10.0	2	$ 5.0
2	1	10.3	10.3	2	5.15
3	2	10.3	20.6	4	5.15
4	2.5	12.875	32.1875	4	8.046875
5	3.125	16.09375	50.292969	4	10.058594

Note: In each part below, the question is to first find the <u>percentage change</u> in Real GDP, then find the <u>percentage change</u> in Real GDP Per Capita.

a. If the quantity of labour remains constant and the productivity of labour rises by 3 percent, what happens to real GDP? Given those changes and a constant population, what happens to per capita real GDP?

↑ 3%, ↑ 3%,

b. If the quantity of labour doubles and the productivity of labour remains constant, what happens to real GDP? Given those changes and a doubling of population, what happens to per capita real GDP?

c. If the quantity of labour rises by 25 percent and labour productivity rises by 25 percent, what happens to real GDP? Given those changes and a constant population, what happens to per capita real GDP?

d. If the quantity of labour rises by 25 percent and labour productivity rises by 25 percent and population rises by 25 percent, what happens to per capita real GDP?

BUSINESS SECTION

International Marketing: The Location Decision: Country Evaluation

Long-term growth, as discussed in Chapter 6, is especially relevant to businesses that want to establish operations in new markets in other countries. Other factors being the same, a company would tend to favour situating in countries that are forecasted to experience rapid long-term economic growth.

In an earlier learning guide chapter the annual percentage increase in Real GDP was mentioned as a common measure used to assess the short-term growth prospect of an economy. The related measure of longer-term growth often reported by international statistical agencies is the average annual rate of growth in real GDP measured as follows.

$$\text{Average Annual Rate of Growth in Real GDP} = 100 \times \left[\left(\frac{\text{Real GDP 2}}{\text{Real GDP 1}} \right)^{\frac{1}{n}} - 1 \right]$$

Where:
- Real GDP 2 refers to the GDP measure for the last year of the growth period.
- Real GDP 1 refers to GDP measure for the first year of the growth period.
- n = # of years included in the growth period.

(LO 6.1)
Application Problem 1
Refer to the table below to answer each of the following.

Real GDP in 1995 prices and at 1995 exchange rates – billions of dollars			
	1995	1998	2000
Canada	579.2	634.2	695.3
Mexico	286.2	337.2	374.0
U.S.	7338.4	8292.8	9038
Australia	376.7	427.9	465.4
Japan	5137.4	5345.3	5458.4

(Source: Frequently Requested Statistics – GDP. OECD. March 2000. Available
http://www.oecd.org/std/gdp.htm)

1. a. Calculate the average annual compounded rate of growth in Real GDP for
    i.   Canada for the period 1995 – 2000 and for the period 1998 – 2000.
    ii. Mexico for the period 1995 – 2000 and for the period 1998 – 2000.
    iii. Australia for the period 1995 – 2000 and for the period 1998 – 2000.
    iv. U.S. for the period 1995 – 2000 and for the period 1998 – 2000.
    v.   Japan for the period 1995 – 2000 and for the period 1998 – 2000.

   b. In the 1995 – 2000 period which country displayed the largest average annual percentage increase in GDP? Where did Canada rank?

   c. In the more recent 1998 – 2000 period, which country displayed the largest average annual percentage increase in GDP? Where did Canada rank?

ANSWERS TO CHAPTER 6

COMPLETION QUESTIONS

1. per capita real GDP
2. rightward
3. sum; the rate of growth of the productivity of those growth rates.
4. save
5. capital
6. must be
7. innovations
8. capital
9. the environment
10. a higher standards of living, less population growth, new technologies
11. lower
12. agricultural, industrial, service.
13. well-defined property rights, saving, investments in human capital, open economies

TRUE-FALSE QUESTIONS

1. F   The basic measure is real GDP per capita.
2. T
3. F   Technology is one very important source of economic growth.
4. T   Savings are a necessary prerequisite for economic growth.
5. T
6. F   There are many government polices that can enhance or inhibit growth.
7. T
8. F   New-growth theorists maintain that incentives are required to bring forth such things.
9. F   As long as incentives to develop new ideas exist, economic growth will occur. Many resources are recyclable and renewable
10. F   Economic growth usually has an impact on the environment.
11. T   Economic growth usually benefits everyone in the society.
12. F   A small change in the growth rate leads to enormous changes in living standards over time.
13. T

MULTIPLE CHOICE QUESTIONS

1.c; Economic growth is defined to be an increase in real GDP per capita. When this occurs this creates the potential for each citizen to be materially better off.

2.b; Since economic growth relates to a situation where the productive capacity of the nation is enhanced, this can be described as a rightward shift in the product possibility curve.

3.c; For any nation economic growth progresses unevenly over time.

4.c; According to the TIP below, one broad contributor to economic growth is increased productivity. Specific factors contributing to increased productivity include technological progress, human capital investment and well-defined property rights. Human capital investment relates to increased education, on the job training and self-learning. Well-defined property rights encourage entrepreneurial activity by fostering incentives to take risks.
TIP: Economic growth = growth rate in capital + growth rate in labour + growth rate in resource productivity.

6.b; Before capital accumulation can take place, the nation must sacrifice current consumption so as to accumulate the savings necessary to create investment in new capital goods.

7.c;   In the long run, nationalization of foreign investment will reduce the incentives to provide new capital investment from residents living in foreign countries. Nationalization will also encourage the nation's own residents to invest their savings in capital investments in other nations.

8.c;   Raising taxes will reduce the incentive to make investments, thus lowering productivity in the long run.

9.c;   While economic growth does provide the potential for every citizen to enjoy a higher income level, it does not assure full employment. A high rate of technological progress and capital accumulation can increase the degree of structural unemployment.

10.b;   The only option that will increase productivity in terms of output produced per worker, is research and development. Higher taxes and the elimination of patents will reduce incentives to accumulate more capital per worker.

11.c;   Only c. is an outcome of economic growth.

12.d;

MATCHING

a and 4;   b and 6;   c and 9;   d and 1;   e and 5;   f and 3   g and 8.

PROBLEMS

1.   a.   rises by 3 percent; rises by 3 percent
      b.   doubles; remains constant
      c.   rises by 56.25 percent (note: this equals the sum of their changes plus their product); rises by 56.25 percent
      d.   rises by 25 percent

BUSINESS SECTION

1.   a.   i.   Canada   3.72%, 4.71%
            ii.   Mexico   5.50%, 5.32%
            iii. U.S.4.25%, 4.40%
            iv.   Australia   4.32%, 4.29%
            v.   Japan   1.22%, 1.05%
      b.   Mexico, Canada ranked 4th
      c.   Mexico, Canada ranked 2nd

CHAPTER 7

MODELLING REAL GDP AND THE PRICE LEVEL IN THE LONG RUN

PUTTING THIS CHAPTER INTO PERSPECTIVE

In Chapters 7 and 8, a basic model of the economy is created. Using this model, we will be able to explore many of the issues that concern us as a nation and as individuals. The fundamental components of this model are the aggregate demand curve and the long-run aggregate supply curve. You must master these curves if you are to understand the modern theory of the price level and modern theories of inflation (the rate at which the price level is rising).

Modern theories of how to combat inflation depend on a thorough understanding of the aggregate demand curve and the long-run aggregate supply curve. This is a key chapter—one that forms the foundation for many discussions in macroeconomics. You should read your text carefully and master this chapter in your Student Learning Guide. Much of what is in this chapter appears in today's headlines; Chapter 7 will help you to make sense of these headlines and to analyse the story behind them.

LEARNING OBJECTIVES

After reading this chapter, you should be able to:

7.1   Understand the concept of long-run aggregate supply.

7.2   Describe the effect of economic growth on the long-run aggregate supply curve.

7.3   Explain why the aggregate demand curve slopes downward and list key factors that cause this curve to shift.

7.4   Discuss the meaning of long-run equilibrium for the economy as a whole.

7.5   Evaluate why economic growth can cause deflation.

7.6   Evaluate likely reasons for persistent inflation in recent decades.

CHAPTER OUTLINE

LO 7.1 - Understand the concept of long-run aggregate supply.
1. An **aggregate supply curve** shows the relationship between planned rates of total production for the entire economy and various price levels.
   a. The **long-run aggregate supply** (LRAS) curve relates the nation's level of real national output of goods and services to the price level, when full information and full adjustments have occurred.
   b. The LRAS curve has the following properties:
      i.   The LRAS curve is vertical at the level of real national output determined by tastes, technology, and the **endowments** of resources that exist in the nation.
      ii. The LRAS curve is vertical in the long run because a higher price level for output will be accompanied by higher costs for producers; hence, after all these adjustments are made, producers have no incentive to increase output merely because the price level is higher.

LO 7.2 - Describe the effect of economic growth on the long-run aggregate supply curve.
2. The LRAS curve shifts rightward over time, as technological improvements occur and as the nation's endowments increase.

LO 7.3 - Explain why the aggregate demand curve slopes downward and list key factors that cause this curve to shift.
3. The aggregate demand curve indicates the various quantities of all goods and services demanded at various price levels.
   a. The aggregate demand curve is downward sloping for at least three reasons.
      i.   When the price level rises (falls), those people who own cash balances will experience a reduction (an increase) in the purchasing power of their wealth; they consequently will plan to spend less (more) on goods and services. This is known as the **real-balance effect**.
      ii. When the price level rises (falls), people want to hold more (less) money in order to make the same transactions; given the supply of money, this increase (decrease) in the relative demand for money will cause interest rates to rise (fall); planned purchases on consumer durables and capital goods will therefore fall (rise). This is known as the **interest rate effect**.
      iii. When the price level rises (falls), domestic residents will export less (more) and import more (less); these two effects (which result from international relative price changes) cause a decrease (an increase) in planned purchases of domestically produced goods and services. This is known as the **open economy effect**.
   b. When the non-price-level determinants of aggregate demand change, the aggregate demand curve shifts. For example:
      i.   If the money supply rises (falls), then the AD curve will shift to the right (left); if taxes fall (rise), the AD curve will shift to the right (left).

    ii. If expectations about the future economic outlook become more (less) favourable, the AD curve will shift to the right (left).

    iii. If a nation's exchange rate decreases (increases), the AD curve will shift to the right (left).

LO 7.4 - Discuss the meaning of long-run equilibrium for the economy as a whole.

4. The long-run equilibrium price level and the long-run equilibrium output (real national income) level are determined at the intersection of the AD curve with the LRAS curve.

LO 7.5 - Evaluate why economic growth can cause deflation.

5. Inflation does not necessarily accompany economic growth.

    a. Increases in a nation's endowments of factors such as labour and capital or improvements in technology shift the LRAS curve rightward.

    b. In the absence of any change in aggregate demand, the price level actually would fall in a growing economy, as it did in the United States in the latter part of the nineteenth century; that is, there would be secular deflation.

LO 7.6 - Evaluate likely reasons for persistent inflation in recent decades

6. Long-run inflation cannot result from economic growth.

    a. In the long run, inflation can result from supply-side factors only if the LRAS curve shifts leftward, which does not occur in a growing economy.

    b. Maintaining a constant long-run equilibrium price level in a growing economy requires the aggregate demand curve to shift outward at the same pace as the outward shift of the LRAS curve; hence, in the long run inflation results when the aggregate demand curve shifts rightward at a faster pace than rightward shifts in the LRAS curve.

KEY TERMS AND CONCEPTS

Aggregate demand	Open economy effect	Interest rate effect
Aggregate supply	Deflation	Endowments
Real balance effect		

COMPLETION QUESTIONS
Fill in the blank or circle the correct term.

(LO 7.1)

1. The long-run aggregate supply curve is (horizontal, vertical), because in the long run there is (full, incomplete) information, and full adjustment to changes in the price level can occur.

(LO 7.2)

2. Economic growth is shown as a shift to the (left, right) of the LRAS curve, and a shift to the (left, right) of the PPC curve.

(LO 7.3)

3. The sum of all planned expenditures in an economy is called (aggregate demand, the aggregate demand curve); the sum of planned production in the economy is called (aggregate supply, the aggregate supply curve).

4. The aggregate demand curve relates planned purchase rates of all goods and services to various _____; the aggregate supply curve relates planned rates of total production for the entire economy to various _____.

5. The aggregate demand curve is _____ sloped due to three effects: _____, _____, and _____.

6. When the price level rises (other things being constant), the real wealth of people who hold cash balances (falls, rises); therefore planned purchases of goods and services will (fall, rise).

7. When the price level rises, people will want to hold (more, less) money; this increase in the demand for money causes interest rates to (rise, fall); such a change in the interest rate causes households to plan to purchase (more, fewer) consumer durables, and businesses to plan to purchase (more, fewer) capital goods.

8. When a nation's price level falls (other things being constant) its exports (rise, fall) and its imports (rise, fall); therefore the planned purchases of its output will (rise, fall).

9. Non-price determinants of aggregate demand include _____, _____, _____, _____and _____.

10. If government spending rises and taxes fall, the AD curve will shift to the (left, right); if the economic forecast is rosy, the AD curve will shift to the (left, right); if the money supply falls, the AD curve shifts to the _____.

(LO 7.5)

11. Economic growth can cause deflation when the LRAS curve shifts (further, less than) the AD curve shifts.

(LO 7.6)

12. If the position of the (aggregate demand, long-run aggregate supply) curve remains unchanged, then economic growth causes the long-run equilibrium price level to (decline, increase).

TRUE-FALSE QUESTIONS

Circle the T if the statement is true, the F if it is false. Explain to yourself why a statement is false.

(LO 7.1)

T F   1. The LRAS curve is vertical because firms and providers of resources can make complete adjustments and information is complete.

T F   2. The aggregate supply curve relates planned rates of total expenditure to various price levels.

(LO 7.2)

T F   3. The LRAS curve is vertical and doesn't shift in a growing economy.

(LO 7.3)

T F   4. Aggregate demand relates planned purchases to price levels.

T F   5. As the price level falls, other things being constant, the purchasing power of cash balances rises.

T F   6. As the price level of a nation rises, other things being constant, the value of its imports and exports both fall.

T F   7. As the price level falls, other things being constant, the demand for money falls and the interest rate rises.

T F   8. If the price level falls, the AD curve shifts to the right.

(LO 7.4)

T F   9. Long-run equilibrium occurs where the LRAS curve intersects the AD curve.

(LO 7.5)

T F   10. Economic growth causes a nation's long-run AS curve to shift to the right, therefore deflation always accompanies economic growth.

T   F   11.   If the aggregate demand curve shifts rightward at a slower pace than rightward shifts in the LRAS curve in a growing economy, then secular deflation occurs.

(LO 7.6)

T   F   12.   A demand shock that shifts the AD curve rightward will probably cause national output to rise and the price level to fall in the long run.

T   F   13.   A key factor causing the long-run equilibrium price level to rise in a growing economy is the accompanying decline in long-run aggregate supply.

MULTIPLE CHOICE QUESTIONS

Circle the letter that corresponds to the best answer.

(LO 7.1)

1.   The LRAS curve
   a.   is a short-run phenomenon.
   b.   shows national output rising with the price level.
   c.   does not shift over time, due to economic growth.
   d.   reflects the price level/national output situation with full information and complete adjustment.

(LO 7.2)

2.   Which of the following certainly will NOT shift the LRAS curve?
   a.   a change in the price level.
   b.   a new oil discovery.
   c.   freer trade among nations.
   d.   economic growth.

(LO 7.3)

3.   Analogy: price is to demand as the price level is to
   a.   aggregate demand.
   b.   aggregate supply.
   c.   interest rates.
   d.   aggregate supply curve.

4.   Aggregate demand includes
   a.   planned production rates by businesses.
   b.   planned saving.
   c.   planned purchases by households and businesses.
   d.   various price levels.

5. The aggregate demand curve
   a. relates planned purchases to various price levels.
   b. is negatively sloped.
   c. includes planned expenditures on consumption, investment, and government-provided goods.
   d. All of the above

6. The aggregate demand curve is negatively sloped because, other things being constant,
   a. as the price level rises, the demand for money falls.
   b. as the price level falls, the purchasing power of cash balances rises.
   c. as the price level falls, the AD curve shifts to the right.
   d. as the price level rises, exports rise.

7. When the price level falls, other things being constant,
   a. the demand for money falls.
   b. the interest rate falls.
   c. household and business planned expenditures rise.
   d. All of the above

8. Which of the following does NOT occur when the price level rises, other things being constant?
   a. Exports rise, imports fall.
   b. The demand for money rises.
   c. The purchasing power of cash balances falls.
   d. Aggregate demand falls.

9. Which of the following does not cause the AD curve to shift?
   a. an increase in taxes.
   b. a decrease in the real interest rate.
   c. a decrease in the price level.
   d. a change in the money supply.

(LO 7.4)
10. Long-run equilibrium occurs
    a. where AD crosses potential output.
    b. because there is excess/shortage of inventory being produced which firms react to.
    c. because of the adjustment of prices and wages.
    d. all of the above.

(LO 7.5)

11.   Which of the following does NOT cause secular deflation?

a.   economic growth.

b.   a decrease in long-run aggregate supply.

c.   a decrease in aggregate demand at a faster pace than a decrease in long-run aggregate supply.

d.   failure of aggregate demand to increase in the face of an increase in long-run aggregate supply.

(LO 7.6)

12.   The most likely cause for persistent inflation is

a.   a leftward shift of the LRAS curve.

b.   a rightward shift of the AD curve.

c.   a decline in productivity of the economy.

d.   not explainable by economists today.

MATCHING

Choose the item in Column (2) that best matches an item in Column (1).

(1)	(2)
(LO 7.1)	
a. aggregate supply	1. change in government spending or taxation
(LO 7.3)	
b. aggregate demand shift	2. endowments
c. aggregate demand	3. changes in imports and exports due to price changes
d. real balances effect	
e. open economy effects	4. planned production
f. interest rate effects	5. changes in the demand for money due to changes in the price level
	6. demand-pull inflation
	7. planned expenditures
	8. unanticipated change in investment expenditures
	9. change in the value of cash balances

PROBLEMS

(LO 7.5), 7.6

1. Consider the graph below, and then answer the following questions.

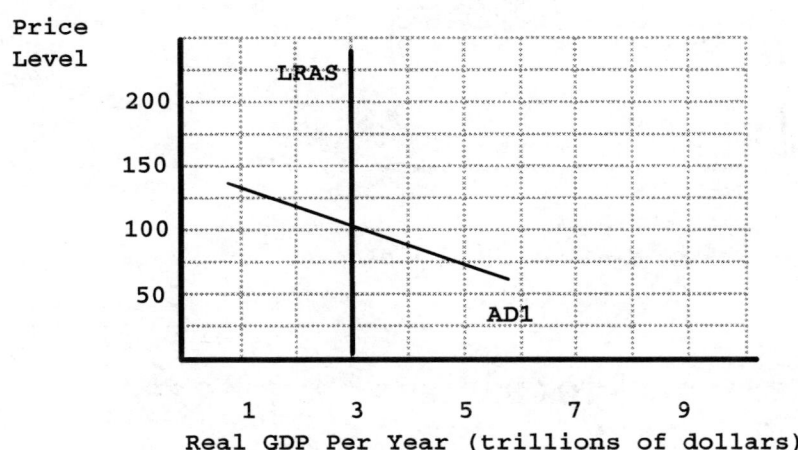

a. What is the current long-run equilibrium level of real GDP? What is the current long-run equilibrium price level?

b. If the economy grows sufficiently that $2 trillion in additional real GDP is forthcoming in the long run, and if aggregate demand remains unchanged, what will be the new long-run equilibrium price level?

2. Consider the diagram on the next page, and suppose that the long-run equilibrium level of real GDP rises by $2 trillion, but the equilibrium price level remains unchanged. Assuming parallel shift(s) of any schedule, draw new schedules showing how this could take place.

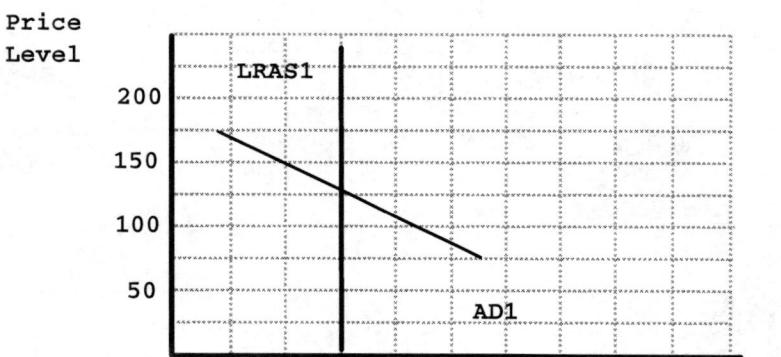

ANSWERS TO CHAPTER 7

COMPLETION QUESTIONS

1. vertical, full
2. right, right
3. aggregate demand; aggregate supply
4. price levels; price levels
5. negatively; real-balance, interest rate, open economy effects
6. falls; fall
7. more; rise; fewer, fewer
8. rise, fall; rise
9. government spending and taxing policies, exchange rates, expectations, money supply, real interest rates
10. right; right; left
11. further
12. aggregate demand, decline

TRUE-FALSE QUESTIONS

1. T
2. F   This is the aggregate demand curve.
3. F   Growth with shift LRAS to the right.
4. T
5. T
6. F   The value of exports falls, imports rise.
7. F   Interest rates fall.
8. F   A lower price level leads to a movement down the AD curve; no shift.
9. T
10. F   It is possible for the AD curve to increase as well, so inflation is also possible.
11. T
12. F   It would likely increase the price level.
13. F   A growing economy is reflected in an increase in AS.

MULTIPLE CHOICE QUESTIONS

1.d; The LRAS curve reflects the price level/national output situation when costs freely adjust to price level changes. In contrast, the SRAS curve assumes costs of production do not adjust to price level changes.

2.a; A change in the price level will not shift the LRAS curve. Only "non-price factors" that affect supply, will cause a shift in the curve.
TIP: The LRAS curve is vertical because if input prices fully adjust to output prices, there is no profit incentive to increase production in the longer run, as the price level increases.
TIP: The LRAS curve is situated at the full-employment level of real GDP. In general, the position of the LRAS curve is determined by tastes, technology and resource endowments.

3.a; Price is to demand as the price level is to aggregate demand. Aggregate demand refers to total demand for all domestic goods and services. The price level refers to the average price of all goods and services.
TIP: While microeconomics focuses on the price and quantity demanded in one market, macro-economics is concerned with variables that relate to the economy as a whole, such as the average price of all goods and the total demand for all goods.

4.c; In general, aggregate demand is the sum of total planned consumption, investment, government and net foreign spending or demand. The only option consistent with this definition of aggregate demand is planned purchases by households and businesses.

5.d; The aggregate demand curve relates different possible average price levels to total planned expenditures. The curve is negatively sloped indicating that as the average price level falls, total planned spending increases.

6.b; One explanation as to why the aggregate demand curve is negatively sloped is described as the Real Balance Effect. This explanation focuses on the direct effect that the average price level has on the purchasing power of the wealth that has been accumulated by households. If the price level falls, the purchasing power of one's wealth in the form of cash balances increases, which in turn can cause total spending to increase.

7.d; When the price level falls, the real value of cash balances increases. To maintain the same level of spending, the demand for money will decline resulting in excess cash balances. Some of this excess money will be used to increase household and business expenditures. The other portion of the excess cash will be used to purchase bonds and finance new loans. This will cause interest rates to decline.

8.a; When the price level rises in Canada relative to her trading partners, foreigners buy fewer Canadian goods and more of their own. This means that Canadian exports will fall, not rise.

9.c; A decrease in the price level will result in a "movement along" the same aggregate demand curve.
TIP: If the price level changes a "movement along" the same aggregate demand curve results. If "non-price factors" affecting aggregate demand changes, this will cause a "shift" in the aggregate demand curve.

10.d; All of these are different ways of representing equilibrium.

11.b; If LRAS decreases, all else equal, this would cause inflation.

12.b; Rising demand is likely to be the cause of persistent inflation in Canada.

MATCHING

a and 4; b and 1; c and 7; d and 9; e and 3; f and 5;

PROBLEMS

1. a. real GDP = 3 trillion, price level = 100
    b. the price level would fall to 75

2.

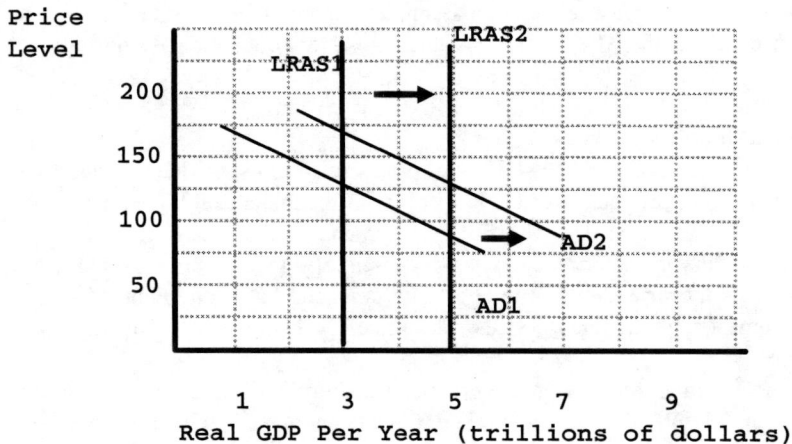

Both curves would have to shift to the right by $2 trillion.

CHAPTER 8

MODELLING REAL GDP AND THE PRICE LEVEL IN THE SHORT RUN

PUTTING THIS CHAPTER INTO PERSPECTIVE

In this chapter you build on the model introduced in the previous chapter. Here, we incorporate economic theory that explains the short-run fluctuations of the economy first discussed in chapter 4. You must master these curves if you are to understand the modern theory of the price level and modern theories of inflation (the rate at which the price level is rising). Such curves also play a prominent role in the explanation of stagflation—the simultaneous existence of high unemployment rates and high inflation rates. Stagflation erupted several times in the 1970s and that phenomenon led economists to rethink old macroeconomic models and to develop new models. The aggregate demand/aggregate supply model can also be used to explain short-run inflation, and we will also explore the effect of having an open economy, and economic growth.

LEARNING OBJECTIVES

After you have studied this chapter you should be able to:

8.1   Explain the concept of the short-run aggregate supply curve.

8.2   Understand what factors cause shifts in the short-run and long-run aggregate supply curves.

8.3   Evaluate the effects of aggregate demand and supply shocks on equilibrium real output in the short run.

8.4   Explain the long-run adjustment process.

8.5   Explain how an open economy affects aggregate demand and aggregate supply.

8.6   Explain short-run inflation and economic growth in the economy

CHAPTER OUTLINE

LO 8.1 - Explain the concept of the short-run aggregate supply curve.

1. The **short-run aggregate supply (SRAS)** curve shows how real national output changes with the price level in the short run, before full adjustment is made and before full information is available.
   a. If the price level rises, while input costs remain the same, profit-per-unit increases so producers have an incentive to increase output;
   b. Producers are able to expand output in the short run in response to price level increase because:
      - firms can use existing workers more intensively.
      - existing capital equipment can be used more intensively.
      - if wage rates don't rise, it is profitable for firms to hire the unemployed or new entrants to the labour force.
   c. At some point the SRAS curve becomes very steep; it becomes harder and harder to find more workers at existing wage rates or to get more effort out of existing machinery as production levels increase.
   d. The SRAS curve, therefore, is positively sloped and becomes steeper and steeper as the price level gets higher.
   e. **Capacity utilization** measures how intensively plant and equipment and machinery are being used. It indirectly measures the desirability of production versus the capability of production.

LO 8.2 - Understand what factors cause shifts in the short-run and long-run aggregate supply curves.

2. Changes in some non-price determinants of aggregate supply lead to shifts in both the LRAS and SRAS. These are:
   a. Any change in our endowments of land, labour or capital.
   b. Any change in the level of technology or knowledge.

3. Some changes in the non-price determinants of aggregate supply lead to shifts in the short-run aggregate supply curve **only**.
   a. If input costs rise (fall), the SRAS curve shifts to the left (right).

LO 8.3 - Evaluate the effects of aggregate demand and supply shocks on equilibrium real output in the short run.

4. The price level and the equilibrium output (real national income) level are determined in the short run at the intersection of the AD and SRAS curves. Firms adjust their level of output and prices because of inventory accumulation or shrinkage.

5. Unanticipated shifts in the AD and the AS curves are called **aggregate demand shocks** and **aggregate supply shocks**, respectively.

6. These shocks create **output gaps**, which is the difference between LRAS and actual GDP.
   a. An **inflationary gap** exists if actual GDP is greater than potential GDP.

    b. A **recessionary gap** exists if actual GDP is less than potential GDP.

LO 8.4 - Explain the long-run adjustment process.

7. The economy will adjust over time (without government intervention) to its potential output if an inflationary or recessionary gap exists.

    a. An inflationary gap leads to excess demand for resource inputs. Over time, these input prices will rise and cause the SRAS curve to shift to the left. Eventually, actual output with equal potential output and the pressure on input prices will cease.

    b. A recessionary gap leads to an excess supply of resource inputs. Over time, these input prices will fall and cause the SRAS curve to shift to the right. Again, actual output will equal potential output and the pressure on input prices will cease.

    c. Many economists believe that wages (the largest input costs in an economy) are "sticky." They theorize that it is harder to lower wages than to raise them for several reasons.

        i. Wage contracts usually run several years, and only allow for workforce adjustment (layoffs), not wage adjustment.

        ii. Employers may be reluctant to reduce wages because of the effect on morale. With a poor morale, efficiency of production may fall. This is called an **efficiency wage**.

        iii. With an inflationary gap, the reverse situation is not true. Workers can always quit their jobs to work for another employer offering a higher wage. Thus wages can adjust upwards more quickly than down.

LO 8.5 - Explain how an open economy affects aggregate demand and aggregate supply.

8. Both aggregate supply and aggregate demand are affected if a nation's exchange rate changes.

    a. If a nation's exchange rate rises in value, its SRAS curve will shift rightward, as imported raw material prices fall, and its AD curve will shift leftward as its imports rise and its exports fall.

    b. The net effect is a lower price level, while the net effect on GDP is indeterminate.

LO 8.6 - Explain short-run inflation and economic growth in the economy

9. There are two types of short-run inflation—demand pull and cost-push.

    a. **Demand-pull** inflation is caused by increases in aggregate demand that are not matched by increases in aggregate supply.

    b. **Cost-push** inflation is caused by continual leftward shifts in the short-run aggregate-supply curve.

10. It is possible to have economic growth without inflation.

    a. Economic growth shifts the short-run and long-run AS curves rightward.

    b. Rightward shifts in the AD curve, therefore, can be offset by rightward shifts in AS curve.

KEY TERMS AND CONCEPTS

Short-run aggregate
 supply curve
Recessionary gap
Capacity utilization

Aggregate supply shock
Demand-pull inflation
Inflationary gap
Efficiency wage

Aggregate demand shock
Cost-push inflation
Output gap

COMPLETION QUESTIONS
Fill in the blank or circle the correct term.

(LO 8.1)

1. If changes in production costs lag behind changes in the price level, producers will have an incentive to produce (more, less) as the price level rises.

2. At very high GDP levels, the SRAS curve becomes very (flat, steep) because it becomes (more difficult, easier) to get more labour at relatively fixed wage-rates.

(LO 8.2)

3. The short-run AS curve will shift if there is a change in any of the following non-price-level determinants of aggregate supply: _____, _____, _____ and _____.

4. If wage-rates fall, the short-run AS curve will shift to the _____; if technological improvements occur and if the prices of raw materials fall permanently, the long-run AS curve will shift to the _____.

5. A temporary increase in an input price shifts only the (LRAS, SRAS).

(LO 8.3)

6. The price level and the equilibrium national output level are determined where the SRAS curve and the AD curve _____.

7. An unanticipated shift in the AD curve is called a _____.

8. If long-run equilibrium does not exist, then either a _____ or a _____ exists.

(LO 8.4)

9. When an inflationary gap exists, the _____ will adjust in the long-run by moving to the _____, moving actual _____ towards potential GDP.

(LO 8.5)

10. Nation A's exchange rate has increased. As a result its SRAS curve will shift to the _____, and its AD curve will shift to the _____; the

net effect is that nation A's price level will _____ and its GDP change will _____.

11. Country Z's exchange rate has weakened. As a result its AD curve will _____ and its SRAS curve will _____; the net effect on country Z is that its GDP change will _____ and its price level will _____

(LO 8.6)

12. Continual leftward shifts in the SRAS causes _____.

13. As economic growth occurs, a nation's short-run AS curve will shift _____ and its long-run AS curve will shift _____. Consequently, if the AD curve shifts rightward during periods of economic growth inflation (will, will not, may not) result.

TRUE-FALSE QUESTIONS

Circle the **T** if the statement is true, the **F** if it is false. Explain to yourself why a statement is false.

(LO 8.1)

T F   1. The short-run aggregate supply curve is positively sloped.

T F   2. If the price level rises and wage rates do not producers have an incentive to produce less.

T F   3. The SRAS curve becomes very flat at higher and higher price levels.

(LO 8.2)

T F   4. If productivity rises and raw material prices fall, then the SRAS curve will shift to the right.

T F   5. Producers can expand output in the short run by adding to their capital stock.

T F   6. A demand shock that shifts the AD curve rightward will probably cause national output to rise and the price level to fall.

(LO 8.3)

T F   7. An increase in wages will increase national output and raise the price level.

T F   8. A decline in investment spending will create a recessionary gap.

(LO 8.4)

T   F   9.   If neither a recessionary nor an inflationary gap exists, then full employment equilibrium exists.

T   F   10.   The long-run adjustment process happens because of an excess of inventory of real GDP.

(LO 8.5)

T   F   11.   If a nation's exchange rate weakens, its SRAS curve will shift leftward, its AD curve will shift rightward, and its price level will rise.

(LO 8.6)

T   F   12.   Cost-push inflation involves continual shifts leftward in the short-run aggregate supply curve.

T   F   13.   Economic growth causes a nation's long-run AS curve to shift to the right, but its short-run AS curve to shift to the left.

MULTIPLE CHOICE QUESTIONS
Circle the letter that corresponds to the best answer.

(LO 8.1)

1.   Concerning the SRAS curve, an increase in the price level
    a.   has no effect on planned production.
    b.   leads to an increase in output if input prices rise proportionally.
    c.   causes a decrease in planned production in the long run.
    d.   causes an increase in planned production.

2.   If the price level rises faster than costs of production rise, then
    a.   profits per unit fall.
    b.   producers have an incentive to increase output.
    c.   the aggregate supply curve shifts to the right.
    d.   the aggregate supply curve shifts to the left.

3.   If unused capacity and significant unemployment exist, then the SRAS curve is
    a.   vertical over a broad range.
    b.   downward sloping.
    c.   horizontal or slightly upward sloping.
    d.   the same as the LRAS curve.

(LO 8.2)

4. Which of the following causes the SRAS curve to shift to the left?
    a. a fall in wage rates.
    b. rises in productivity.
    c. technological improvements.
    d. increase in raw material costs.

5. Which of the following will not shift the LRAS curve?
    a. a change in the price level.
    b. a new oil discovery.
    c. freer trade among nations.
    d. economic growth.

6. A temporary rise in production costs
    a. shifts the LRAS curve rightward.
    b. shifts the SRAS curve leftward.
    c. shifts the AD curve leftward.
    d. shifts the AD curve rightward.

(LO 8.3)

7. Assume SRAS, LRAS and AD all intersect at one point. At this intersection point
    a. the equilibrium price level is determined.
    b. the equilibrium national output level is determined.
    c. economy-wide equilibrium exists.
    d. All of the above.

8. An unanticipated rightward shift in the AD curve
    a. is a supply shock.
    b. is a demand shock.
    c. will cause the output level to fall.
    d. will cause the price level to fall.

9. Massive technological changes in the computer industry probably will cause the
    a. SRAS curve to shift upward.
    b. LRAS curve to shift rightward.
    c. AD curve to shift leftward.
    d. AD curve to shift rightward because the price level will rise.

10. Both unemployment and the price level rise if the
    a. AD curve shifts to the right.
    b. AD curve shifts to the left.
    c. SRAS curve shifts to the left.
    d. SRAS curve shifts to the right.

11. Which of the following is most unlike the others?
    a. Rosy economic outlook.
    b. Rise in a nation's exchange rate.
    c. Tax decreases.
    d. Increase in money supply.

(LO 8.4)

12. Wages are more difficult to lower than to raise for all of the following reasons *except*
    a. Workers can always quit their jobs to work for someone else, but wage contracts don't allow wages to be lowered in the short-run.
    b. Lowering wages may reduce morale and the efficiency of production.
    c. Government standards don't allow wages to be renegotiated downwards.
    d. Wage contracts allow for layoffs but not for reductions in wage rates.

13. The long-run adjustment process eliminates an inflationary gap because
    a. Excess inventory encourages firms to reduce production and prices.
    b. Excess demand for resources causes prices of inputs to rise.
    c. Firms reduce capacity to eliminate output capability.
    d. Governments decrease the supply of money to reduce aggregate demand.

(LO 8.5)

14. If a nation's exchange rate rises (all else equal), its
    a. SRAS curve shifts leftward, due to input cost reductions.
    b. AD curve shifts rightward, due to falling imports.
    c. price level will fall.
    d. GDP will rise, unambiguously.

15. If a nation's exchange rate falls, its
    a. SRAS curve shifts leftward, due to input cost increases.
    b. AD curve shifts rightward, due to increased exports and decreased imports.
    c. price level rises.
    d. All of the above.

(LO 8.6)

16. When economic growth occurs, a nation's
    a. short-run AS curve shifts leftward
    b. short-run and long-run AS curves shift rightward
    c. long-run AS curve becomes horizontal
    d. price level must rise

MATCHING
Choose the item in Column (2) that best matches an item in Column (1).

(1)   (2)

(LO 8.1)
a. capacity utilization   1. difference between actual and potential GDP
(LO 8.3)   2. potential GDP greater than actual GDP
b. aggregate demand shock   3. actual GDP greater than potential GDP
c. aggregate supply shock   4. intensity of use of machinery and equipment
d. inflationary gap   5. increase in AD not matched by increases in
e. output gap   SRAS
                                        6. higher wages increases efficiency
(LO 8.4)   7. changes in SRAS
f. efficiency wage   8. increases in LRAS
(LO 8.6)   9. changes in AD
g. demand-pull inflation

PROBLEMS

(LO 8.2)
1. Consider the graph below, then answer the questions that follow. National Income figures are in hundreds of billions of dollars.

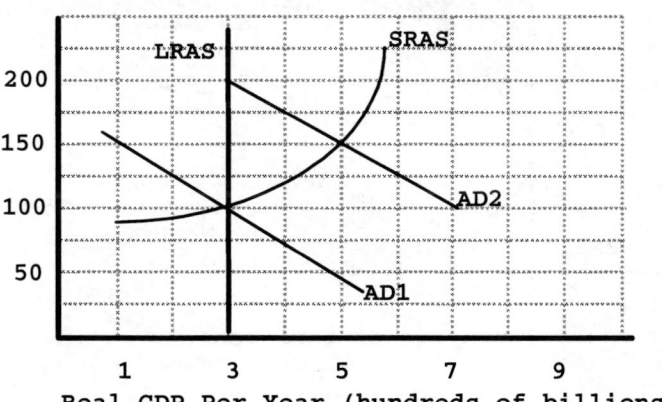

a. What is the equilibrium price level, given the AS and AD1 curves? What is the equilibrium level of real national income? Is the economy at full employment? Why?

(LO 8.3)
b. What factors could cause the AD1 curve to shift to AD2?

c. Given AD2, what will be the new short run equilibrium price level? Why?

d. When AD1 shifts to AD2 what would be the percentage change in the short-run equilibrium price level? What type of inflation is said to occur in this situation?

e. Given AD2, what will be the new short-run equilibrium level of real national income. Why?

f. If full employment exists at the real national income level of $300 billion, what type of gap exists at the new equilibrium level (with AD2)? Briefly explain.

2. Consider the graph below, then answer the questions that follow. Real GDP per year is in hundreds of billions of dollars.

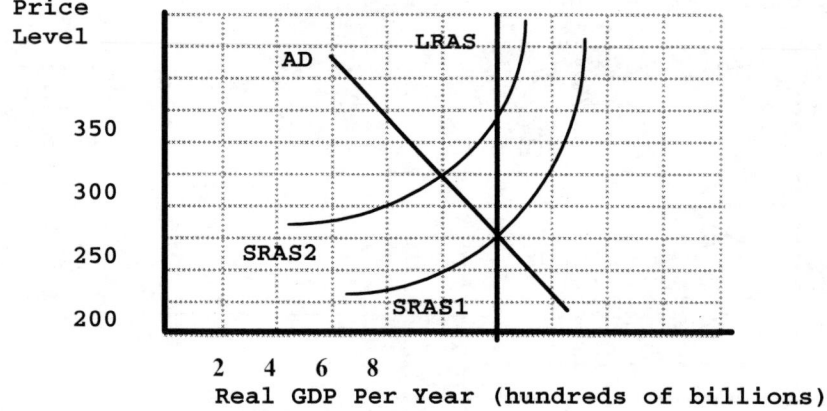

(LO 8.2)

a. What is the equilibrium price level, given the SRAS1 and AD curves? What is the equilibrium level of real GDP? Is the economy at full employment? Explain.

b. What factors could cause the SRAS1 curve to shift to SRAS2?

(LO 8.3)

    c.   Given SRAS2 and the AD curve, what will be the new short-run equilibrium price level?

    d.   Given SRAS2 and the AD curve, what will be the new short run equilibrium level of real GDP?

(LO 8.6)

    e.   When the short run aggregate supply curve shifts from SRAS1 to SRAS2, what type of inflation is said to occur?

    f.   What factors could cause the LRAS curve to shift rightward?

(LO 8.3)

    3.   Using the co-ordinate system below, answer the questions that follow.

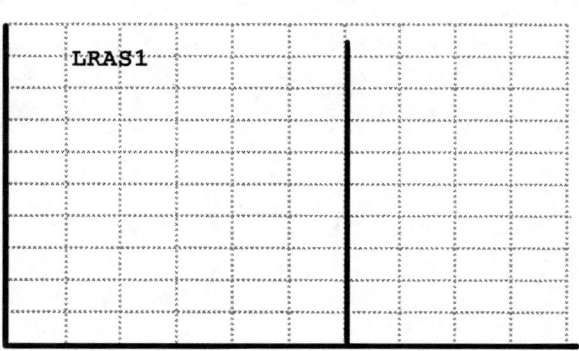

Real GDP Per Year (trillions of dollars)

    a.   Assuming a flexible price level and an open economy draw an equilibrium situation using the short run AS/AD model.

    b.   Assume that this nation's exchange rate has weakened, draw in the new AD and the new SRAS curves.

    c.   What happens to GDP and the price level?

    4.   Assuming the economy is operating at long-run potential output, predict what happens to the equilibrium price level and the equilibrium real national income level as a result of:

    a.   productivity increases.

    b.   an increase in the labour participation rates.

    c.   a significantly lower marginal tax rate.

    d.   economic growth.

    e.   a temporary rise in raw material prices.

    f.   an increase in population.

    g.   a decrease in raw material prices.

    h.   a decrease in government spending.

    i.   an improvement in expectations about the future economic outlook.

    j.   an increase in the price of oil.

    k.   technological improvements.

    l.   a temporary increase in investment spending.

    m. a permanent increase in investment spending.

BUSINESS SECTION

(LO 8.2)
Finance: The Top-Down Strategy and the TSE Sub-indices

You may recall, from an earlier chapter of the learning guide, according to the fundamental stock analysis approach, the single most important factor affecting a stock price is the expected profitability of the company who issued the stock. The investor's profit expectations are affected by both macroeconomic and microeconomic factors.

The Top-Down investment strategy is one common way of applying the fundamental stock analysis approach in order to make stock purchase or sale decisions. The first step of the Top Down investment strategy is to assess the macro (national) economic environment. As an example, suppose that after completing the first step, an investor decides to invest in Canada, on the Toronto Stock Exchange. This decision would likely have been based on studying the macro trends in the Canadian economy, including the behaviour of the TSE 300.

Once an investor decides to invest in the Canadian stock market, the next step is to decide which sectors or industries to invest in. To help make this decision, the investor may examine the behaviour of various sub-indices of the TSE 300. Some of these sub-indices are listed below:

- Merchandising—food stores, department stores, specialty stores.
- Consumer Products—food processing, tobacco, distilleries, breweries, etc.
- Industrial Products—construction materials, transportation equipment, autos and parts.
- Paper and Forest Products—heavily dependent on exports.
- Financial Services—banks, trust companies, investment companies

The following problem illustrates how the theory in Chapter 10 can help an investor understand and predict the sub-index behaviour so as to determine which sectors of the economy to invest in.

Application Problem 1:

For each of the following events, predict which component of aggregate demand will be affected. In turn, identify which one of the TSE sub-indices listed above is most likely to be positively affected by the event in question.

1. a. Canadian interest rates decline.

    b. The Canadian dollar depreciates.

    c. The U.S economy experiences a rapid growth rate.

    d. As the baby boom population reaches middle age, the savings rate increases.

    e. The Canadian government lowers the personal income tax.

    f. Many key Canadian industries are operating at close to full capacity.

2. Which one of the sub indices is least likely to be sensitive to business cycle fluctuations? Briefly explain. (look back to Example 5-2)

ANSWERS TO CHAPTER 8

COMPLETION QUESTIONS
1. more
2. steep, more difficult
3. wage-rates, productivity, technology, raw-material prices
4. right; right
5. SRAS
6. intersect
7. demand shock
8. recessionary gap; expansionary gap
9. SRAS, left, real GDP
10. right; left; fall; be indeterminate (not determinable)
11. shift rightward; shift leftward; be indeterminate; rise
12. cost-push inflation
13. rightward; rightward; may not

TRUE-FALSE QUESTIONS

1. T
2. F   They have an incentive to produce more.
3. F   It becomes very steep as labour becomes more difficult to obtain at constant wage rates.
4. T
5. F   By assumption, this option is not available in the short run.

6.   F   The price level will rise too
7.   F   This will shift SRAS (only) to the left, lowering actual national output.
8.   T   AD will shift left, and assuming we are at potential to being with, create a recessionary gap.
9.   T
10.   T   While excess inventory may happen as part of the chain of events, the primary cause is a change in the cost of inputs.
11.   T
12.   T
13.   F   Both shifts rightward in a growing economy.

MULTIPLE CHOICE QUESTIONS

1.d;   The SRAS curve assumes that input prices remain constant as output prices increase. Therefore, in the short run, as the price level increases, it becomes profitable for firms to expand production.

2.b;   If the price level rises faster than costs of production rise, then the firm can increase profit by increasing output. The upward sloping SRAS curve describes this situation.

3.c;   If significant unemployment exists, the SRAS curve is horizontal or slightly upward-sloping. This indicates a situation where a small increase in output prices can induce a large increase in production. This reflects the ease with which employers can hire inputs when widespread excess capacity exists.

4.d;   An increase in raw material costs would decrease firms expected profits at any given price level. In turn this would shift the SRAS curve leftward, reflecting a decrease in supply.
        TIP: As the degree of excess capacity decreases the SRAS curve will rise more steeply.

5.a;   A change in the price level will not shift the LRAS curve. Only "non price factors" that affect supply, will cause a shift in the curve. It is assumed that input prices are fixed in the short run.

6.b;   A temporary rise in production costs will reduce the profits of firms, at the current price level. In turn, this will decrease firms willingness to supply goods and services causing the SRAS curve to decrease or shift leftward.

7.d;   In the long run, equilibrium is where the SRAS curve, the LRAS curve, and the AD curve all intersect.

8.b;   A shift in the AD curve is called a demand shock, while a shift in aggregate supply is called a supply shock.

9.b;   Massive technological changes in the computer industry will cause an increase in supply which, in turn, will shift the aggregate supply curve to the right.

10.c;   If the SRAS curve shifts to the left, the price level will increase and the real GDP will decrease. If real GDP decreases, unemployment will rise.

11.b;   A rise in a nation's exchange rate will make domestically produced goods more expensive to foreigners and hence, will reduce foreign demand for domestically produced goods. This will result in a decrease in real GDP making this factor the only answer option pointing to a decline in future real GDP.

12.c;   Governments in most countries allow free-bargaining, which can result in lower wage rates.

13.b;   While b, c, and d all could eliminate a gap, only b is identified with the long-run adjustment process.

14.c;   If a nation's exchange-rate rises, foreign demand for this nation's goods and services will decline. Assuming an upward sloping aggregate supply curve, this decrease in aggregate demand will cause the equilibrium price level to fall.

15.d;   If a nation's exchange rate falls, this will increase the cost of imports to domestic firms but decrease the cost of domestic exports to foreign buyers. As a result the SRAS will shift leftward due to the increased cost of imported inputs. In addition, as exports increase, the aggregate demand curve will shift rightward, causing the price level to increase (assuming an upward sloping aggregate supply curve).

16.b;   When economic growth occurs, both the SRAS and LRAS curves will shift rightward.
        TIP: It is possible to have economic growth with or without inflation. If the aggregate demand curve shifts outward to the right at the same speed as the aggregate supply curve shifts outward (economic growth) no inflation will result.

MATCHING

a and 4;   b and 9;   c and 7;   d and 3;   e and 1;   f and 6;   g and 5

PROBLEMS

1.   a.   100, $300 billion, yes it is at full employment since the economy is on the LRAS curve.
     b.   Increase in government expenditures, decrease in taxes, increase in money supply, increase in population, rosier expectations, decline in the exchange rate, decrease in real interest rates.
     c.   150, because a general shortage of goods and services now exists at the previous price level.
     d.   50% increase, demand pull inflation.
     e. $500 billion per year, as firms have a profit incentive to produce more with higher prices, every thing else (like input prices) staying the same.
     f.   Expansionary gap, as the short-run equilibrium national income exceeds the full employment national income level.
2.   a.   150, $600 billion, yes the economy is at full employment as it is on the LRAS curve.
     b.   temporary change in input prices such as a temporary increase in oil prices or wage rates.
     c.   250.
     d. $500 billion per year.
     e.   cost-push inflation.
     f.   increases in resource endowments, education, international trade and technology.
3.   a.

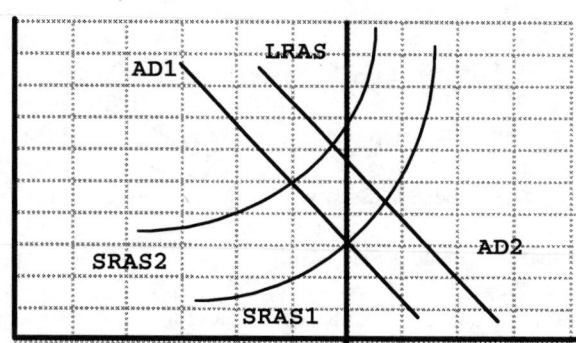

Real GDP Per Year (hundreds of billions)

     b.   The AD curve should shift rightward; the AS curve should shift leftward.
     c.   Effect on GDP is indeterminate; price level should rise.
4.   a.   The SRAS and LRAS curves shift to the right; therefore national output rises, and the price level falls.
     b.   The SRAS and LRAS curve shifts to the right; therefore national output rises, and the price level falls.
     c.   The SRAS and LRAS curve shifts to the right; therefore national output rises, and the price level falls.
     d.   The SRAS and LRAS curve shifts to the right as potential output increases; national output rises, and the price level falls.
     e.   Temporary rise in price level, temporary reduction in national output.
     f.   The AD curve shifts to the right; therefore national output and the price level rise. SRAS may also rise if more people participate in the labour force.
     g.   The SRAS curve shifts to the right temporarily; therefore the price level falls and national output rises.
     h.   The AD curve shifts to the left; national output falls and the price level falls.
     i.   The AD and LRAS curves shifts to the right; therefore national output rises, and the price level may rise or fall.

    j.   The SRAS curve shifts to the left; Canada as an exporting nation would also see an increase in AD. The change in output is uncertain, although the price level would increase.

    k.   The SRAS and LRAS curves shift to the right; therefore national output rises; and the price level falls.

    l.   The AD curve shifts to the right; therefore national output and the price level rise in the short run.

    m.   LRAS shifts as well as AD; national output rises, the effect on the price level is uncertain.

BUSINESS SECTION

1.   a.   Investment increases; positive effect on Industrial Products
        b.   Net exports increases; positive effect on Paper and Forest Products
        c.   Net exports increases; positive effect on Paper and Forest Products
        d.   Consumption declines; positive effect on Financial Services.
        e.   Consumption increases, positive effects on both Merchandising and Consumer Products
        f.   Investment increases; positive effect on Industrial Products.

2.   The Consumer Products sub-index is least likely to be sensitive to business-cycle fluctuations as this sub-index includes necessity expenditures that cannot be postponed such as food, beverage and addictive products.

CHAPTER 9

CONSUMPTION, INVESTMENT, AND THE MULTIPLIER

PUTTING THIS CHAPTER INTO PERSPECTIVE

In this chapter we analyse in detail the model developed by John Maynard Keynes, introduced in the Appendix to Chapter 8. Recall that Keynes' model assumed high levels of excess capacity and unemployment; hence the price level is assumed constant. Keynes' model provides important insights into many important aspects of the economy. Using a "break even" type model, it particularly analyses; the consumption, saving, and investment functions; how equilibrium is determined, and how shifts in the planned expenditures curve lead to multiplier effects.

LEARNING OBJECTIVES

After you have studied this chapter you should be able to:

9.1   Distinguish between saving and savings and explain how saving and consumption are related.

9.2   Explain the key determinants of consumption and saving in the Keynesian model.

9.3   Identify the primary determinants of planned investment.

9.4   Describe how equilibrium national income is established in the Keynesian model.

9.5   Evaluate why autonomous changes in total planned expenditures have a multiplier effect on equilibrium national income.

9.6   Understand the relationship between total planned expenditures and the aggregate demand curve.

CHAPTER OUTLINE

LO 9.1 - Distinguish between saving and savings and explain how saving and consumption are related.

1. The sum of consumption expenditures and saving, equals disposable income, by definition.
   a. Saving, consumption, and income are flows which; therefore, are measured per unit of time; savings and wealth are stocks whose values are measured at a given moment in time.
   b. Investment, which is a flow, includes expenditures by firms for capital goods.

LO 9.2 - Explain the key determinants of consumption and saving in the Keynesian model.

2. John Maynard Keynes maintained that planned real consumption and planned real saving were determined by real disposable income. He called these relationships the **consumption function** and the **saving function**.
   a. For the household, the consumption function is typically plotted as a curve with the value of consumption expenditure on the vertical axis and real disposable income on the horizontal axis; the planned saving curve can be derived by subtracting the planned consumption curve from the 45-degree reference line.
   b. **Autonomous consumption** is that consumption that is independent of income. It is the value of the vertical intercept on the consumption function; if consumption is positive at zero national income, then dis-saving must exist over the lower range of the consumption function.
   c. The **marginal propensity to consume** (MPC) equals the change in real consumption divided by the change in real disposable income; the marginal propensity to save (MPS) equals the change in real saving divided by the change in real disposable income.
   d. The MPC + MPS = 1.
   e. When real disposable income changes, a movement along the consumption curve results; when there is a change in the non-income determinants of consumption, the consumption curve shifts.

3. The non-income determinants of consumption include wealth, future income, inflationary expectations, and population.
   a. If wealth increases, the consumption function shifts upward; if wealth decreases, it shifts downward.
   b. If households expect better times ahead, the consumption function shifts upward; expected worse times will shift it downward.
   c. An expectation that the inflation rate will fall may shift the consumption function downward.
   d. An increase in population shifts the consumption function upward; a decrease in population shifts it downward.

LO 9.3 - Identify the primary determinants of planned investment.

4. Investment includes business expenditures on plants and equipment and on inventories; such expenditures are more variable than household consumption expenditures because expectations play a more important role in investment expenditures. The relationship between investment and these variables and planned real investment expenditure is called the **planned investment function**.
    a. An inverse relationship exists between investment expenditures and the interest rate.
    b. Non-interest rate determinants of investment spending include expectations, innovation and technology, and business taxes.
        i.   If the future looks rosier, then more investment expenditures will be made at any interest rate; the investment curve will shift to the right.
        ii. Improvements in technology and innovation shift the planned investment curve to the right.
        iii. If business taxes rise, the planned investment curve shifts to the left; a reduction in such taxes shifts it to the right.

LO 9.4 - Describe how equilibrium national income is established in the Keynesian model.

5. Real consumption depends on real disposable income and it is also related to real national income; the latter relationship is more convenient for our analysis.
    a. A portion of the consumption function is autonomous, or independent, of real national income.
    b. Net investment is dependent on the interest rate; for simplicity we assume that it is autonomous, or independent, of national income.
    c. When all types of expenditure are added together, including government and foreign sector spending, the resulting total is called total planned expenditures.
    d. The **total planned expenditures curve** (TPE) models the relationship between all types of spending in the economy and the level of national income.

6. The **equilibrium level** of **real national income** occurs at that income level where the total planned expenditures curve intersects the **45-degree reference line**.
    b. Once the equilibrium real national income level is determined, the employment level is also determined because a functional relation exists between those two variables in the short run.
    c. At all other income levels, dis-equilibrium exists.
        i.   If total planned expenditures exceed real national income, then business inventories will fall involuntarily and businesses will find it profitable to increase output and employment.
        ii. If total planned expenditures are less than real national income, then business inventories will rise involuntarily and businesses will find it profitable to decrease output and employment.

LO 9.5 - Evaluate why autonomous changes in total planned expenditures have a multiplier effect on equilibrium national income.

7. When **autonomous expenditures** change, the planned expenditures curve shifts and there will be a **multiplier** effect.
    a. If autonomous consumption, autonomous investment, autonomous government expenditures, or net exports change, the total planned expenditures curve shifts by an identical amount.
    b. Equilibrium real national income per year will change by a multiple of the change in autonomous expenditure, in the same direction. This multiple is the value of the multiplier.

8. The multiplier effect exists because one person's expenditure is another person's income, and changes in autonomous spending lead to successive rounds of spending and income creation.
    a. The multiplier equals the reciprocal of the proportion of **leakages**.
    b. The steeper the slope of the total planned expenditure curve, the greater is the multiplier; the higher is the proportion of leakages, the smaller is the multiplier.
    c. Because of the multiplier effect, fluctuations in economic activity will be magnified.
    d. Economists estimate the multiplier is between 1.0 and 1.9 in Canada, and about 2.0 in the Unites States. The United States has a higher multiplier because it imports much less into its economy than Canada.
    e. The multiplier is smaller when the price level can change, and the SRAS is positively sloped.

LO 9.6 - Understand the relationship between total planned expenditures and the aggregate demand curve.

9. The aggregate demand curve and the total planned expenditures curve are closely related.
    a. The total planned expenditure curve is created assuming that the price level is constant.
    b. If the price level varies, then a new total planned expenditure curve is drawn for each price level; as prices rise, the total planned expenditure curve falls, and vice versa.

KEY TERMS AND CONCEPTS

Consumption	Saving	Consumption function
Marginal propensity to consume	Marginal propensity to save	Marginal propensity to import
Wealth	Investment	Autonomous consumption
Dis-saving	Capital Goods	Autonomous spending
Consumption goods	Multiplier	Lump-sum tax
45-degree reference line	Equilibrium	Total Planned Expenditure
		Marginal propensity to spend

COMPLETION QUESTIONS
Fill in the blank or circle the correct term.

(LO 9.1)

1.   The sum of planned consumption and planned saving equals _____, by definition; when real disposable income rises, planned real consumption _____ and planned real saving _____.

2.   Investment in economics means expenditure on _____ which are also called _____ goods.

(LO 9.2)

3.   The marginal propensity to consume (MPC) equals the change in consumption (divided by, plus, minus) the change in real disposable income; one minus the MPC equals the _____.

4.   The amount of consumption that is (dependent on, independent of) income is called autonomous consumption; when autonomous consumption exists, the vertical intercept of the consumption function is (negative, zero, positive), and the MPC (falls, remains constant, rises) as real disposable income rises.

5.   Dis-saving exists when consumption expenditures (equal, are less than, exceed) income.

6.   The consumption function will shift if autonomous consumption changes due to changes in such non-income determinants of consumption as _____, _____, _____, and _____.

(LO 9.3)

7.   Investment varies (directly, inversely) with changes in the interest rate; the planned investment curve shifts if there are changes in _____, _____, or _____.

(LO 9.4)

8.   Along the 45-degree reference line, total planned expenditures equal real _____; where the planned expenditures line intersects the 45-degree reference line (equilibrium, disequilibrium) exists; where those curves do not intersect, _____ exists.

9.   In the model in which government and foreign transactions are ignored, household planned consumption expenditures plus business investment expenditures equal _____.

10.   If total planned expenditures exceed real national income, business inventories will _____ involuntarily and businesses will find it profitable to (increase,

decrease) output and employment; if total planned expenditures are less than real national income, business inventories will _____ involuntarily and businesses will find it profitable to _____ output and employment.

11. If autonomous government purchases of goods and services (G) are added to the total planned expenditures curve, the total planned expenditures curve will shift (upward, downward) and equilibrium real national income per year will (rise, fall).

12. If exports and imports are added to the total planned expenditure curve and imports exceed exports, then net exports are a (positive, negative) number and equilibrium real national income will (rise, fall) by an amount (greater than, equal to, less than) net exports.

13. Non-income determinants of net exports include: _____, _____, and _____.

(LO 9.5)
14. Changes in autonomous expenditure result in a greater effect on equilibrium national income through a process called the _____ effect.

15. The multiplier can be calculated as the reciprocal of the proportion of _____.

16. The three types of leakages are _____, _____, and _____.

(LO 9.6)
17. A change in the price level will cause a (shift of, move along) the TPE curve and a (shift of, move along) the aggregate demand curve.

TRUE-FALSE QUESTIONS
Circle the **T** if the statement is true, the **F** if it is false. Explain to yourself why a statement is false.

(LO 9.1)
T   F   1.   Saving is a stock variable.

T   F   2.   Consumption and saving together equal disposable income.

(LO 9.2)
T   F   3.   The MPS plus the MPC equals 10, by definition.

T F   4.   If autonomous consumption is positive, then the vertical intercept of the consumption curve is positive.

T F   5.   In the Keynesian model, the MPC falls and the MPS rises as national income rises.

T F   6.   In the Keynesian model, if wealth rises, the consumption function shifts upward.

T F   7.   If real disposable income rises, the consumption function will shift upward.

T F   8.   Autonomous consumption and autonomous investment vary directly with real national income.

T F   9.   Government expenditures are about 20% of real national income.

(LO 9.4)

T F   10.   The 45-degree reference line indicates planned expenditures at each level of real national income.

T F   11.   The equilibrium level of real national income is found at the point at which the planned expenditures curve intersects the 45-degree reference line.

T F   12.   If total planned expenditures exceed real national income, then business inventories will fall and businesses will increase output.

T F   13.   In the short run, employment and real national income (output) are directly related.

T F   14.   If autonomous expenditures rise, then the total planned expenditures curve will shift upward.

(LO 9.5)

T F   15.   If autonomous expenditures rise by $1 billion, national income will probably rise by more than $1 billion.

T F   16.   If the proportion of leakages is 25%, a $1-billion increase in autonomous expenditures will cause national income to rise by $4 billion, if the SRAS curve is horizontal.

(LO 9.6)

T F   17.   If the price level falls, the total planned expenditures curve will shift upward.

MULTIPLE CHOICE QUESTIONS
Circle the letter that corresponds to the best answer.

(LO 9.1)
1. *Analogy*: Saving is to income as _____ is to wealth.
   a. income
   b. savings account balances
   c. investment
   d. consumption

2. Saving plus consumption equal
   a. investment.
   b. aggregate demand.
   c. disposable income.
   d. 1.

(LO 9.2)
3. The consumption function
   a. has an autonomous component that varies with income.
   b. indicates that real consumption falls as real income rises.
   c. shifts if autonomous consumption changes.
   d. is the same as the autonomous investment function.

4. Autonomous real consumption
   a. varies directly with real disposable income.
   b. varies inversely with real disposable income.
   c. changes with changes in wealth.
   d. equals planned saving.

5. The 45-degree reference line
   a. indicates planned expenditures.
   b. is a line along which planned expenditures equal real national income.
   c. is the consumption function.
   d. is the autonomous investment function.

6. Autonomous consumption
   a. varies with disposable national income.
   b. varies with wealth.
   c. changes lead to movements along a given consumption curve.
   d. if positive, means that the vertical intercept of the consumption function is zero.

7.   If autonomous consumption is positive, then
    a.   the vertical intercept of the consumption function is positive.
    b.   the MPC falls as real disposable income rises.
    c.   dis-saving occurs at very low real disposable income levels.
    d.   a. and c. are true.

8.   If the MPC = 0.8 then the
    a.   slope of the TPE = 0.2.
    b.   marginal propensity to save = 0.2.
    c.   marginal propensity to import = 0.2.
    d.   vertical intercept of the consumption function is positive.

9.   If real disposable income rises by $100 and consumption rises by $75, then
    a.   the MPS = 0.75.
    b.   the MPC = 0.25.
    c.   the MPS = 0.25.
    d.   the MPC = $75.

10.   Which of the following causes the consumption function to shift?
    a.   an increase in real disposable income.
    b.   a decrease in real disposable income.
    c.   an increase in wealth.
    d.   an increase in investment.

(LO 9.3)
11.   If planned investment is autonomous, then
    a.   it is independent of real national income.
    b.   it is independent of the interest rate.
    c.   it varies directly with real national income.
    d.   it varies inversely with real national income.

(LO 9.4)
12.   At that level of income where the total planned expenditures curve intersects the 45-degree reference line (ignoring G and X-M)
    a.   equilibrium exists.
    b.   unplanned inventory changes equal zero.
    c.   planned saving equals planned investment.
    d.   All of the above.

13.   Changes in autonomous expenditures
    a.   affect the 45-degree reference line.
    b.   shift the planned expenditures curve.
    c.   are movements along the total planned expenditures curve.
    d.   lead to equal increases in real national income.

14. Which of the following will cause an increase in autonomous net exports for country Xu.
    a. significant decrease in the national income of a foreign trading partner.
    b country Xu decreases tariffs on foreign goods.
    c. the exchange rate for country Xu depreciates.
    d. interest rates in country Xu increase.

15. If total planned expenditures exceed real national income, then
    a. business inventories will rise involuntarily.
    b. business inventories will fall involuntarily.
    c. equilibrium exists.
    d. real national income will fall.

16. If total planned expenditures are less than real national income, then
    a. business inventories will rise involuntarily.
    b. business inventories will fall involuntarily.
    c. equilibrium exists.
    d. real national income will rise.

17. Which of the following is most unlike the others?
    a. consumption function.
    b. investment function.
    c. 45-degree reference line.
    d. total planned expenditures curve.

18. If business inventories rise involuntarily, then
    a. equilibrium exists.
    b. total planned expenditures are less than real national income.
    c. real national income will rise.
    d. businesses will hire more labour.

19. In the short run, total employment and real national income/output
    a. are inversely related.
    b. are directly related.
    c. are independent of each other.
    d. reflect the law of demand.

(LO 9.5)
20. The multiplier
    a. relates changes in autonomous expenditures to changes in equilibrium real national income.
    b. deals with shifts in the planned expenditures curve.
    c. implies that economic fluctuations are magnified.
    d. All of the above

21. As the MPC rises, the multiplier
    a. falls.
    b. rises.
    c. is unaffected.
    d. changes in an unpredictable way.

22. If the proportion of leakages is 1/2, then (ignoring price level effects)
    a. the multiplier is 1/2.
    b. changes in autonomous income lead to equal changes in national income.
    c. shifts in the planned expenditures curve lead to a change in equilibrium real national income that equals twice the value of the shift.
    d. the APC must fall as real income falls.

(LO 9.6)
23. When the price level rises,
    a. the planned expenditures curve shifts downward.
    b. the 45-degree reference line shifts upward.
    c. autonomous expenditures rise.
    d. the multiplier effect is increased.

24. If the total planned expenditures curve shifts downward when the price level rises, and upward when the price level falls, then
    a. the multiplier effect is lessened.
    b. the economy can pull out of a recession faster.
    c. economic fluctuations due to shocks will be lessened.
    d. All of the above

MATCHING

Choose the item in Column (2) that best matches an item in Column (1).

(1)   (2)

(LO 9.2)
a. MPS
b. MPC
c. autonomous consumption

(LO 9.3)
d. determinant of investment

(LO 9.4)
e. build up of inventories
f. equilibrium

(LO 9.5)
g. reciprocal of proportion of leakages

1. planned expenditures equal national income
2. falling national income
3. multiplier
4. planned expenditures are less than national income
5. interest rate
6. proportion of added income that is saved
7. non-interest-rate determinants of investment
8. non-income determinants of consumption
9. change in consumption divided by change in income

WORKING WITH GRAPHS

(LO 9.2)

1.   Using the graphs provided, answer the questions that follow.

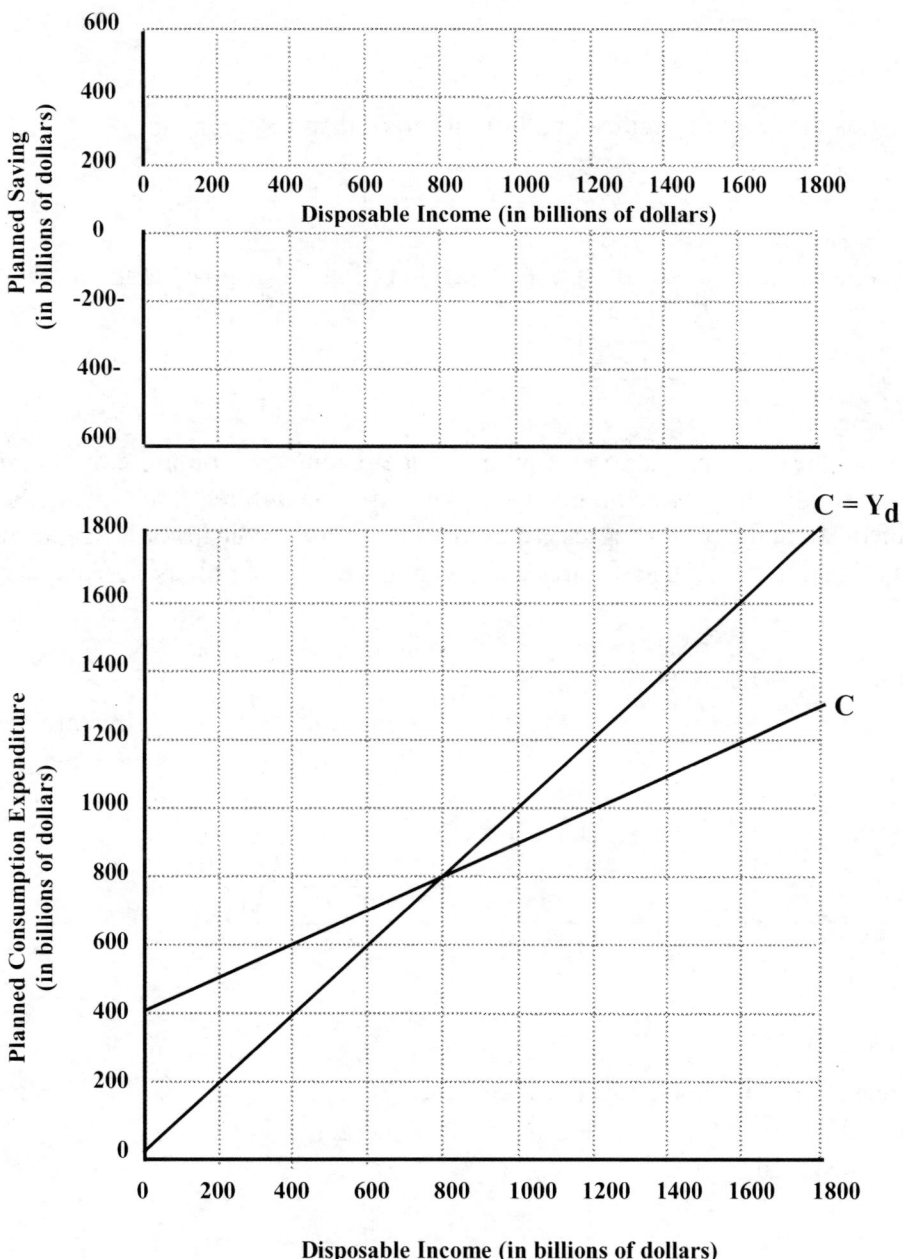

a.   Graph the saving function in the space provided.

b.   What is the break-even level of disposable income?

c.   What is the MPC? What is the MPS?

d.   What is the level of savings at $800 billion of disposable income?

e.   What is the level of consumption at $1600 billion of disposable income?

(LO 9.4)
2.   Given the following information about a hypothetical economy, complete the table below and then represent this economy in a planned expenditures diagram in the graph provided. Include a 45-degree reference line and indicate the level of equilibrium national income. (The figures are given in billions of dollars per year.)

$$C = \$200 + .80Y \qquad I = \$160$$

Y	I	C	S	Total Planned Expenditures	Inventory Changes
800	_____	_____	_____	_____	_____
900	_____	_____	_____	_____	_____
1500	_____	_____	_____	_____	_____
1800	_____	_____	_____	_____	_____
2000	_____	_____	_____	_____	_____
2400	_____	_____	_____	_____	_____

where: C = planned consumption   S = planned saving
          Y = real national income   I = planned investment
          Taxes are assumed to be 0

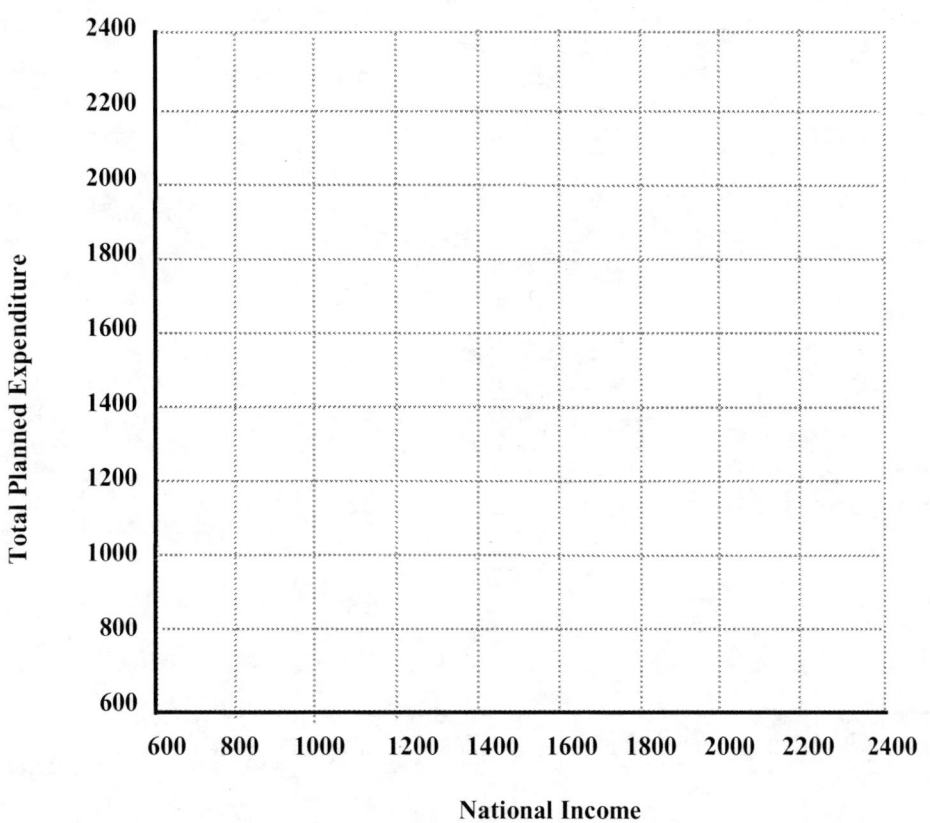

(LO 9.4 & 9.5)

3.   Consider the graphs on the following pages, then answer the questions that follow. (Note that G = government spending and X-M = net imports.)

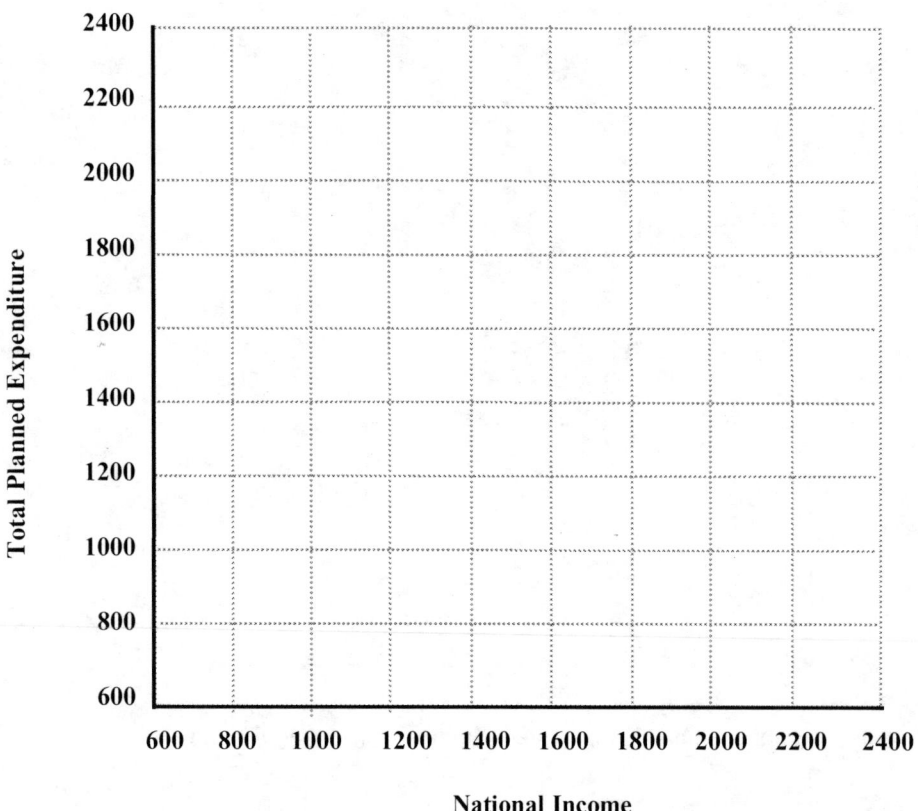

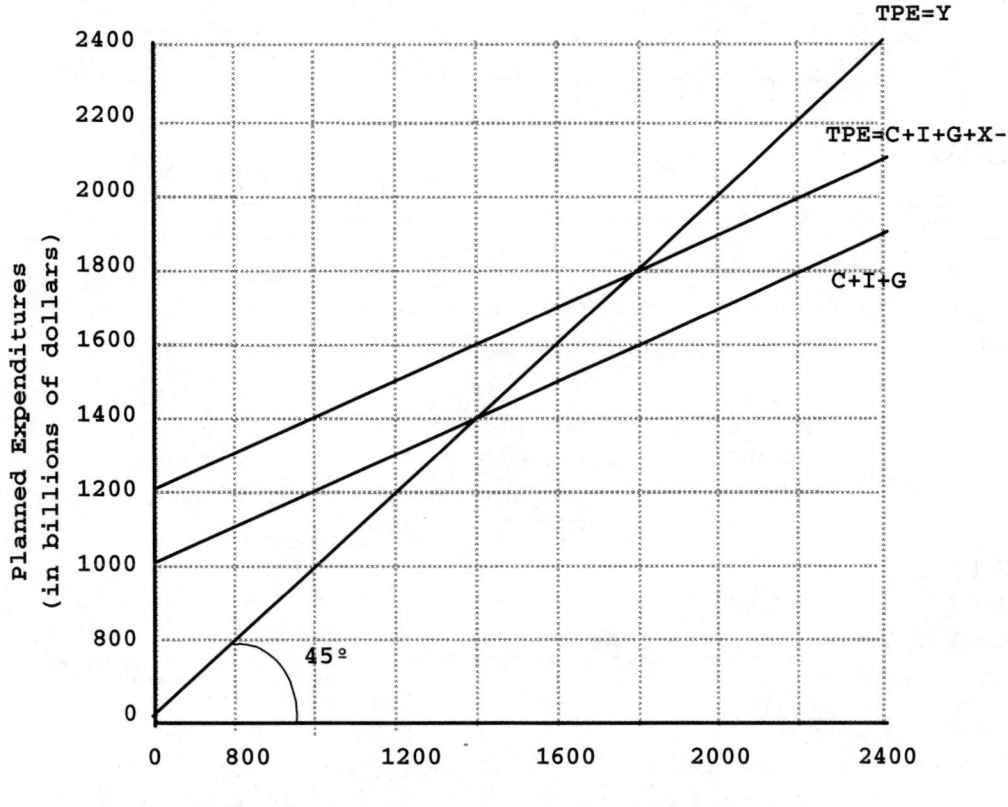

a.   What is the value of net exports?

b.   What is the MPC for this economy?

c.   What is the value of the equilibrium level of real national income?

d.   What is the multiplier for this economy?

(LO 9.6)
4.   Draw a LRAS and an AD curve. Then show what happens if the money supply is increased, other things constant. Explain your answer briefly.

(LO 9.6)

5.   Draw an AS and an AD curve, using the Keynesian Range model assumptions. Then show what happens if government expenditures are increased, other things constant.

PROBLEMS

(LO 9.4 & 9.5)

1.   Suppose that for a particular economy, MPS = ¼__ (assume there are no other leakages to taxes or imports). Complete the following table under the assumption that autonomous investment has just increased by $2000 (using the simple Keynesian model).

	Change in Income	Change in Consumption	Change in Saving
Round 1	2000	_____	_____
Round 2	1500	_____	_____
Round 3	_____	_____	_____
All other rounds	_____	_____	_____
Total	_____	_____	_____

(LO 9.5)

2.   Answer the following assuming a simple Keynesian economy:

    a.   If the MPE = 3/4, and the current equilibrium level of real national income is $1240 billion, what will be the new equilibrium level of income if autonomous investment falls by $10 billion?

    b.   Given the same initial equilibrium level of real national income and the same decrease in investment, what would be the new equilibrium if MPE is 4/5 rather than 3/4?

(LO 9.2, 9.4 & 9.5)

3.   Consider the domestic economy described in the table below. Assume that planned investment (I), government spending (G), and net exports (X-M) are all completely autonomous. Also assume that I = $55, G = $30, X = $15. Lump sum taxes = $40. All figures are in billions dollars per year. Assume that the SRAS curve is horizontal.

Real GDP	Taxes	Disposable Income	Planned Consumption	Planned Saving	Total Planned Expenditures	Unplanned Inventory Change
250	40	?	180	?	?	?
300	40	?	220	?	?	?
350	40	?	260	?	?	?
400	40	?	300	?	?	?
450	40	?	340	?	?	?

a   Fill in the blanks in the table above.

b.   Calculate the MPC and MPS.

c.   Determine the equilibrium level of real GDP.

d.   Calculate the multiplier.

e.   If autonomous investment (I) increases by $5 billion per year calculate the change in equilibrium real GDP.

(LO 9.4)

4.   For each event below, predict whether the event will most likely increase or decrease planned consumption (C) or planned investment (I) or net exports (X-M) in country Y.

a.   the real GDP of country Z, a major trading partner of country Y decreases significantly.

b.   interest rates in country Y decrease.

c.   personal taxes in country Y are significantly decreased.

d.   country Y's foreign exchange rate appreciates.

e.   industry profits are expected to increase significantly in the next decade.

f.   households begin the current year already heavily in debt.

g.   the government lowers business taxes.

h.   households expect inflation to escalate in the future.

i.   the government increases the general level of tariffs on foreign goods.

BUSINESS SECTION

(LO 9.3)
Financial Management: The Multiplier Concept and Government Financial Support

Financial management focuses on acquiring and investing the firm's financial resources. When a project undertaken by a private firm results in a significant multiplier effect on a local economy, the firm might be successful in acquiring financial support from the local government authorities. The following example suggests one way that a firm can apply the multiplier concept, introduced in Chapter 9, in order to estimate the maximum amount of government financial support to seek from the local government.

Sample Example
Peter Skalbania is considering the purchase of a major league baseball team in an eastern Canadian city in order to prevent the team from moving to the U.S. Peter projects that the annual operating costs will be $92 500 000 per year. At best, Pete expects that the business venture will break even each year. Based on economic analysis undertaken by the city's department of economic development, Pete estimates that keeping the team in the city entails an annual multiplier effect of 1.1. If Pete purchases the team, he has to sign an agreement to keep the team in the city for 10 years. Determine the maximum amount of financial support that Pete could seek from the local government, assuming an interest rate of 9%.

Step 1: Estimate the 3rd party or external community benefit based on the 1.1 multiplier. This is equivalent to the total of the 2nd, 3rd, 4th,.....nth, round expenditure effects:

3rd party benefit = (1.1) x (92 500 000) – 92 500 000 = $9 250 000 per year.

Step 2: Find the present value of an annuity consisting of 10 annual 3rd party benefits worth $9 250 000 each, as described below.

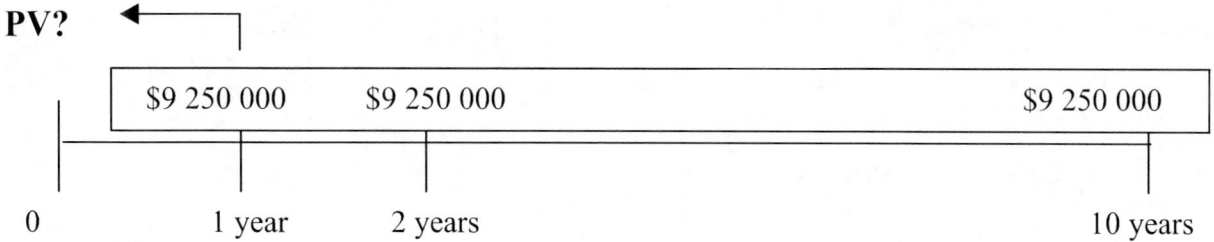

Recall, from a chapter in your microeconomics text that the present value formula is as follows:

$$PV = = \$R\left(\frac{1-(1+i)^{-n}}{i}\right) = \$9{,}250{,}000 \times \left(\frac{1-(1+.09)^{-10}}{.09}\right) = \$59\ 363\ 333.74$$

NOTE: Why is this the *maximum* amount that Pete can reasonably expect from the government? One key reason is that Pete will still be able to sell the team in 10 years and keep the proceeds from the likely capital gain from this sale. In addition, there would be no net external community benefit, if Pete captured all of the 3rd party benefit.

Business Application Problem 1

A western Canadian city has approached Ridaway Rodeos in a bid to host the new North Pacific Championship Rodeo. Ridaway projects that the annual operating costs will be $2 400 000 per year. At best, while the Rodeo event is projected to just break even, it will result in an annual 1.6 multiplier effect on the city's economy. If the bid to host the rodeo is successful, it will stay in the city for the next 10 years. Determine the maximum amount of financial support that Ridaway could seek from the local government, assuming an interest rate of 10%.

ANSWERS TO CHAPTER 9

COMPLETION QUESTIONS

1. disposable income; rises, rises
2. machines and buildings, capital
3. divided by; MPS
4. independent of; positive, remains constant
5. exceed
6. expectations, wealth, population, personal taxes
7. inversely; profit expectations, innovation and technology, business taxes
8. national income; equilibrium; dis-equilibrium
9. total planned expenditures
10. fall; increase; rise; decrease
11. upward; rise
12. negative; fall; greater than
13. exchange rates, trade policies. national income levels in other countries

14.   multiplier
15.   leakages
16.   savings; taxes; imports
17.   shift of; move along

TRUE-FALSE QUESTIONS

1.   T
2.   T
3.   F   The MPC plus the MPS equals 1.0.
4.   T
5.   F   The MPC and MPS are assumed to be constant.
6.   T
7.   F   No shift, just a movement along (increase) the consumption function.
8.   F   Autonomous here means independent of income.
9.   T
10. F   At every point along the 45-degree line; planned expenditures equal national income.
11. T
12. T
13. T
14. T
15. T   Because of the multiplier effect.
16. T   The multiplier formula is 1/proportion of leakages.
17. T

MULTIPLE CHOICE QUESTIONS

1.b;   Both saving and income are "rates" or flow variables relating to the current period. Both savings account balances and wealth are stock variables that are measured at a point in time.
2.c;   Savings plus consumption equals disposable income or household income received after personal taxes and deductions.
3.c;   The consumption function will shift if autonomous or non-real-income factors change.
       TIP: Factors that would shift the consumption function include changes in wealth, consumer debt levels, personal income taxes and expected future prices.
4.c;   Autonomous real consumption refers to planned consumption which depends on factors other than disposable income. The best answer is "changes with changes in wealth".
       TIP: Wealth is a stock variable which consists of the total value of the financial assets, such as; bank balances, stocks and bonds owned, that households have accumulated at the start of the current period or year. Disposable income is a flow variable, which measures the rate of after-tax income received by households during the current period or year.
5.b;   The 45-degree reference line is a line along which planned expenditures equal real national income. At that income level all income is consumed.
6.b;   Autonomous consumption will vary with non-disposable income factors such as wealth, population, personal taxes and future price expectations.
7.d;   If autonomous consumption is positive, this implies that the consumption function will be a curve with a positive intercept.
       TIP: Since we assume that the slope or MPC of the typical consumption function is less than one, the consumption function will have a slope less than the 45-degree line. This implies that at low levels of national income there will be negative saving and as national income increases the APC will decrease.
8.b;   If the MPC = .8, then the MPS = 1 – MPC = .2. That is, any increase in income is either consumed or saved. Thus MPC + MPS = 1.
9.c;   If consumption rises by $75 when real disposable income rises by $100, the MPC = .75. This implies that the MPS = 1 - .75 = .25

10.c; Only autonomous factors can cause the consumption function to shift, which rules out changes in real disposable income. An increase in wealth is the only option that relates to an autonomous factor affecting consumption.

11.a; If planned investment is autonomous, then it is independent of real national income. In other words planned investment is assumed to be affected by factors other than real national income such as the real interest rate and profit expectations.

12.d; When the total planned expenditures curve intersects the 45 degree line, this means that planned expenditure equals planned production. Equilibrium occurs at this point as planned savings equals planned investment so that no unplanned inventory investment will take place. Businesses will continue to produce the same production or real GDP rate in the next period (year).

13.b; Changes in autonomous expenditures shift the planned expenditures curve as they are caused by factors other than changes in disposable income.

14.c; If the exchange rate for country Xu depreciates, this will make country Xu's goods cheaper to foreigners. Therefore, exports will increase, causing net exports to rise.

15.b; If total planned expenditures exceed real national income (production), then business inventories will fall involuntarily. This will cause businesses to increase the rate of production (real national income) in the next period (year).

16.a; If total planned expenditures are less than real national income (production) then business inventories will rise involuntarily. This will cause businesses to decrease the rate of production (real national income) in the next period (year).

17.c; The 45-degree line is the only answer option that is not a planned expenditure.

18.b; If business inventories rise involuntarily, then this reflects a situation where total planned expenditures are less than current production or real national income. In this case businesses will reduce the production rate in the near future leading to layoffs and a reduction in real national income.

19.b; In the short run, it is assumed that firms will hire more labour in order to increase production and real national income.

20.d; The multiplier implies that autonomous business fluctuations in expenditures will cause magnified fluctuations in real national income.

21.b; As the MPC rises, the multiplier will increase. This is because the induced increases in planned expenditures in the 2nd, 3rd, 4th…. nth rounds will be higher.

22.c; If the proportion of leakages is ½ or .5, then the multiplier is 1/.5 = 2. This means that if the planned expenditures curve shifts vertically by a given amount, the equilibrium increase in real national income will increase by twice the given amount.

23.a; When the price level rises, the planned expenditures curve will shift downward due to a decrease in real wealth, higher interest rates and a decline in foreign demand for the more expensive Canadian goods.

24.d; Due to the dampening effects that price level changes have on planned expenditures, the multiplier effect will be lessened. Which means that "shocks" will cause smaller fluctuations in equilibrium real national income.

TIP: In a recession, since prices tend to fall, this will partially offset the decline in planned spending and hence make the recession less severe.

MATCHING

a and 6;   b and 9;   c and 8;   d and 5;   e and 4;   f and 1;   g and 3

WORKING WITH GRAPHS

1.   a.

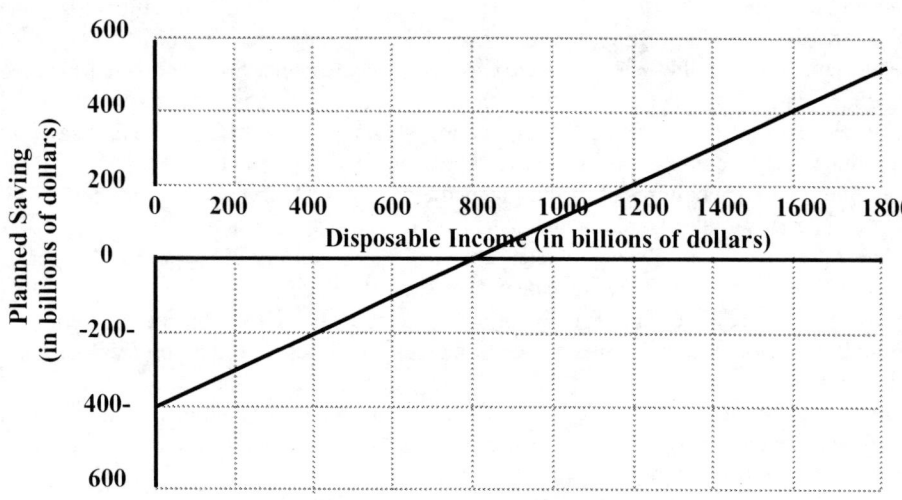

b. $800 billion   c. 1/2; 1/2   d. 0   e. 400

2.

Y	I	C	S	Total Planned Expenditures	Inventory Changes
800	160	840	-40	1000	-200
900	160	920	-20	1080	-180
1500	160	1400	100	1560	-60
1800	160	1640	160	1800	0
2000	160	1800	200	1960	40
2400	160	2120	280	2280	120

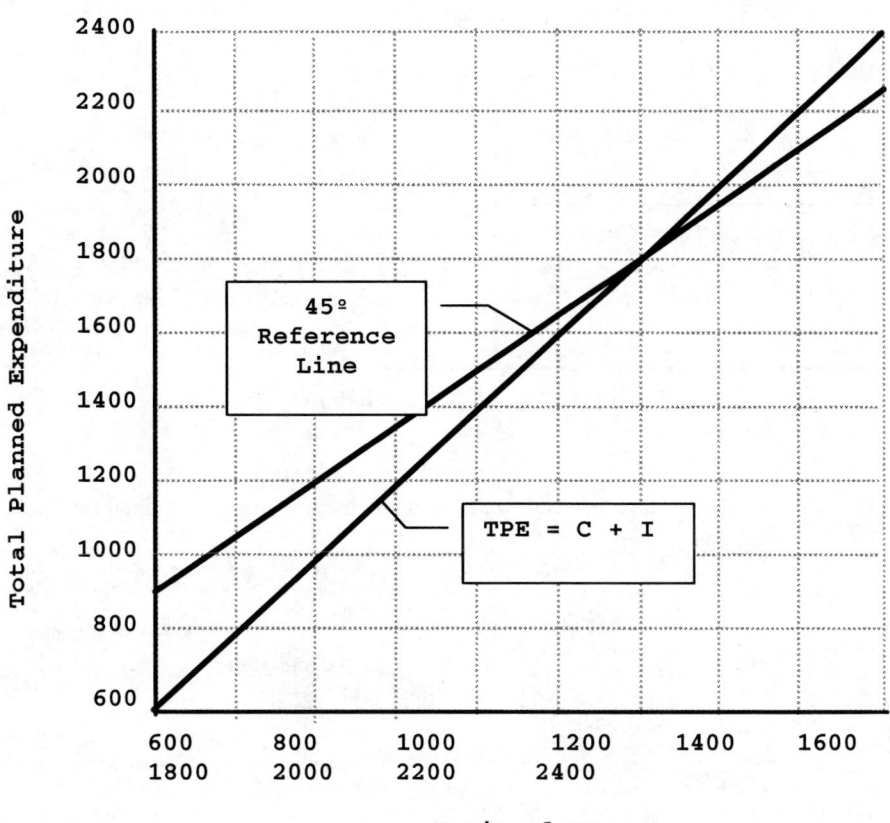

3.   a. $200 billion;   b. 0.5;   c. $1800 billion;   d. 2.0

4.

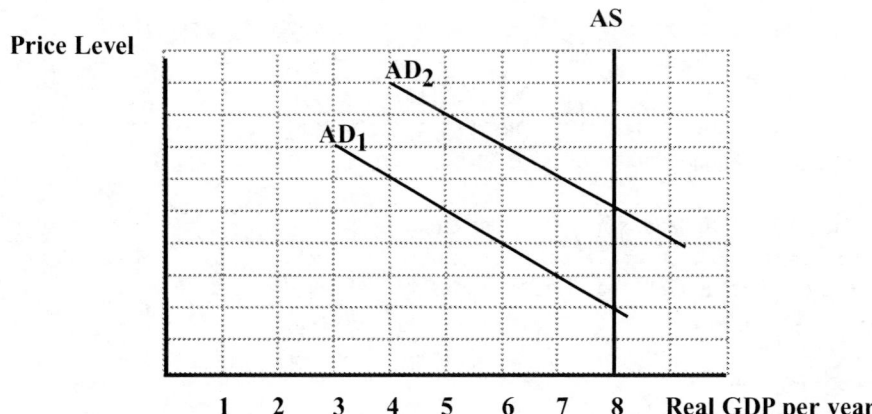

A money supply increase shifts the AD1 curve to AD2, which causes the price level to rise; real national output remains at the full employment/full capacity level.

5.

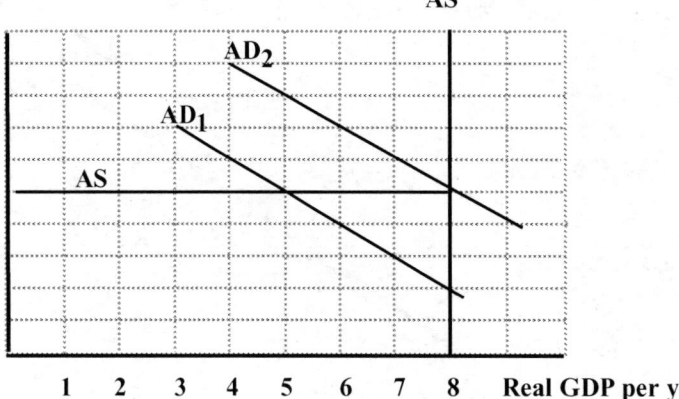

An increase in G shifts the AD1 curve to AD2; real national income rises, but the price level remains constant in the Keynesian Range.

PROBLEMS

1.		Change in Income	Change in Consumption	Change in Saving
	Round 1	2000	$1500.00	$500.00
	Round 2	1500	1125.00	375.00
	Round 3	1125	843.75	281.25
	All other rounds	3375	2531.25	843.75
	Total	$8000	$6000.00	$2000.00

2.   a. $1200 billion
      b $1190 billion

3   a.   Disposable Income: 210, 260, 310, 360, 410.
           Planned Saving: 30, 40, 50, 60, 70.
           Total Planned Expenditures: 280, 320, 360, 400, 440.
           Unplanned Inventory Changes: -30, -20, -10, 0, +10.
      b.   MPC = 0.8, MPS = 0.2.
      c. $400 billion per year. (Unplanned inventory changes = 0)
      d.   Multiplier = 1/0.2 = 5
      e.   Total change in equilibrium GDP = 5x5=$25 billion.

4.   a.   decrease in net exports.
      b.   increase in investment.
      c.   increase in consumption.
      d.   decrease in net exports.
      e.   increase in investment.
      f.   decrease in consumption.
      g.   increase in investment.
      h.   increase in consumption in the current year.
      i.   net exports increase as imports decrease.

BUSINESS SECTION

Step 1: Total annual 3rd party, external community benefit = (1.6)(2 400 000) – 2 400 000 =$1 440 000 per year

Step 2: Over 10 years: PV= $1,440,000 \times \left(\dfrac{1 - (1 + .10)^{-10}}{.10} \right)$ = $8 848 176.63

CHAPTER 10

THE PUBLIC SECTOR

PUTTING THIS CHAPTER INTO PERSPECTIVE

To date you have learned that scarcity is a human condition, that economists study how resources are allocated to satisfy wants, and that there are many potential determinants of how resources are rationed in specific situations. In Chapter 10 we analyze how governments influence resource use—or more specifically, how individuals and groups use the institution of government to influence resource use.

It is important to master this chapter because our overall goal is to understand how resources are rationed in the Canadian economy. The role of the government in our economy has grown tremendously since World War II; some maintain that it is nearly as important as the price system in determining resource use in Canada.

It is generally agreed that the price system is an efficient resource allocator. Typically the value of output will be maximized (opportunity costs will be minimized) if the price system is permitted to allocate resources to satisfy wants. Nevertheless, the resource allocation that results from a price system is not always efficient. In this chapter you learn that if externalities exist, then the price system will transmit *incorrect* signals, and resource misallocation will result as the economy overproduces or underproduces specific goods and services. Similarly, because of the "free rider" problem, the price system will underproduce public goods. For these reasons the government has an *economic* function to perform; it can help to correct resource misallocation by providing the correct signals to economic agents.

The government has important *political* functions to perform also; it affects the output of merit and demerit goods and it redistributes income if the political process decides that the income distribution that results from the price system is unfair.

Chapter 10 provides a brief overview of the *Theory of Public Choice*, which focuses on how government decisions are made. In general, public choices are made through collective decision-making actions of voters, politicians, political parties, interest groups, and bureaucrats.

In analyzing collective decision making it is important to note various similarities and differences between the private market sector and the public sector. Similarities include scarcity, competition, and similarity of individuals. Key differences between the private and public sectors are: government goods at zero price, possible use of force, and voting vs. spending. In a political system, *majority rule* prevails, whereas the market system is run by *proportional rule*.

Bureaucrats and special interest groups can have a disproportionate amount of power in terms of public sector decisions due to *rational ignorance* on the part of voters. Rational voters will often remain at some level of ignorance about government programs and policies because the additional cost of obtaining information outweighs the additional benefits to the typical voter. However for the special interest group(s) involved, the extra benefits of obtaining additional information may far exceed the extra costs.

It is impossible to analyze the public sector without understanding the role of taxes and government expenditures. In this chapter we distinguish between marginal and average tax rates and analyze the effects of raising tax revenues through various types of tax systems. The major types of government expenditures incurred at different levels of government is examined.

LEARNING OBJECTIVES

After you have studied this chapter you should be able to:

10.1.1 Explain externalities and the 4 other economic functions of government.
10.1.2 Describe the two main political functions of government and how decision making differs depending on whether the individual is in the public or private sector.
10.1.3 Distinguish between average and marginal tax rates and explain the Canadian tax system.

CHAPTER OUTLINE

LO 10.1 Explain externalities and the 4 other economic functions of government.
1. The government provides many economic functions that affect the way in which resources are allocated.
    a. If a benefit or cost, associated with an economic activity, *spills over* to **third parties**, the price system will misallocate resources; and **market failure** in the form of externalities occurs**.** A proper role for government is to correct such **externalities** or spillovers.
        i. If a negative externality exists, the price system will over-allocate resources to that industry; the government can correct this by taxing, charging **effluent fees**, or regulating such activities.
        ii. If a positive externality exists, the price system will under-allocate resources to that industry; the government can correct this by financing additional production, by providing special subsidies**,** or by regulation.

b. A legal system that defines and enforces **property rights** is crucial to the process of buyers and sellers engaging in contracts in markets.

c. Because a competitive price system transmits correct signals, an important role for government is to promote competition and prevent the occurrence of **monopoly**. **Anti-combines legislation** attempts to promote competition.

d. A price system will underallocate resources to the production of **public goods**.

    i. Characteristics of public goods or **government goods** include:

      -They are usually indivisible.

      -They can be used by more people at no additional cost.

      -Additional users of public goods do not deprive others of any of the services of the good.

      -It is difficult to charge individual users a fee based on how much they themselves consume of the public good.

    ii. Because public goods must be consumed collectively, individuals have an incentive to take a **free ride** and not pay for them.

    iii. Because the price system underproduces public goods, a proper role of government may be to ensure their production.

e. In recent years the government has taken on the economic role of ensuring economy-wide stability: full employment, price stability, and economic growth.

LO 10.2 Describe the 2 main political functions of government and how decision making differs depending on whether the individual is in the public or private sector.

2. The government provides political functions that also affect resource allocation.

a. Governments subsidize the production of **merit goods** and tax or prohibit the production of **demerit goods**.

b. By combining a progressive tax structure with **transfer payments**, the government attempts to redistribute income from higher to lower income groups. (Although many "loopholes" frustrate such a policy.)

3. In order to understand how resources are allocated by governments, economists have developed the **public choice model**, which analyses **collective decision making**, which involves the actions of voters, politicians, bureaucrats, political parties, and special-interest groups.

4. There are similarities and dissimilarities in how resources are allocated in the private sector vs. the public (government) sector.

a. As is true for private economy decision makers, all participants in the political marketplace follow the dictates of rational self-interest.

b. In the private marketplace firms specialize in the production of private goods, while governments provide political goods at a zero price; in the private sector buyers can reveal the intensity of their wants via a **proportional rule** (dollar votes), whereas in the political sector an all or nothing **majority rule** is followed, hence the composition of output would be different under each system.

5. **Bureaucrats** are non-elected governmental officials who organize special interest groups and defend the rights of such "clients."
    a. Because performance in government is often measured by the number of clients served, bureaucrats have an incentive to expand the size of their clientele.
    b. Bureaucratic rewards do not depend on profits (as would be the case in the private sector); therefore their rewards appear not so much in high salaries but in job perks which provide further incentives for **bureaucrats** to protect their jobs.
    c. Due to rational ignorance on the part of voters, bureaucrats and special interest groups can disproportionately affect the allocation of resources.

LO 10.3 Distinguish between average and marginal tax rates and explain the Canadian tax system.

6. Governments tax in order to obtain revenues to finance expenditures.
    a. The **marginal tax rate** is the change in the tax payment divided by the change in income.
    b. The **average tax rate** equals the total tax payment divided by total income.

7. There are three main types of taxation systems.
    a. Under a **proportional taxation** system, as a person's income rises, the percentage of income paid (rate of taxation) in taxes remains constant.
    b. Under a **progressive taxation** system, as a person's income rises, the percentage of income paid in taxes rises.
    c. Under a **regressive taxation** system, as a person's income rises, the percentage of income paid in taxes falls.

8. The federal government imposes income taxes on individuals and corporations, and it collects sales taxes and other taxes.
    a. The most important tax in the Canadian economy is the personal income tax, where the level of taxation paid is based on individual annual income.
    b. The difference between the buying and selling price of an asset, such as a share of stock or a plot of land, is called a **capital gain** if a profit results, and a **capital loss** if it doesn't.

9. The corporate income tax is a moderately important source of revenue for the various governments in the Canadian economy.
    a. Corporate stockholders are taxed twice: once on corporate income and again when dividends are received or when the stock is sold.
    b. The incidence of corporate taxes falls on people—consumers, workers, management, and stockholders—not on such inanimate objects as "corporations."

10. An increasing percentage of federal tax receipts is accounted for each year by taxes (other than income) levied on payrolls, such as Canada Pension contributions and Employment Insurance.

11. Major sources of revenue for provincial and local governments are income, sales, excise and property taxes.

12. Federal government outlays are made mostly for interest on the public debt; elderly benefits, transfers to provinces and Employment Insurance benefits. Provincial and local government expenditures allocate more funds to health, education, and social services than to other categories.

13. A value-added tax assesses a tax on the difference between what the firm sells its final product for and the value of the goods that it bought and used to produce the final product.

14. Alternatives to our current federal progressive income tax system are (1) a flat tax, (2) a national sales tax or a value-added tax, and (3) a consumption tax.

KEY TERMS AND CONCEPTS

Market failure	Merit goods	Proportional tax
Externality	Demerit goods	Progressive tax
Effluent fee	Theory of public choice	Regressive tax
Third parties	Bureaucracy	Tax incidence
Property rights	Collective decision-making	Capital gain
Private goods	Bureaucrats	Capital loss
Exclusion principle	Proportional rule	Tax bracket
Principle of rival consumption	Majority rule	Average tax rate
Free-rider problem	Incentive structure	Retained earnings
Public good	Marginal tax rate	
Monopoly	Transfer payments	
Anti-combines legislation	Government, or political goods	

COMPLETION QUESTIONS
Fill in the blank or circle the correct term.

(LO 10.1)

1. Positive and negative externalities are examples of market _____.

2. If externalities are an important result of an economic activity, then the price system is (inefficient, efficient).

3. If Mr. Johnson buys an automobile from General Motors, then those people not directly involved in the transaction are considered _____.

4.   Pollution is an example of a (negative, positive) externality.

5.   When there are spillover costs, a price system will (under, over) allocate resources to the production of the good in question.

6.   If third parties benefit from a good, then (negative, positive) externalities exist, and the price system (under, over) allocate resources to the production of the good in question.

7.   A government can correct negative externalities by imposing (taxes, subsidies)

8.   A government can correct positive externalities by _____, _____, _____.

9.   Anti-combines legislation, in theory, is supposed to (decrease, promote) competition in the private sector.

10. Public goods have four distinguishing characteristics. They are usually (divisible, indivisible); they can be used by more people at _____ additional cost; additional users (do, do not) deprive others of the services of a public good; it is very (easy, difficult) to charge individuals based on how much they used the public good.

11. A free-rider has an incentive to (pay, not pay) for a public good.

12. The five economic functions of federal government in our capitalistic system are _____, _____, _____, _____, _____.

(LO 10.2)

13. Demerit goods are goods for which society wants to (decrease, increase) production.

14. Important political functions of government include (encouraging, discouraging) the production of demerit goods and _____ income from higher income to lower income groups.

15. Many government, or political, goods are provided to consumers at a (zero, positive) price; but the opportunity cost to society of providing government goods is (zero, positive).

(LO 10.3)

16. The public choice model assumes that even though regulators and bureaucrats are (like, unlike) the rest of us, they face a (similar, different) incentive system.

17. The public choice model assumes that politicians, bureaucrats, and regulators pursue (society's, their own) self-interest.

18. Private sector buyers can reveal the intensity of their wants via (majority, proportional) rule through _____ votes; in the political sector the all or nothing (majority, proportional) rule is followed; we can conclude that the composition of output will (differ, be the same) under those two rules of supplying goods to customer/clients.

19. Bureaucrats are (elected, non-elected) governmental officials whose clients are _____ groups; bureaucrats' rewards take the form of _____.

20. Because information to voters (is, is not) free and because voters will not be concerned with expenditure programs that affect them only slightly, voters often choose to be (rationally informed, rationally ignorant).

21. Fundamental to the theory of public choice is the idea that voters, bureaucrats, and politicians follow the dictates of rational _____, just as do private decision-makers.

22. If the price of an asset rises after its purchase, the owner receives a _____ gain; if the price falls, the owner suffers a _____ loss.

23. The marginal tax rate applies only to the (lowest, highest) tax bracket reached.

24. The corporate income tax is paid by one or more of the following groups: _____, _____, and _____.

25. A flat tax is a (proportional, regressive) tax.

26. A consumption tax (encourages, discourages) saving.

TRUE-FALSE QUESTIONS
Circle the **T** if the statement is true, the **F** if it is false. Explain to yourself why a statement is false.

(LO 10.1)
T F 1. In the Canadian economy the government plays only a minor role in resource allocation, because the country is capitalistic.

T F 2. If externalities, or spillovers, exist, then a price system misallocates resources, so that inefficiency exists.

T   F   3.   If a negative externality exists, buyers and sellers are not faced with the true opportunity costs of their actions.

T   F   4.   If a positive externality exists when good A is produced, a price system will underallocate resources into the production of good A.

T   F   5.   One way to help correct for a negative externality is to tax the good in question, because that will cause the price of the good to fall.

T   F   6.   A price system will tend to overallocate resources to the production of free goods, due to the free rider problem.

T   F   7.   If third parties are hurt by the production of good B and they are not compensated, then too many resources have been allocated to Industry B.

T   F   8.   Governments provide a legal system, but this important function is not considered an economic function.

T   F   9.   One aim of anti-combines legislation is the promotion of competition.

(LO 10.2)
T   F   10.   Deciding what is a merit good and what is a demerit good is easily done and does not require value judgements.

T   F   11.   Scarcity exists in the market sector, but not in the public sector.

(LO 10.3)
T   F   12.   The public choice model assumes that regulators and bureaucrats are mostly concerned with their own—not the public's—self-interest.

T   F   13.   The public choice model indicates that households will be provided the same goods by elected representatives as they would by the private sector.

T   F   14.   It is often rational for voters to remain ignorant of political issues and of candidates.

T   F   15.   Bureaucrats can often exert great influence on matters that concern themselves.

T   F   16.   In the private marketplace, dollar votes indicate majority, not proportional rule.

T   F   17.   In a progressive tax structure, the average tax rate is greater than the marginal tax rate.

T   F   18.   Positive economics confirms that a progressive taxation system is more equitable than a regressive taxation system.

T F   19.   In Canada the tax system that yields the most revenue to all governments combined is the corporate income tax.

T F   20.   When corporations are taxed, consumers and corporate employees are also affected.

T F   21.   A flat tax is regressive.

MULTIPLE CHOICE QUESTIONS

Circle the letter that corresponds to the best answer.

(LO 10.1)

1.   Market failure exists if
   a.   Mr. Smith cannot purchase watermelons in his town.
   b.   buyers and sellers must pay the true opportunity costs of their actions.
   c.   third parties are injured and are not compensated.
   d.   the government must provide merit goods.

2.   Which of the following will properly correct a negative externality that results from producing good B?
   a.   subsidizing the production of good B
   b.   letting the price system determine the price and output of good B
   c.   forcing sellers of good B to pay the true opportunity costs of their actions.
   d.   banning the production of good B

3.   Which of the following statements concerning externalities is true?
   a.   If a positive externality exists for good A, A will be overproduced by a price system.
   b.   If externalities exist, then resources will be allocated efficiently.
   c.   Efficiency may be improved if the government taxes goods for which a positive externality exists.
   d.   The output of goods for which a positive externality exists is too low, from society's point of view.

4.   Which of the following is not an economic function of government?
   a.   income redistribution
   b.   providing a legal system
   c.   ensuring economy-wide stability
   d.   promoting competition

5.   A price system will misallocate resources if
   a.   much income inequality exists.
   b.   demerit goods are produced.
   c.   externalities exist.
   d.   All of the above

6. Which of the following does not belong with the others?
    a. positive externality
    b. negative externality
    c. demerit good
    d. public good

7. The exclusion principle
    a. does not work for public goods.
    b. does not work for private goods.
    c. causes positive externalities.
    d. makes it easy to assess user fees on true public goods.

8. Which of the following is **NOT** a characteristic of public goods?
    a. indivisibility
    b. high extra cost to additional users
    c. exclusion principle does not work easily
    d. difficult to determine how each individual benefits from public goods

9. The free rider problem exists
    a. for private goods.
    b. for goods that must be consumed collectively.
    c. only if people can be excluded from consumption.
    d. All of the above

10. If Mr. Ayres loves good A, he can convey the intensity of his wants if good A is
    a. a private good.
    b. a public good.
    c. not subject to the exclusion principle.
    d. expensive

(LO 10.2)
11. Merit and demerit goods
    a. are examples of public goods.
    b. are examples of externalities.
    c. indicate market failure.
    d. are not easily classified.

12. If the government taxes group A and gives to group B, then economic incentives for
    a. group A may be reduced.
    b. group B may be reduced.
    c. both may change so as to reduce output.
    d. All of the above.

13.   Which of the following characterizes collective, but not market, decision making?
   a.   the legal use of force
   b.   a positive price usually is charged to users
   c.   intensity of wants is easily revealed
   d.   proportional rule

14.   People who work in the public sector
   a.   are more competent than other workers.
   b.   are less competent than other workers.
   c.   face a different incentive structure than many workers in the private sector.
   d.   would behave in the same way if they worked for a small private business.

(LO 10.3)
15.   The public-choice theory assumes that voters, bureaucrats, and politicians usually
   a.   attempt to pursue their self-interest.
   b.   are concerned with society's interests.
   c.   exhibit behaviour not subject to economic analysis.
   d.   are indifferent to what voters want.

16.   Voters often find it rational to remain ignorant of issues and candidates because
   a.   ignorance is bliss.
   b.   politicians don't care what voters want anyway.
   c.   information is costly to obtain.
   d.   they don't have to pay for expenditures anyway.

17.   Voters tend to be
   a.   very knowledgeable about the issues.
   b.   ignorant of many political issues.
   c.   very knowledgeable about a candidate's political platform.
   d.   willing to spend much time and effort to become knowledgeable.

18.   Bureaucrats
   a.   often can exert great influence on matters concerning themselves.
   b.   seldom can exert great influence on matters concerning themselves.
   c.   cannot influence public demand; they only have political influence.
   d.   refrain from exerting political influence because they are concerned with society's interests.

19.   According to the public choice model, people enter politics mostly to
   a.   maximize their income and wealth.
   b.   do good for society.
   c.   help the poor.
   d.   eliminate economic rents.

20. In a progressive tax structure,
    a. the marginal tax rate exceeds the average tax rate.
    b. equity exists.
    c. the average tax rate falls as income falls.
    d. All of the above

21. If Mr. Romano faces a 90 percent marginal tax rate,
    a. the next dollar he earns nets him ninety cents.
    b. his total tax payments equal 90 percent of his total income.
    c. he has a strong incentive to not earn extra income.
    d. his average tax rate must be falling.

22. A proportional tax system
    a. is unfair.
    b. cannot be consistent with people's ability to pay such taxes.
    c. means that upper income people pay smaller percentages of their income in taxes than do lower income people.
    d. requires upper income people to pay more tax dollars than lower income people pay.

23. Which of the following statements is true?
    a. Under a regressive tax structure the average tax rate remains constant as income
    rises.
    b. If upper-income people pay more taxes than lower income people, equity must exist.
    c. The Canadian federal personal income tax system is progressive.
    d. Sales taxes tend to be progressive in nature.

24. The tax incidence of the corporate income tax falls on
    a. corporate stockholders.
    b. corporate employees.
    c. consumers of goods and services produced by corporations.
    d. All of the above

25. Which of the following statements about CPP premiums is **NOT** true?
    a. Since it is a compulsory levy it is considered to be a tax.
    b. The CPP premium rate is predicted to decrease due to demographic trends.
    c. Both employees and employers pay CPP premiums.
    d. It is a payroll tax.

26. Which of the following is most unlike the others?
    a. income tax
    b. sales tax
    c. consumption tax
    d. value added tax

27. A consumption tax
  a. is placed on earnings.
  b. is progressive.
  c. encourages saving.
  d. reduces the nation's growth rate.

MATCHING

Choose the numbered item in Column (2) that best matches the term or concept in Column (1).

(1)

(LO 10.1), 10.2, 10.3

a. spillover
b. positive externality
c. negative externality
d. anti-combines legislation
e. government good
f. demerit good
g. public choice theory
h. rational ignorance
i. intensity of wants revealed

(2)

1. pollution
2. externality
3. national defence
4. alcohol
5. eliminate monopoly
6. flu shots
7. proportional rule
8 self-interested politicians
9. information is too costly to obtain
10. progressive tax
11. regressive tax

WORKING WITH GRAPHS

(LO 10.1)

1. Consider the graph below, then answer the questions. Assume S represents industry supply and S' includes pollution costs to society as well as industry private costs.

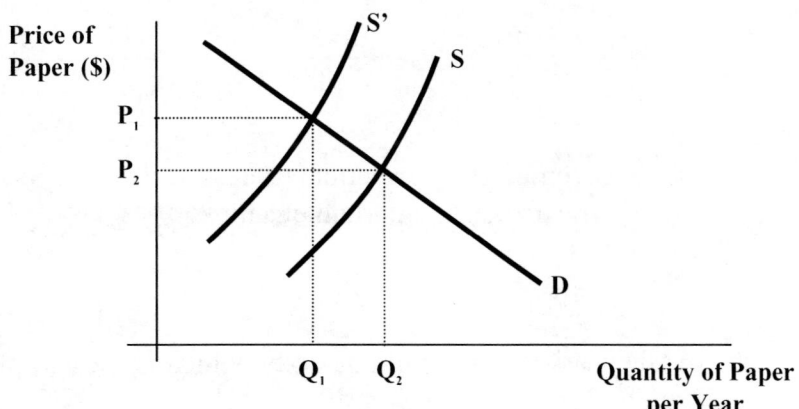

a. If no governmental intervention takes place, what will be the market equilibrium price? The market equilibrium quantity?

b. At the market equilibrium quantity (Q_2), which are higher: private costs or social costs?

c. From *society's* point of view, what is the price that reflects the true opportunity costs of paper? From that same point of view, what is the optimal quantity of paper?

d. Considering your answers in the above three questions, will a price system produce too little, or too much paper.

e. Does a negative externality or a positive externality exist?

(LO 10.2)

2. Consider the graph below, then answer the questions that follow. Assume that D represents private market demand and that D' represents benefits that accrue to third parties as well as private benefits.

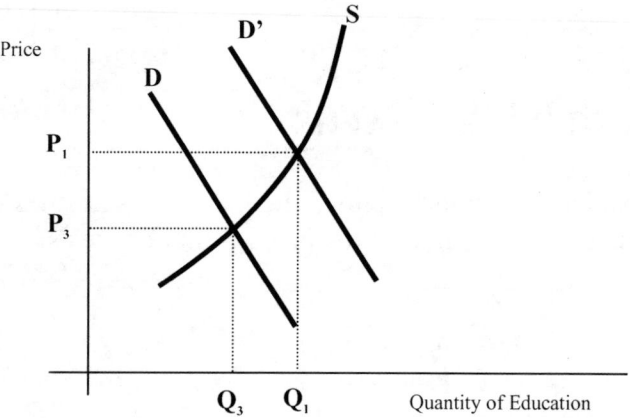

a. If no government intervention occurs, what will be the market equilibrium price? The market equilibrium quantity?

b. At the market equilibrium quantity, which is greater, private benefits or social benefits?

c. From *society's* point of view, what is the optimal price and the optimal quantity of education?

d. In this example, does the price system provide too much, or too little education?

e. Is there a positive externality or a negative externality for this good?

(LO 10.1)

3. Suppose you know the demand and supply of fertilizer locally, and you have graphed them as shown in the graph that follows. The fertilizer plant that operates in your town is also producing pollution. This pollution is a constant amount per unit of output (proportional to output) at the plant. If the government decides to try to combat the pollution problem by imposing *a $20-per-tonne tax on fertilizer produced*:

a. Show graphically, on the graph provided below, what will happen to the fertilizer market.

b. Will the level of pollution in your town be reduced? If so, by how much? If not, can you offer a solution to the pollution problem?

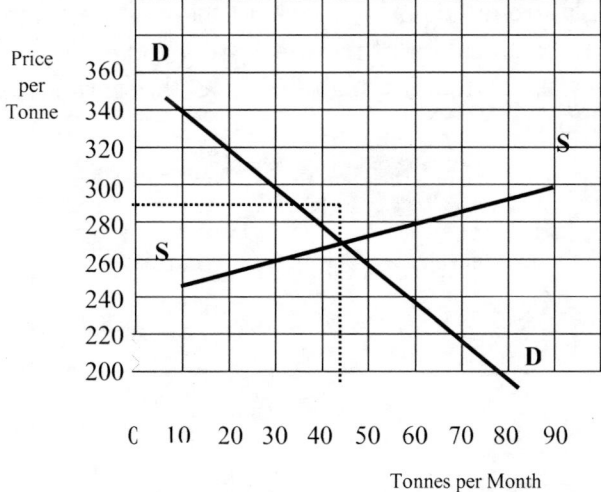

PROBLEMS
(LO 10.1 and 10.2)

1.   In the text the following economic and political functions of government were examined: *providing legal system, promoting competition, correcting externalities, providing public goods, stabilizing the economy, encouraging merit goods, discouraging demerit goods, redistribution.*   Match each of the following government activities to one (or more) of the functions listed above. Write in the matching function(s) in the blank space provided below.

a) Providing aid to welfare recipients   _____
b) Passing anti-combines laws   _____
c) Subsidizing the arts   _____
d) Prohibiting the sale and possession of drugs   _____
e) Providing national defense   _____
f) Enforcing a progressive tax structure   _____
g) Enforcing contracts   _____
h) Providing public education to children   _____
i) Prosecuting fraud   _____
j) Providing funds for AIDS research   _____
k) Creating jobs to reduce unemployment   _____

(LO 10.1)

2.   One important purely economic function of government is to promote competition, which presumably makes the price system more efficient. During the 1970s the OPEC oil cartel was able to restrict output dramatically, which permitted the cartel to charge much higher prices and earn higher profits. How did consumers, businesses, and other governments react to the higher relative price of oil? Were such actions rational, from the point of view of the individuals involved? Did such decisions lead to a misallocation of resources from *society's* point of view? (Hint: the OPEC price was artificially high because the cartel reduced output and repressed competition.)

(LO 10.3)

3. Complete the following table for three taxes and then indicate what type of tax each is.

Income	Tax 1		Tax 2		Tax 3	
	Tax paid	Average tax rate	Tax paid	Average tax rate	Tax paid	Average tax rate
$ 1000	$ 30	_____	$ 10	_____	$ 100	_____
3000	90	_____	60	_____	270	_____
6000	180	_____	180	_____	480	_____
10,000	300	_____	400	_____	700	_____
15,000	450	_____	750	_____	900	_____
20,000	600	_____	1200		1000	_____
30,000	900	_____	2100	_____	1200	_____

4. Suppose the above table had a fourth tax as shown below. Find the average and marginal tax rates and explain what type of tax it would be.

Income	Tax paid	Average tax rate	Marginal tax rate
$ 1,000	$ 30	_____	_____
3,000	120	_____	_____
6,000	300	_____	_____
10,000	500	_____	_____
15,000	600	_____	_____
20,000	700	_____	_____
30,000	900	_____	_____

BUSINESS SECTION

(LO 10.3)
Accounting: Personal Income Tax Planning Strategies

The *marginal tax rate (MTR)* relating to the highest tax bracket of an individual tax payer is frequently used to determine the tax savings that can be achieved by pursuing possible legal tax planning strategies. The following two formulae are frequently used:

Formula 1:   **Extra Dollar Tax Payable = MTR x Extra Income Earned**

Formula 2:   **Extra Dollar Tax Savings = MTR x Extra Deductions Claimed**

The table on the next page compares the "top marginal tax rates" that apply to individuals earning an annual taxable income of $50,000 in the different Canadian provinces in 2000. The marginal tax rates that are displayed combine both the federal and provincial personal income tax rates for each province.

(Source: *EY/Personal RRSP Calculator 2000,* Ernst and Young, Feb 28, 2001. On-line. Internet. March 1, 2001. (Available: http://www.tax.ca/taxtools/tools/2000taxcalc.cfm?p=1&c=1)

Province	*Top Marginal Tax Rates in Percent*		
Province	*Dividends*	*Capital Gains*	*Other Income*
British Columbia	21.83%	18.70%	37.40%
Alberta	21.63%	18.25%	36.50%
Saskatchewan	25.68%	20.94%	41.88%
Manitoba	27.02%	20.61%	41.22%
Ontario	20.19%	17.31%	34.62%
Quebec	26.76%	21.69%	43.38%
New Brunswick	23.85%	20.11%	40.21%
Nova Scotia	26.63%	19.98%	39.95%
P.E.I	22.97%	19.69%	39.38%
Newfoundland	24.17%	20.72%	41.43%

The Other Income category in the table above would apply to forms of income such as employment income, interest income, and self-employment income. According to formula 1 and the table above, if a resident of BC and earns an extra $1000 of employment or interest income then his/her extra tax payable would be: $1000 x .3740 = $374

Some of the common tax planning strategies used to minimize an individual's personal income tax payable is described below. Make sure that you consult your General Tax Guide as well as Revenue Canada to ensure that these strategies apply to your province.

Strategy 1: Earning income which is taxed at rates below the "Other Income" tax rate.

Business Application Problem 1
At the start of 2000 Bill Dawson, a resident of Manitoba, transferred funds from his savings account to purchase stocks. As a result, Bill earned extra dividends in 2000 worth $10 000. How much did Bill save by earning $10 000 of dividend income instead of $10 000 of interest income?

Business Application Problem 2
In 2000, Mona Bullock, a Nova Scotia resident decided to give up $8 000 worth of part time employment income in order to better manage her existing savings. In 2000, Mona managed to earn an extra $8 000 of capital gains by frequently buying and selling stock. How much did Mona save by earning $8 000 of capital gains income instead of $8 000 of employment income?

Strategy 2: Deferring Income: Registered Retirement Savings Plan (RRSP)

Business Application Problem 3

Rachel Manovickz, a resident of Ontario, used funds from her employment earnings in 2000 to deposit $5000 into a RRSP. By doing this, Rachel was able to claim an extra $5000 deduction on her income-tax return. Calculate the extra tax savings that will accrue in 2000 due to this RRSP. Will Rachel ever have to pay tax on this $5000 of employment income?

Strategy 3: Claim the maximum allowable tax deductions and tax credits.

Business Application Problem 4

On his 2000 Saskatchewan tax return Perry Cuomo decided to claim $3000 worth of moving costs he incurred when moving between cities to start a new job. Calculate the extra tax savings resulting from this extra deduction.

ANSWERS TO CHAPTER 10

COMPLETION QUESTIONS

1. failure
2. inefficient
3. third parties
4. negative
5. over
6. positive; under
7. taxes
8. subsidizing production, financing production, regulation
9. promote
10. indivisible; zero; do not; difficult
11. not pay
12. providing a legal system, promoting competition, correcting externalities, providing public goods, ensuring economy-wide stability.
13. decrease
14. discouraging, redistributing
15. zero; positive
16. like; different

17. their own
18. proportional, dollar; majority; differ
19. non-elected; special interest; perks such as a large staff, pensions
20. is not; rationally ignorant
21. self interest
22. capital; capital
23. highest
24. stockholders, consumers, employees
25. proportional
26. encourages

TRUE-FALSE QUESTIONS

1. F   Even in capitalist countries the government plays a major role.
2. T
3. T
4. T
5. F   A tax will cause the price of the good to *rise*, which is a movement in the correct direction.
6. F   The free-rider problem deals with goods that are *scarce*, but for which the exclusion principle does not work well. The price system will underallocate resources to public goods.
7. T
8. F   It is an economic function because by enforcing contracts government can promote incentives to buy and sell which makes markets operate effectively.
9 . T
10. F   Whether or not a good is a merit good requires value judgements about good or bad.
11. F   Scarcity exists in the public sector too; after all, the government uses and allocates scarce goods.
12. T
13. F   The goods will differ because proportional rule in the private sector can reveal intensity of wants, while majority rule cannot.
14. T
15. T
16. F   Dollar votes indicate a proportional rule system.
17. F   For average taxes to rise with income (a progressive tax) the marginal tax rate must exceed the average tax rate.
18. F   "Equitable" is a normative statement based on value judgements.
19. F   No, the personal income tax does so.
20. T
21. F   It is proportional.

MULTIPLE CHOICE QUESTIONS

1. c;   When injured third parties are not compensated this results in overproduction of the product in question, a symptom of market failure
2. c;   When buyers and sellers are forced to pay the full opportunity costs of their actions it is in their best interests to refrain from allocating too many resources to the production and consumption of the good in question
3. d;   In a positive externality situation, the producing firm is not compensated for the the benefits conferred on third parties. Therefore this product is underproduced from a social view.
4. a;   Income redistribution is a political function as it is normative in nature.
5. c;   When externalities exist the market system misallocates resources by either overallocating resources or underallocating resources in the market.
    TIP: The market overallocates resources to the production of a good which entails external costs. The market underallocates resources to the production of a good which entails external benefits.
6. c;   A demerit good is the only situation which relates to the political function.

7. a;   Since it is very difficult, if not impossible to exclude non payers from benefiting from a public good, the exclusion principle does not work in these cases.

8. b;   The principle of rival consumption does not apply to public goods. In other words, if one individual consumes some of the benefits from national security, this does not reduce the amount of benefit that is available to another consumer.

9. b;   If goods are consumed collectively, non payers can still benefit from the public good. This means that there is no incentive to pay for the provision of the good.
TIP: Due to the free rider problem, the private sector would not produce a desirable public good. Because of this type of market failure, the government must provide the public good.

10. a;   If good A is a public good it is not subject to the exclusion principle. This means that Mr Ayres has no incentive to convey the intensity of his wants as it is impossible to deny him the benefits even if he does not pay for good A.
TIP: Principle of rival consumption implies that if one consumer wants to consume more of a private good this means that less of the good will be available to other consumers. In order to obtain more of the private good the consumer will have to convey his/her intensity of wants by paying a higher price.

11. d;   These goods are not easily classified as it depends on whether the political system deems these goods desirable or undesirable. These classifications can change over time.

12. d;   If group A is taxed, the reduced after tax income may reduce A's incentives. If group B receives the proceeds of the taxes without earning them, this also may reduce incentives.

13. a;   All governments are able to engage in the legal use of force to ensure individuals adhere to collective decisions. As an example, governments can seize your assets if you refuse to pay your taxes.

14. c;   Due to the absence of the profit motive and competition, there is less of an incentive to be efficient in the public sector. Bureaucrats often have an incentive to expand the size of their department.

15. a;   The public choice theory assumes that voters, bureaucrats, and politicians attempt to pursue their self interest. As an example since bureaucrats are often rewarded based on the size of their clientele, they are motivated to increase the size of the government department.

16. c;   For many public issues, voters decide to remain at some level of ignorance as the extra benefits from obtaining more information may not be worth the extra cost.

17. b;   Voters tend to be ignorant of many issues, for rational reasons; the extra benefits from obtaining more information may not be worth the extra cost.
TIP: *Rational ignorance* explains why voters often choose to be uninformed about a public issue as the extra benefits from obtaining more information may not be worth the extra cost. Rational ignorance can explain how a minority of politicians, bureaucrats and interest groups can have a disproportionate amount of political power.

18. a;   Due to rational ignorance, bureaucrats can organize and coach their clientele (interest groups) so as to influence the amount of funding granted and the activities in which they engage.

19. a.   Due to rational ignorance, people may be tempted to enter politics as a means to maximize income and wealth.

20. a;   With progressive taxes, since the marginal tax rate exceeds the average tax rate, the average tax rate increases as taxable income increases.

21. c;   A 90% marginal tax rate means that for each additional dollar of income earned, Mr Romano only can take home $.10. He would have a strong incentive not to earn additional income.

22. d.   An example of a proportional tax would be a 20% flat tax. This means that an individual earning $10 000 would pay $2 000 in taxes. A person earning $100 000 would pay $20 000 in taxes.

23. c;   The personal income tax is progressive. As ones taxable income increases, the percentage of income paid in taxes also increases.

24. d;   To the extent that due to the corporate income tax, consumers pay higher prices, employees earn lower wages and shareholders receive a reduced profit. All these groups "pay" for this tax.

25. b;   The CPP premium rate is predicted to increase due to the demographic trend of an aging population.

26. a;   The income tax is unlike the other taxes as it is not based on the sale or consumption of goods. Rather, it is based on one's income level.

27. c;   A tax on consumption encourages savings as this is one way one can avoid the tax.

MATCHING

a and 2;   b and 6;   c and 1; d and 5;   e and 3;   f and 4;   g and 8;   h and 9; i and 7

WORKING WITH GRAPHS

1. a. $P_2; Q_2$
    b. social costs
    c. $P_1; Q_1$
    d. too much
    e. negative

2. a. $P_3; Q_3$
    b. social benefits
    c. $P_1; Q_1$
    d. too little
    e. positive

3. a. The supply curve after the tax is imposed shifts to S_1—that is, upward by $20 at each quantity. This is shown in the graph below.

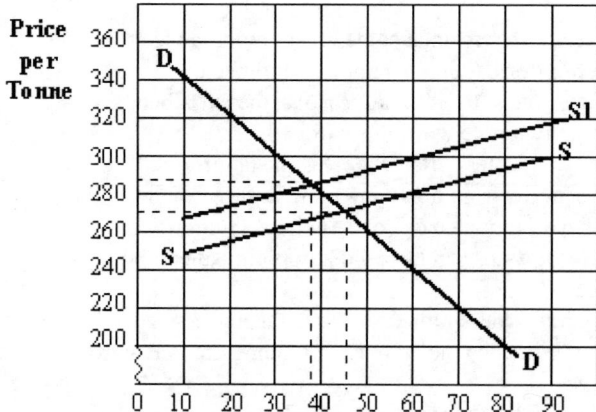

   b. The equilibrium quantity falls from 45 tonnes per month to below 40 tonnes per month as a result. Thus the quantity of fertilizer produced has declined by more than 10 percent. This means that the output of pollution has declined by more than 10 percent, because the output of pollution is a constant per unit of output of fertilizer. The result of the analysis should not be extended in a general fashion without regard to other possible effects that a tax of this nature might have. We might also wish to consider other factors before imposing a pollution tax. Among these factors are the effects of the increased price of the fertilizer,

the likely reduction in employment as a result of the reduced quantity of
fertilizer produced, and the ability of alternative methods of pollution control to
achieve the same results.

PROBLEMS

1. a. redistribution
    b. promoting competition
    c. providing merit goods
    d. discouraging demerit goods
    e. providing public goods
    f. redistribution
    g. providing legal system
    h. correcting positive externality
    i. providing legal system
    j. correcting negative externality
    k. stabilizing economy

2. Consumers joined car pools, drove less often, bought smaller cars, and endured less comfortable temperatures at home; businesses invested in the production of such oil substitutes as solar energy, nuclear energy, shale oil, coal, etc.; governments subsidized the production of gasohol and shale oil, etc. Such actions were rational because they were responses to a perceived increase in the relative price of oil and its distillates. From society's point of view, such actions led to a misallocation because the lack of competition caused the price system to transmit an incorrect signal. The signal was that oil had become more scarce—but the signal was induced by an artificial restriction of supply.

3. Tax 1: 3 percent; 3 percent; 3 percent; 3 percent; 3 percent; 3 percent; 3 percent; proportional
    Tax 2: 1 percent; 2 percent; 3 percent; 4 percent; 5 percent; 6 percent; 7 percent; progressive
    Tax 3: 10 percent; 9 percent; 8 percent; 7 percent; 6 percent; 5 percent; 4 percent; regressive

4. ATR: 3 percent; 4 percent; 5 percent; 5 percent; 4 percent; 3.5 percent; 3 percent
    MTR: 3 percent; 4.5 percent; 6 percent; 5 percent; 2 percent; 2 percent; 2 percent

    The average tax rate for this tax initially rises and then falls, as does the marginal tax rate. As a result, this tax is progressive up to an income of $6 000, proportional from there to $10 000, and regressive for levels of income above $10 000. Thus this tax is a combination of all three types of taxes as income varies. Can you graph the ATR and MTR for this tax? What specific taxes might behave in this manner?

BUSINESS SECTION

1. (.4122x$10 000) - (.2702x$10 000) = 4122 – 2702 = $1420 of savings
2. (.3995x$8000) – (.1998x$8000) =3196 – 1598.40 = $1597.60 of savings
3. (.3462x5000) = $1731 of savings in 2000. In later years, when Rachel withdraws the funds from her RRSP she may have to pay the related tax, depending on her income.
4. (.4188x$3000) = $1256.40 savings

CHAPTER 11

FISCAL POLICY AND THE PUBLIC DEBT

PUTTING THIS CHAPTER INTO PERSPECTIVE

In recent years, the public debt problems experienced by all Canadian governments have been brought under control, with governments in Canada now running balanced budgets, or small surpluses. However, we do have a large outstanding debt remaining from many years of deficit spending (and borrowing) that occurred from the mid 1970s to the late 1990s. Behind these debts were the decisions of politicians, and the public who elected them, to create many social support programs and to raise taxes to support these programs. Many federal and provincial governments were later elected (and failed) to bring the deficits of their governments under control during that time period, and only since 1995 have government deficits been dramatically declining.

Getting the deficit problem under control has meant painful restructuring of many of Canada's government programs. Taxes were raised, and funding for many programs, including government investment in education, has been cut back. In the most recent budgets, there have been some reductions in taxes again as governments have been able to run modest surpluses, and some of the debt has been paid back.

You have already learned how macroeconomic equilibrium is determined. In Chapter 8 it was pointed out that that there is nothing in a capitalistic (free enterprise) economy that assures full employment or price stability. The existence of recessionary gaps and inflationary gaps implies that equilibrium and unemployment (or inflation) can exist simultaneously.

Here you learn that if we wish to pursue the normative economics goals of full employment and price stability, then fiscal policy can be employed. Fiscal policy is the deliberate changing of government expenditures and/or taxes in order to attain such national economic goals as full employment, price stability, economic growth, and an international payments equilibrium. (In later chapters we develop the analysis of the other major stabilization tool, monetary policy, which can be employed to attain those same national goals.)

This chapter indicates how fiscal policy may be employed to counteract inflationary gaps and recessionary gaps. It also indicates that fiscal policy measures can be offset by indirect effects (changes in interest rates and the Ricardian equivalence theorem), direct effects (government expenditures that compete with the private sector cause an offsetting reduction in business investment) and net export effects (deficit spending leads to an offsetting reduction in net exports as higher domestic interest rates cause the country's exchange rate to rise).

You also learn in this chapter that changes in marginal tax rates affect the labour-leisure trade-off, the household saving-investment trade-off, and business investment decisions. (We will explore this issue in more depth later in the book).

Fiscal policy analysis is a rather complex business. We must be careful to distinguish between *discretionary* fiscal policy (in which conscious stabilization policies are pursued by policymakers) and automatic fiscal policy. The latter occurs automatically, without any conscious policy-making decisions, as a result of a progressive tax structure, employment insurance, the corporate income tax, and other taxes.

An important, if sad, lesson to be learned in this chapter is that fiscal policy is very difficult to implement. First there are the technical problems. Is the data accurate? How much crowding out will occur? How long or how variable are the various fiscal policy time lags? Then there are the political questions. If you leave this chapter with the feeling that fiscal policy is more an art than a science, then you are on the right track.

LEARNING OBJECTIVES

After you have studied this chapter you should be able to:

11.1   Use the aggregate demand/aggregate supply model to evaluate the effects of fiscal policy.

11.2   Explain the relationship between government budgets and the accumulated debt and describe the current situation for Canadian governments.

11.3   Explain the relationship between a government deficit and a current account deficit.

11.4   Discuss ways in which crowding out, direct expenditure offsets, the net export effect, supply-side economics, and the Ricardian equivalence theorem may offset the effectiveness of fiscal policy.

11.5   Explain how fiscal policy time lags complicate the use of fiscal policy to eliminate GDP gaps.

11.6   Describe how certain aspects of fiscal policy function as automatic stabilizers for the economy.

CHAPTER OUTLINE

LO 11.1 - Use the aggregate demand/aggregate supply model to evaluate the effects of fiscal policy.

1. **Fiscal policy** is the discretionary changing of government expenditures and/or taxes in order to achieve such national economic goals as high employment and price stability.
    a. If a recessionary gap exists, then expansionary fiscal policy is in order; if government expenditures increase (or lump-sum taxes fall), the aggregate demand curve shifts rightward and the recessionary gap can be eliminated, at a higher price level.
    b. If an inflationary gap exists, then contractionary fiscal policy is called for; if government expenditures decrease (lump-sum taxes increase), the aggregate demand curve shifts leftward and the inflationary gap can be eliminated, at a lower price level.
    c. If the economy is already operating on LRAS, shifts in the AD curve lead to *temporary* increases (decreases) in real GDP which are untenable because they are off LRAS; in the long run input owners revise their expectations upward (downward) and the SRAS curve shifts leftward (rightward); in the long run GDP will be at the LRAS level and the price level change will be greater than the change in the short run.

LO 11.2 - Explain the relationship between government budgets and the accumulated debt and describe the current situation for Canadian governments.

2. The **budget balance** is the amount of revenue collected minus spending. A **budget deficit** occurs when revenue is less than spending, and a **budget surplus** occurs when revenues exceed spending.
    a. Government spending must be paid for by one of three methods, taxes, borrowing, or money-financing.
    b. Governments borrowed heavily as they expanded in size through the 1970s until the mid-1990s.

3. The **public debt** is the total value of all outstanding federal government securities.
    a. The **net public debt** equals the gross public debt minus all government assets.
    b. The ratio of annual interest payments on the public debt to national income increased steadily from 1973 to 1995; it has since declined by about 1/3, but is still double the ratio of the mid 1970s.

LO 11.3 - Explain the relationship between a government deficit and a current account deficit.

4. Empirical evidence implies that a linkage may exist between our nation's federal deficits and its international trade deficit.
    a. Theoretically, higher budget deficits cause higher, domestic interest rates, which in turn induces foreigners to purchase our federal (and private) debt; hence

foreigners may substitute purchases of our debt for purchases of our export goods, thereby contributing to a trade deficit.

LO 11.4 - Discuss ways in which crowding out, direct expenditure offsets, the net export effect, supply side economics, and the Ricardian equivalence theorem may offset the effectiveness of fiscal policy.

5. There are various reasons why fiscal policy may not be as effective as we might hope.
    a. If government expenditures are financed by borrowing (**deficit spending**) then the interest rate may rise, which will cause a reduction in (a) business investment and (b) household expenditures on such durable goods as housing and automobiles. This is called the **crowding out effect**.
    b. The **net export effect** may also offset fiscal policy; deficit spending may cause the interest rate to rise, which induces foreigners to purchase domestic Canadian assets, which causes the relative price of the domestic currency to rise; in turn net exports fall, which partially offsets an inflationary fiscal policy.
    c. **Combined government spending** may not result in much change in total government expenditure because of the reluctance of smaller governments to finance their expenditures through debt.
    d. **Supply side** effects can result from fiscal policy effects of changing tax rates; changes in marginal tax rates may affect the labor-leisure tradeoff, the household saving-consumption decision, and business investment.
    e. If households perceive deficit spending as an increase in their future tax liabilities, the **Ricardian equivalence theorem** predicts that they will save more, hence the AD curve may not shift at all: household current consumption falls by the amount that G rises.

LO 11.5 - Explain how fiscal policy time lags complicate the use of fiscal policy to eliminate GDP gaps.

6. In practice, fiscal policy is a slow-moving policy.
    a. The **recognition**, **action**, and the **effect time lags** reduce the effectiveness of fiscal policy because the policy may not have any effect on the economy until the problem has resolved itself.

LO 11.6. - Describe how certain aspects of fiscal policy function as automatic stabilizers for the economy.

7. A progressive income tax and employment insurance are two examples of **automatic**, or **built-in stabilizers**; they are not discretionary, and they move the economy automatically toward high employment levels.

8. The fact that fiscal policy is available to use during severe recessions may be enough to stabilize and buoy expectations so that investment spending is smoother than it otherwise would be.

KEY TERMS AND CONCEPTS

Fiscal policy   Expansionary policy   Contractionary policy
Budget Surplus   Budget Balance   Budget Deficit
Gross public debt   Net public debt   Trade Deficit
Crowding out effect   Net Export effect   Ricardian equivalence theorem
Recognition time lag   Supply side economics   Automatic, or built-in
Action time lag   Effect time lag   stabilizers

COMPLETION QUESTIONS
Fill in the blank or circle the correct term.

(LO 11.1)

1. Discretionary fiscal policy is defined as a _____ change in taxes and/or government spending in order to change equilibrium national income and employment.

2. If a recessionary gap exists, it can be offset by (contractionary, expansionary) fiscal policy; such a policy entails (decreasing, increasing) government expenditures or (decreasing, increasing) taxes, which will cause the aggregate demand curve to shift (leftward, rightward); national output should (fall, rise) and the price level should (fall, rise).

3. If an inflationary gap exists, it can be eliminated if government expenditures (decrease, increase) or if taxes are (decreased, increased); this will cause the AD curve to shift (leftward, rightward) and national income will (fall, rise).

4. If the economy is already operating on its long run aggregate supply curve, then fiscal policy actions that shift the AD curve will cause real national income to change (temporarily, permanently) and the price level will change (more, less) in the long run, relative to the short run.

(LO 11.2)

5. A government's revenues minus its spending is called the _____.

6. If government expenditures exceed its tax revenues a _____ exists; if such an excess is financed by borrowing from the private sector, then we say that _____ spending has occurred, and the _____ debt will (fall, rise).

7. The net public debt subtracts government financial _____; hence, it is more relevant than the gross public debt.

8.   The provincial governments in Canada, collectively, have debt that is approximately (one quarter, one half) of the debt of the federal government.

9.   The ratio of annual interest payments on the public debt to national income has (doubled, tripled, quadrupled) since 1975.

(LO 11.3)

10. A linkage may exist between government budget deficits and a nation's _____ deficit; deficits may cause domestic interest rates to rise, which induces foreigners to substitute purchases of our federal _____ for purchases of our exports. Other things constant a trade _____ will emerge.

(LO 11.4)

11. If government expenditures are financed by borrowing, a federal budget (deficit, surplus) will result, which may cause the interest rate to (fall, rise), which in turn will cause business investment and household consumption on (durable, nondurable) goods to (fall, rise); hence fiscal policy effects will be (reduced, increased).

12. Crowding out is less likely to occur if deficit spending is made when the economy is operating at (low, high) levels of unemployment.

13. To the extent that government expenditures compete with the private sector, then such expenditures will (induce more, discourage) business investment expenditures; hence fiscal policy effects of an increase in G will be (reduced, enlarged).

14. If Canadian deficit spending causes the Canadian interest rate to rise, foreigners will want to purchase Canadian_____, which will lead to a(n) (decrease, increase) in the international demand for the dollar; hence Canadian exports will (fall, rise) and Canadian imports will (fall, rise); hence the inflationary effects of an increase in G will be (reduced, enlarged) by this net export effect.

15. Supply side effects can result from fiscal policy tax changes; if marginal tax rates rise this can induce laborers to substitute _____ for _____, and households might be induced to save (less, more) because the after tax return to saving will fall; because the after-tax return on investment will fall, we expect business to invest (less, more).

16. If households perceive government deficit spending as an increase in their future tax liabilities, they may save (less, more) according to the_____ theorem; hence fiscal policy effects will be (reduced, increased).

17.   If the public perceives that deficit spending creates future tax liabilities, and if people wish to leave money to their heirs, then current saving may well (decrease, increase); hence the net effect of deficit spending on interest rates is (to lower them, to raise them, uncertain).

(LO 11.5)

18.   Discretionary fiscal policy is (easy, difficult) to conduct because it usually takes (little, much) time for Parliament to enact such policy.

19.   There are three time lags that hamper fiscal policy: _____, _____, and _____. The existence of time lags makes conducting fiscal policy (easier, harder) for policymakers.

(LO 11.6)

20.   If government expenditures or taxes change over the business cycle without deliberate action taken by Parliament, then this is referred to as automatic fiscal policy, or built-in _____; examples of automatic fiscal policy include _____ and _____; automatic fiscal policy (increases, decreases) the magnitude of business cycle fluctuations.

21.   Because of automatic stabilizers, when the economy is in an expansion phase government transfers (rise, fall) and tax revenues (rise, fall); hence expansions (other things constant) generate government budget (surpluses, deficits).

22.   The existence of automatic stabilizers makes our economy (less, more) stable; they also make it (difficult, easy) to distinguish discretionary from automatic fiscal policy.

TRUE-FALSE QUESTIONS

Circle the T if the statement is true, the F if it is false. Explain to yourself why a statement is false.

(LO 11.1)

T   F   1.   If an inflationary gap exists, fiscal policy calls for increased G and/or reduced taxes.

T   F   2.   If a recessionary gap exists, proper fiscal policy requires a federal government budget surplus or a larger surplus if one already exists.

T   F   3.   If an economy is already operating on its LRAS curve, an inflationary fiscal policy will, eventually, cause the price level to rise by less than it would if the economy had been operating at a SRAS curve.

(LO 11.2)

T   F   4.   Our federal government can finance its expenditures by taxing, borrowing, or by creating money.

T   F   5.   Deficits emerge if the government borrows from other domestic agencies to finance its expenditures.

T   F   6.   When a deficit is incurred, the public debt rises.

T   F   7.   Deficits and surpluses are stock concepts, while the public debt is a flow concept.

(LO 11.3)

T   F   8.   Government budget deficits can cause trade deficits.

(LO 11.4)

T   F   9.   If budget deficits cause interest rates to rise, crowding out of private investment can result.

T   F   10.   If government expenditures are financed by borrowing, a federal deficit is created that could cause interest rates to rise.

T   F   11.   If interest rates rise as a result of deficit spending, inflationary fiscal policy effects will be magnified.

T   F   12.   If federal deficit spending causes interest rates to rise, households will purchase more consumer durables and businesses will invest more.

T   F   13.   If interest rates rise as a result of deficit spending, then foreigners may want to purchase more Canadian assets, which would cause the value of the Canadian dollar to rise on international exchange markets.

T   F   14.   If fiscal policy is pursued by raising marginal tax rates, laborers may choose to work less and businesses might choose to make fewer investments.

T   F   15.   If households perceive an increase in federal deficit spending as an increase in their future tax liabilities they may save more now, which would reduce the effects of inflationary fiscal policy.

(LO 11.4)

T   F   16.   Federal budget deficits can cause trade deficits.

(LO 11.5)

T   F   17.   Because of the time lags involved in fiscal policy, policymakers can more easily achieve national economic goals, because they have more time to solve the problem.

(LO 11.6)

T   F   18.   Discretionary fiscal policy requires Parliamentary approval while automatic stabilizers do not.

T   F   19.   The income tax system is an automatic stabilizer because it is changed by the government whenever a recession or expansion occurs.

MULTIPLE CHOICE QUESTIONS

Circle the letter that corresponds to the best answer.

(LO 11.1)

1.   Fiscal policy
   a.   deals with manipulating exchange rates.
   b.   is relatively easy to conduct.
   c.   deals with discretionary spending and tax policies.
   d.   calls for stabilizing changes in the money supply.

2.   If taxes fall, then
   a.   the planned expenditures curve shifts downward.
   b.   the aggregate demand curve shifts to the right
   c.   the aggregate supply curve shifts to the left
   d.   national income will fall

3.   If a recessionary gap exists, proper fiscal policy could entail
   a.   increased government spending.
   b.   decreased taxes.
   c.   deficit spending.
   d.   All of the above.

4.   If government expenditures rise to counteract a recessionary gap
   a.   the AD curve shifts rightward.
   b.   the AD curve shifts leftward.
   c.   taxes must rise to finance such expenditures.
   d.   the price level will fall.

5. If an inflationary gap exists
   a. contractionary fiscal policy is called for.
   b. G should rise to cause the price level to fall.
   c. inflationary fiscal policy is called for.
   d. taxes should fall, to stimulate the economy.

6. If a recessionary gap exists, then
   a. the equilibrium income exceeds the full-employment income level.
   b. it can be filled by increases in G or decreases in taxes, or some combination of both.
   c. it can be filled by decreases in G or increases in taxes, or some combination of both.
   d. the economy is in an expansion phase.

7. If the economy is operating on its short-run aggregate supply curve and an inflationary gap exists
   a. a contractionary fiscal policy is called for.
   b. leftward shifts in AD that cause some unemployment will be helpful.
   c. contractionary fiscal policy will eventually change only the price level.
   d. All of the above

8. If an inflationary gap exists, it can most efficiently be eliminated by some combination of
   a. increases in G, decreases in taxes.
   b. decreases in G, decreases in taxes.
   c. decreases in G, increases in taxes.
   d. increases in G. increases in taxes.

(LO 11.2)
9. Our federal government can finance larger expenditures by
   a. reducing its sales of government bonds.
   b. running trade deficits.
   c. taxing.
   d. All of the above.

10. When the federal government finances its deficit by borrowing
   a. the public debt rises.
   b. the money supply rises.
   c. taxes must rise.
   d. the public debt falls.

(LO 11.3)

11.   Which of the following will NOT (at least partially) offset fiscal policy?
    a.   the multiplier effect
    b.   G financed by increased taxes
    c.   G financed by borrowing (deficit spending)
    d.   automatic stabilizers

12.   Which of the following can offset an expansionary fiscal policy?
    a.   higher interest rates resulting from deficit spending
    b.   private investment falling in areas competing with government expenditures
    c.   perceptions by households that larger deficits imply increased future tax liabilities
    d.   All of the above

13.   Which of the following may well result from higher interest rates brought on by deficit spending?
    a.   increased purchases of consumer durable goods
    b.   increased business investment
    c.   a rising exchange rate for the domestic economy
    d.   All of the above

14.   If marginal tax rates rise
    a.   labourers may choose less income (work), which is taxed, and more leisure, which is not taxed.
    b.   the tax base could shrink.
    c.   productivity could fall eventually, as business investment falls.
    d.   All of the above

15.   Which of the following will probably **NOT** occur if the federal deficit rises?
    a.   Interest rates will fall.
    b.   Foreigners will wish to purchase our debt.
    c.   Foreigners will tend to import less of our goods.
    d.   Canadian exports will fall.

(LO 11.4)

16.   Which of the following usually occur together?
    a.   trade deficits and government surpluses.
    b.   trade deficits and government deficits.
    c.   trade surpluses and government deficits.
    d.   there is no correlation between trade balances and government budget balances.

(LO 11.5)

17.   Choose the statement that is NOT true.
    a.   Time lags make fiscal policy difficult.
    b.   Fiscal policy is conducted solely by the executive branch of the Canadian government.
    c.   Crowding out reduces the impact of an inflationary fiscal policy.
    d.   The Ricardian equivalence theorem implies that fiscal policy may be quite ineffective.

(LO 11.6)

18.   Fiscal policy
    a.   if discretionary, does not require Parliament's enactment.
    b.   is difficult to implement because of time lag problems
    c.   if automatic, is destabilizing.
    d.   All of the above

MATCHING

Choose an item in Column (2) that best matches an item in Column (1).

(1)	(2)
a. recessionary gap	1. Ricardian equivalence
b. inflationary gap	2. change in tax law
c. discretionary fiscal policy	3. taxes less than government spending
d. budget balance	4. employment insurance
e. net public debt	5. expansionary policy
f. deficit spending	6. contractionary policy
g. crowding out	7. supply side policies
h. time lags	8. conscious attempt to achieve high employment and price stability
i. automatic stabilizer	9. recognition, action, effect
j. stabilization policy	10. result of higher interest rates
	11. value of outstanding government securities
	12. revenue minus spending

WORKING WITH GRAPHS

(LO 11.1)

1.   Consider the graph on the next page, then answer the questions that follow.

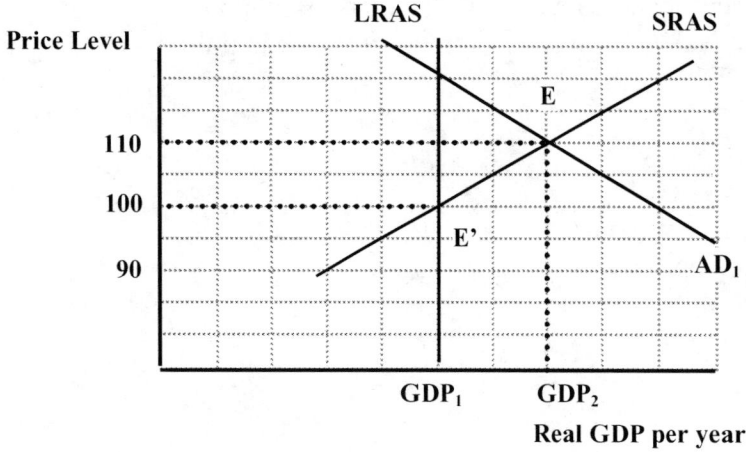

a.   What is the short-run equilibrium level of real GDP? What type of gap exists? Is this real income level sustainable?

b.   What type of fiscal policy would you recommend? Be specific.

c.   Continuing (b) above, you want the new AD curve to shift through what point?

d.   The long-run result of your fiscal policy is to cause what to happen to real GDP? To the price index?

(LO 11.2)

2.   Consider the graph on the next page, then answer the questions that follow.

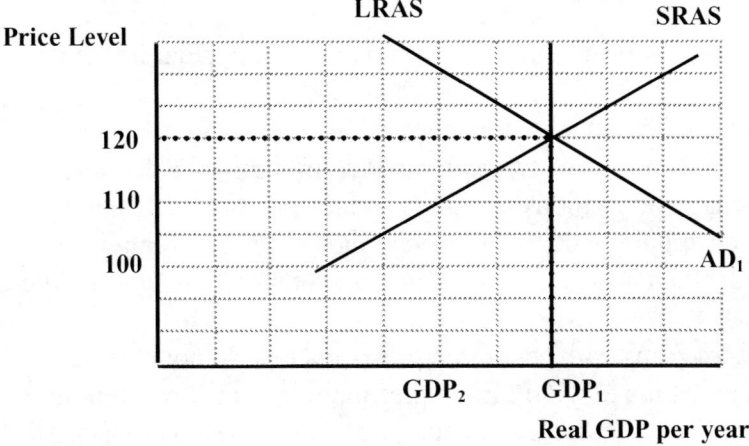

a.   What is the short-run equilibrium level of real GDP? The long-run equilibrium level of real GDP? The short-run equilibrium price level?

b.   Assume that it is desirable to get the short-run equilibrium price level to 110. What type of fiscal policy would you suggest? (Be specific) You want the new AD curve to come through what point? What will be the new short-run level of real GDP? Is this level sustainable? Why not?

c.   Continuing (b) above, what will happen to the short-run aggregate supply curve? Why?

d.   What will be the long-run level of real GDP?

BUSINESS SECTION

Finance: Fiscal Policy, Interest Rates, and the Stock Market

It is appropriate at this point to provide an outline of four types of financial investments.

- *Cyclical stocks* – stocks of firms with economic prospects that change noticeably due to fluctuations in real GDP. These firms typically operate in industries that are sensitive to interest rates and and/or industries that produce postponeable goods such as consumer durables and capital goods. Examples include firms operating in industries related to residential construction, commercial construction, automobiles, machinery and equipment.
- *Defensive stocks* – stocks of firms with economic prospects that do not change significantly with fluctuations in real GDP. Examples include firms operating in industries such as food and beverages, medical care, nursing homes, pharmaceuticals and utilities.
- *Export-driven stocks* – stocks of firms that earn a significant portion of their revenues from exports to other countries. Examples include lumber and forest products, pulp and paper, oil and gas and automobiles.
- *Government bonds* – a financial asset that is issued by the government to borrow funds from the public. At this point, we assume that the major reason investors purchase government bonds is to earn regular (semi-annual or annual) interest income.

(LO 11.4)
Application Problem 1

Suppose the Canadian economy is currently at its LRAS (i.e., peak of the business cycle). For political reasons, the Canadian government increases the deficit, by increasing spending on social programs.

1. a. Predict what will happen to interest rates. Provide two reasons for your prediction.

    b. Will the inflationary fiscal policy more likely induce investors to switch some of their investments from stocks to bonds or from bonds to stocks? Explain.

    c. How will the inflationary fiscal policy likely affect the investor's choice between cyclical stocks vs. defensive stocks. Explain.

    d. Will the inflationary policy likely have any affect on the stock prices of export driven stocks? Explain.

ANSWERS TO CHAPTER 11

COMPLETION QUESTIONS

1. deliberate, or conscious
2. expansionary; increasing; decreasing; rightward; rise, rise
3. decrease, increased; leftward, fall
4. temporarily, more
5. budget balance
6. budget deficit; deficit, public, rise
7. assets
8. one half
9. doubled
10. trade; bonds, deficit
11. deficit; rise; durable; fall; reduced
12. high
13. discourage; reduced
14. assets; increase; fall; rise; reduced
15. leisure; income resulting from working; less; less
16. more, Ricardian equivalence; reduced
17. increase; uncertain
18. difficult; much
19. recognition, action, effect; harder
20. stabilizers, progressive taxes, employment insurance; decreases
21. fall, rise, surpluses
22. more; difficult

TRUE-FALSE QUESTIONS

1. F   An inflationary gap calls for reduced G and/or increased taxes.
2. F   A recessionary gap calls for deficit spending
3. F   The price level will change by more because output won't change.
4. T
5. F   While gross debt rises, net debt will remain unchanged.
6. T
7. F   Deficits and surpluses are flow concepts, while the debt is stock concept.
8. T
9. T
10. T
11. F   No, higher interest rates will cause offsetting expenditure reductions in the private sector.
12. F   No, less of such expenditures will occur in response to a higher interest rate.
13. T   This is the net export effect.
14. T   These are possible supply-side effects.
15. T   This is called Ricardian equivalence.
16. T   This is a logical conclusion of the net export effect.
17. F   Time lags make fiscal policy more difficult because of the uncertainty they generate.
18. T   Parliament has approved these policies in the past, and does not need to re-legislate.
19. F   It is automatic because the government does NOT have to change policies.

MULTIPLE CHOICE QUESTIONS

1.c.;   Fiscal policy deals with discretionary actions or changes relating to government expenditures and/or taxes in order to achieve national economic goals such as economic stability.

2.b;   If personal taxes fall, disposable personal income will increase, causing planned consumption expenditures to increase. This will increase planned spending and shift the aggregate demand curve to the right.

3.d;   If a recessionary gap exists, Keynesians would suggest that the government would have to increase total planned expenditures by increasing government expenditures and/or decreasing taxes, thereby leading the budget in the direction of a deficit.

TIP: When the government pursues discretionary actions, which either increase total government spending and/or decrease total taxes, these actions are often described as inflationary policies as they increase total planned spending and short run equilibrium GDP.

4.a;   If government expenditures increase, this will cause an increase in aggregate demand. Graphically, an increase in aggregate demand is shown as a shift rightward in the aggregate demand curve.

5.a;   If an inflationary gap exists, this means that the short run equilibrium GDP level exceeds the long run equilibrium level as given by LRAS. Since this situation can result in an undesirable rate of inflation, governments often prescribe recessionary fiscal policy in order to shift the aggregate demand curve leftward. This policy is appropriate if the inflationary gap is caused by excessive aggregate demand.

TIP: When the government pursues discretionary actions, which either decrease total government spending and/or increase total taxes, these actions are often described as recessionary policies as they decrease total planned spending and short run equilibrium GDP.

6.b;   A recessionary gap can be filled or closed by increasing government expenditures and/or decreasing taxes. These policies will increase aggregate demand.

7.d;   If an inflationary gap exists, the economy is operating at a level which exceeds LRAS or full employment real GDP. To avoid a possibly undesirable rate of inflation, governments often pursue contractionary fiscal policy, which results in a leftward shift in aggregate demand. If the inflationary gap is due to excessive aggregate demand, the contractionary policy will eventually just reduce the price level.

8.c;   If an inflationary gap exists, the government can, in the long run, achieve a lower price level by decreasing government expenditures and/or increasing taxes. These policies will decrease total planned spending and shift the aggregate demand curve leftward.

9.c;   The only answer option that would help to finance a higher level of government expenditures is an increase in taxes.

10.a;   When the federal government finances its deficit by borrowing this will cause the public debt to rise. If, instead, the government had increased taxes, there would

11.a;   The multiplier effect strengthens the affect that fiscal policy will have on the economy. The other answer options listed tend to weaken or offset fiscal policy.

12.d;   Answer options a. and b. relate to the Crowding Out Effect. In this situation inflationary policy financed by borrowing from the public results in higher interest rates, which in turn crowds out private planned investment and offsets inflationary fiscal policy. Answer option c. describes the Ricardian equivalence theorem.

TIP: The Ricardian equivalence theorem implies that the perceived future tax liabilities resulting from an increased fiscal deficit will cause an increase in the rate of current saving which will offset inflationary fiscal policy.

13.c;   If a Canadian fiscal deficit increases Canadian interest rates offered on Canadian government bonds, this can result in an increase in the foreign demand for Canadian dollars. As a result, the Canadian dollar would rise , which would reduce net exports and offset inflationary fiscal policy. This situation is called the net export effect.

14.d;   According to supply side economists, if marginal tax rates rise ones incentive to work is significantly decreased. This negative incentive effect will decrease productivity and reduce real GDP. In turn, the nation's tax base (GDP) will shrink.

15.a;   If the federal deficit rises, according to the "crowding out effect", interest rates will tend to rise, not fall.
TIP:In order to increase the deficit, the federal government will have to sell more bonds. A key way that the federal government entices the general public to buy these additional bonds is to raise the interest rates offered with these new bonds.

16.b;   Empirical evidence shows that growing federal deficits tend to be followed by growing   current account deficits. Assuming that part of this increased deficit is financed through new borrowing abroad, this evidence is understandable. When the federal government starts to pay out the interest to foreign investors this outflow will contribute to a current account deficit and a lower Canadian dollar.

17.b.   In addition to the federal government, fiscal policy is conducted by other levels of government. The Canadian constitution provides fiscal powers to each provincial government.

18.b;   Discretionary fiscal policy can be difficult to implement because of time lag problems.
TIP: Discretionary fiscal policy can entail three time lags – recognition time lag, action time lag and effect time lag.

MATCHING

a and 5;   b and 6;   c and 2;   d and 12;   e and 11;   f and 3;   g and 10;   h and 9;   i and 4; j and 8

WORKING WITH GRAPHS

1.   a.   GDP2; inflationary gap; no, because it is above the full-employment level of real GDP
     b.   contractionary; Reduce G and/or increases taxes.
     c.   E'
     d.   Fall to GDP1; fall to 100
2.   a.   GDP1;GDP1; 120.
     b.   contractionary; reduce G, increase taxes; (GDP2,110; GDP2; No, because it is below the real GDP consistent with LRAS.
     c.   It will shift rightward as factors of production become accustomed to the lower price level and long-run adjustment takes place.
     d.   GDP1

BUSINESS SECTION

1.   a.   Interest rates will increase due to the crowding out effect and due to increased inflation.
     b.   The inflationary policy is more likely to induce investors to switch some of their investments from stocks to bonds due to the higher interest rates offered on the bonds.
     c.   With the economy already at the peak of the cycle, and with interest rates on the rise, investors would expect the economy to move into a contraction or recession. This expectation would likely motivate investors to switch some of their cyclical stocks to defensive stocks.
     d.   The prices of export driven stocks will likely fall in Canada. This is due to the net export effect. As Canadian interest rates increase, foreign demand for Canadian dollars will increase in order to buy the attractive high interest rate Canadian bonds. This will cause the Canadian dollar to appreciate. In turn, the higher Canadian dollar will reduce demand for Canadian exports, reducing the profit expectations in this sector. However, the appreciated Canadian dollar will lower costs and increase profits for companies who do a lot of importing.

CHAPTER 12

MONEY AND THE BANKING SYSTEM

PUTTING THIS CHAPTER INTO PERSPECTIVE

Chapter 12 is the first chapter in Part Five: Money, Monetary Policy, and Stabilization. Until now, we have analyzed how the equilibrium level of real national income and employment are determined in the short run and how fiscal policy can be used to eliminate contractionary gaps and expansionary gaps.

The aim of Chapter 12 is to introduce you to the concepts essential to an explanation of where money fits into macroeconomics—the main goal of Part Five. Chapter 12 explains that anything that serves the essential functions of money, namely, a medium of exchange, a unit of account, and a store of value is money. And Chapter 12 distinguishes between different definitions of the money supply. Each definition stresses a different function of money and a different point of view as to the role that money plays in the economy.

In order for policymakers to achieve such national economic goals as full employment, price stability, economic growth, and an equilibrium in the international balance of payments, it is necessary that they fully understand how the banking system operates. This is what Chapter 12 attempts to do.

This chapter introduces a lot of new terms, and you should resist the temptation to memorize. Unless you are advised differently by your teacher, you should try merely to understand the main distinctions between, in particular, M1 and M2. Each component in M1 is a medium of exchange; each can be used *directly* to purchase goods and services. Each item in M2 (which includes all the items in M1) has liquidity as a distinguishing feature; each item in M2 can be converted easily into other assets without loss of nominal value and with small transaction costs. In other words, the *nominal* value of M2 items is not subject to capital losses (or gains); as changes occur in the economy, M2 items maintain their nominal (but not necessarily real) values.

Keep in mind that the two methods reflect differing approaches as to the essential feature of money. The M1 approach views money as a medium of exchange; if money is essentially a medium of exchange, then as the money supply rises or falls we should expect total expenditures to rise and fall respectively.

On the other hand, the M2 approach maintains that the essential feature of money is that it is the most liquid asset. People hold a variety of assets in their asset portfolios and reach an equilibrium when they have an optimal amount of money and other (less liquid) assets. When this equilibrium is disturbed as a result of changes in the money supply, their asset portfolios become "too liquid" or "too illiquid" and their behaviour changes in a predictable way.

Thus M1 and M2 reflect different theories of the essential nature of money and therefore two different theories about how changes in the supply of money affect the macroeconomy.

LEARNING OBJECTIVES

After you have studied this chapter you should be able to

12.1   Define the functions of money.

12.2   Explain what "backs" the Canadian dollar.

12.3   Describe the various definitions of the money supply.

12.4   Describe the Canadian financial system.

CHAPTER OUTLINE

LO 12.1 - Define the functions of money
1.   There are three traditional functions of **money**, and anything that serves these three functions is money.
   a.   Money is a **medium of exchange**; money is that for which people exchange their productive services or that which they give for goods and services.
   b.   Money is a **unit of account**; the monetary unit is used to value goods and services relative to each other.
   c.   Money acts as a **store of value**; money is an **asset** that is a convenient store of generalized purchasing power.

2.   **Liquidity** is the degree to which an asset can be acquired or disposed of without loss in terms of nominal value and with small transactions costs.
   a.   Money is the most liquid of all assets.
   b.   Different goods have served as money throughout history.

LO 12.2 - Explain what "backs" the Canadian dollar.

3. Today Canada is on a **fiduciary monetary system**.
    a. The dollar is money in Canada because it is acceptable by virtually everyone in exchange for goods and services.
    b. The dollar is money in Canada, **fiat money**, because it is declared by the government to be legal tender.
    c. Another reason the dollar is money in Canada is because it has predictability of value in the future.

LO 12.3 - Describe the various definitions of the money supply.

4. There are three measures of the Canadian money supply.
    a. **M1** stresses that the essence of money is that it is a medium of exchange.
        i.   M1 includes *currency*—monetary coins and paper money outside the banks.
        ii. M1 also includes **chequable deposits** (accounts on which people can write cheques) at the chartered banks.
    b. Although credit cards seem to act as a medium of exchange, they are not really money.
    c. **M2** stresses that money is a highly liquid asset; such assets have an unchanging *nominal* value.
        i.   M2 includes all the items in M1.
        ii. M2 also includes personal **savings deposits** in chartered banks.
        iii. M2 also includes **non-personal notice deposits** made by firms in chartered banks.
    d. **M2+** includes M2 plus the deposits held at the financial institutions that are not chartered banks.

LO 12.4 - Describe the Canadian financial system.

5. The current Canadian banking structure includes *commercial banks (chartered banks)*, and **near banks**.

6. Financial institutions act as **financial intermediaries**; that is, they perform the function of transferring funds from savers to investors.

KEY TERMS AND CONCEPTS

M1	Savings deposits	Assets
M2	Non-personal notice deposits	Liabilities
M2+	Store of value	Fiat money
Medium of exchange	Fiduciary monetary system	Liquidity
Barter	Financial intermediaries	Chequable deposits
Money	Money supply	Near bank
Unit of account	Financial intermediation	

COMPLETION QUESTIONS
Fill in the blank or circle the correct term.

(LO 12.1)

1.   Because money is accepted for goods and services, it is used as a _____;
      it also performs the functions of _____, and a
      _____.

2.   _____ is the most liquid of all assets, because it maintains its
      (nominal, real) value.

3.   For an exchange to take place in a barter economy, a _____ coincidence
      of wants must exist; when a money system replaces a barter economy,
      specialization (decreases, increases) transaction costs.

4.   The opportunity cost of holding money is foregone _____ earnings;
      the benefit to holding money is increased _____.

5.   When inflation occurs, the price level (rises, falls), and the value of a unit of
      money (rises, falls).

(LO 12.2)

6.   Canada is on a _____ monetary system, which means the dollar is
      backed by (gold, faith that it can be exchanged for goods); items are used as
      money because of their _____ and _____ of value.

(LO 12.3)

7.   M1 includes _____ and _____; each can be used as a
      _____.

8.   M2 includes _____ plus _____ and _____; each of which is
      characterized as having a high degree of _____ because they
      maintain their nominal value.

9.   M2+ includes _____ plus _____.

10.   Near monies include _____ and _____.

(LO 12.4)

11.   Chartered banks are (commercial, government) banks, while near banks include
      _____; _____, and _____.

12.   Financial intermediaries perform the function of transferring household
      _____ to business _____.

TRUE-FALSE QUESTIONS

Circle the **T** if the statement is true, the **F** if it is false. Explain to yourself why a statement is false.

(LO 12.1)

T   F   1.   Exchange in a money economy requires a double coincidence of wants.

T   F   2.   In a money economy, specialization is encouraged and transaction costs fall, relative to a barter economy.

T   F   3.   An asset is liquid if it can be disposed of at a low transaction cost without loss of nominal value.

T   F   4.   There is no opportunity cost to holding money, because it is the most liquid of all assets.

T   F   5.   When the price level falls, the value of money rises.

T   F   6.   Barter economies are more efficient than money economies.

(LO 12.2)

T   F   7.   In Canada the dollar is backed by gold and silver.

T   F   8.   The fiduciary money system is "backed" by acceptability and predictability of value.

(LO 12.3)

T   F   9.   The components of M1 are less liquid than the components of M2.

T   F   10.   The components of M2 all are used as a medium of exchange.

T   F   11.   Credit cards are officially counted in M2.

T   F   12.   The value of M2 always exceeds the value of M1.

T   F   13.   Currency is the highest percentage of M1.

T   F   14.   M1 and M2 is the same thing.

T   F   15.   M2 always exceeds the value of M2+.

(LO 12.4)

T   F   16.   Financial intermediation is the process of transforming business investments into household saving.

MULTIPLE CHOICE QUESTIONS

Circle the letter that corresponds to the best answer.

(LO 12.1)

1. Which of the following is a function of money?
   a. medium of exchange
   b. unit of account
   c. store of value
   d. All of the above

2. Which of the following is an advantage of money over barter?
   a. permits more specialization of labour
   b. does not require a double coincidence of wants
   c. reduces transaction and storage costs
   d. All of the above

3. Barter
   a. increases specialization of labour.
   b. makes money less useful.
   c. increases transaction costs.
   d. eliminates the need for a double coincidence of wants.

(LO 12.2)

4. Under a fiduciary monetary standard, money is backed by
   a. gold.
   b. public faith that money can be exchanged for goods and services.
   c. precious metals that can be exchanged for goods and services.
   d. the chartered banks' assets.

(LO 12.3)

5. Which is not considered money?
   a. chequable deposits
   b. demand deposits
   c. credit cards
   d. currency

6. Which of the following is a characteristic of M2?
   a. high liquidity
   b. medium of exchange
   c. significant changes in nominal value
   d. real value does not vary during inflationary periods

7. Which of the following assets are probably the least liquid?
   a. savings account balances
   b. shares of stock in a major corporation
   c. office building
   d. Canada Savings Bond

8. Which of the following is most **UNLIKE** the others?
    a. currency
    b. passbook savings account
    c. chequing accounts
    d. demand deposit

9. Which of the following is **NOT** a component of M1?
    a. savings deposits
    b. demand deposits
    c. currency
    d. All of the above

10. Which of the following is not a part of M1?
    a. demand deposits
    b. credit card limits
    c. currency
    d. chequable deposits

11. *Analogy*: M1 is to *medium of exchange* as M2 is to _____.
    a. unit of account
    b. store of value
    c. barter approach
    d. double coincidence of wants

12. Near monies
    a. are used as a medium of exchange.
    b. are highly liquid.
    c. include currency and demand deposits.
    d. All of the above

13. Currency
    a. is not a component of M2.
    b. earns no interest.
    c. is illiquid.
    d. cannot be used in transactions.

(LO 12.4)
14. Which of the following is NOT a near bank?
    a. trust company
    b. caisses populaires
    c. credit union
    d. chartered bank

15. Regarding Canadian financial institutions,
    a. they are becoming less similar.
    b. the distinctions among them are becoming blurred.
    c. very few changes have occurred since the 1970s.
    d. they all have pretty much the same composition of assets and liabilities.

MATCHING
Choose the item in Column (2) that best matches an item in Column (1).

(1)	(2)

a. M1   1. ease of conversion into money
b. barter   2. savings deposit
c. currency   3. coins and paper money
d. bank liability   4. medium of exchange
e. liquidity   5. double coincidence of wants
                      6. unit of account
                      7. store of value

PROBLEMS

(LO 12.3)

1. Below you are given hypothetical figures in billions of dollars for various financial assets.

Currency	23.2
Money market mutual funds	14.7
Non-personal notice deposits in chartered banks	24.3
Personal savings deposits in chartered banks	237.5
Certificates of deposits	81.9
Chequable deposits in chartered banks	33.2

a. Find the value of M1.

b. Find the value of M2.

2. Below are rates of return, in percent, recorded for different investments available on a given date:

i.	Personal savings account (min. $3,000 -$5000 balance)	.25%
ii.	Personal savings account (min. $5,000 - $10,000 balance)	1.25%
iii.	Canada savings bond - 1 yr. term	3.00%
iv	Investment certificate - 1yr. term (min $1,000)	3.70%
v.	Investment certificate - 5 yr. term (min. $1,000)	4.50%
vi.	Federal government bond - 25 yr. term	5.96%
vii.	Corporate bond - 25 yr. term	6.54%

a. Why does the second personal savings account listed above offer a higher rate of interest (1.25%) compared to the first savings account listed (.25%)?

b.   Why does the 1-year Canada savings bond offer only 3% interest, compared to the I-year term guaranteed investment certificate rate of 3.70% available through a chartered bank?

c.   Why does the 25-year corporate bond offer a higher rate of interest (6.54%) than the 25-year federal government bond (5.96%)?

BUSINESS SECTION

(LO 12.1)
Finance: Mutual Funds

A mutual fund can be viewed as a company that manages investments for a diverse group of investors. The mutual fund company raises funds by issuing (selling) units (shares) to many investors. These funds are then invested in a variety of securities issued by governments and by companies. While there are many type of mutual funds, one broad way of classifying these funds is according to their primary investment objective as follows.

Growth funds aim to provide the investor with significant capital gains in the future by investing in equities such as common stocks. *Fixed–income funds* seek to provide a consistently high level of annual income by purchasing bonds, mortgages, and preferred shares. Money market funds provide investors with a high level of security by investing in liquid investments such as government treasury bills.

The value or price of a mutual fund unit is called the Net Asset Value Per Unit (NAV/unit) calculated as follows: (we will ignore possible commission or "load" fees that may be added to the cost or sale):

$$NAV/unit = \frac{Total\ Assets\ of\ Fund - Total\ Liabilities\ of\ Fund}{Total\ Number\ of\ Units\ Outstanding}$$

Application Problem 1: Net Asset Value Per Unit (NAV/unit)

CanInvest is a Canadian equity growth fund that currently owns common stocks in a variety of sectors including communications and media, consumer products, metals and minerals, oil and gas, utilities and paper and forest products. CanInvest's assets and liabilities, as of December 31, 2004 is shown below.

Assuming that as of December 31, 2004, there are 15 065 221 units (shares) outstanding, calculate the Net Asset Value per Unit for CanInvest.

Assets

| All stock investments at market value | $220 978 150.00 |
| Other Assets | $4 567 230.00 |

Total Liabilities (includes fees, redemptions, distributions payable) $ 790 120.00

ANSWERS TO CHAPTER 12

COMPLETION QUESTIONS

1. medium of exchange; unit of account, store of value
2. money, nominal
3. double; decreases
4. interest; liquidity
5. rises, falls
6. fiduciary; faith that it can be exchanged for goods; acceptability, predictability
7. currency, chequable deposits, medium of exchange;
8. M1; personal savings deposits, non-personal notice deposits, liquidity
9. M2; deposits at near banks
10. time deposits, short term government securities
11. commercial; credit unions, caisses populaires, trust companies
12. savings, investors

TRUE-FALSE QUESTIONS

1. F   That statement is true for a barter economy.
2. T
3. T
4. F   The opportunity cost of holding money is foregone interest.
5. T
6. F   Barter economies require a double coincidence of wants and they limit opportunities for specialization.
7. F   Canada is on a fiduciary monetary standard.
8. T
9. F   They are more liquid.
10. F   They are all highly liquid, but some are not a medium of exchange.
11. F   Credit cards, by definition, are not a part of M2.
12. T
13. F   Chequable deposits are.
14. F   M2 includes non-chequable deposits (savings deposits).
15. F   M2+ includes M2 plus deposits at near banks
16. F   It is the process of transferring household saving to business investment.

MULTIPLE CHOICE QUESTIONS

1.d;   To say that money serves as a medium of exchange is to say that generally, sellers will accept it as payment for market transactions. The unit of account function refers to the practice of using the monetary unit as a measuring yardstick to compare the relative value of goods and services. A third key function of money is that it is a convenient store of value due to its liquidity.

2.d;   This question describes some of the advantages that a money system has over a barter system. In a money system, a double coincidence of wants is not required in order to facilitate an exchange of goods and services. The existence of money reduces the transaction costs associated with means of payment uncertainty—individuals no longer have to hold a diverse collection of goods as an exchange inventory. Finally, to the extent that money facilitates exchange, it permits greater specialization of labour.

3.c;   Barter increases transaction costs associated with means of payment uncertainty. In a barter system each individual has to hold a diverse collection of goods as an exchange inventory.

4.b;   Under a fiduciary monetary standard, money is backed by public faith that money can be exchanged for goods and services. The paper money that people hold is not backed by precious metals such as gold or silver.

5.c;   A credit card transaction is not considered to be an addition to the money supply. It is really a loan to you by the issuer of the card, such as a bank or a store. You still must rely on a demand deposit or chequable deposit to pay off the loan created by the credit card transaction.

   TIP: The narrowest definition of the money supply is called M1 that focuses on the medium exchange function of money. M1 includes currency and demand deposits.

6.a;   M2 refers to a broader measure of money, which includes M1 and other very liquid assets, such as personal saving accounts and non-personal notice deposits.

   TIP: A liquid asset is one that can be acquired or disposed of without high transaction costs and with relative certainty as to its value.

7.c;   An office building is likely the least liquid of the assets listed. If you had to unexpectedly dispose of an office building you would be faced with very high transaction costs as well as uncertainty as to the final value that you will be able to negotiate.

8.b;   Passbook savings account is the only item listed that does not serve directly as a medium of exchange.

9.a;   Since M1 consists of currency and demand deposits, a savings account is not a component of M1.

10.b;   Credit card limits is not considered to be money. Instead credit card transactions are really loans that eventually are paid through the use of chequing deposits.

11.b;   M1 is to medium of exchange as M2 is to store of value. In other words, while M1 includes items used as a medium of exchange such as currency and demand deposits, M2 includes personal savings accounts and non-personal notice deposits, which serve as a store of value.

12.b;   Near monies are highly liquid assets which are included in definitions of the money supply alternate to M1 and M2. As an example M2+ includes M2 plus near bank deposits.

13.b;   Currency earns no interest. It is desirable due to its widespread acceptance as a medium of exchange.

14.d;   In the text, when we refer to banks we mean the chartered banks. When we refer to near banks we refer to other financial institutions that offer chequable deposits such as credit unions, trust companies, and caisses populaires.

15.b;   The distinction between financial institutions such as chartered banks, trust and mortgage companies, credit unions, and insurance companies has become more blurred as the laws governing these institutions change.

MATCHING

a and 4;   b and 5;   c and 3;   d and 2;   e and 1

PROBLEMS

1.   a.   M1 = $56.4 billion   b.   M2 = $318.2 billion
2.   a.   Since, with the second savings account you are required to commit a higher minimum balance, there is a higher opportunity cost involved, so you will "demand" a higher rate.

   b.   Since the 1 year Canada savings bond can be cashed in at any time without penalty, it is more liquid, which makes it attractive, despite the lower rate offered.

   c.   With the corporate bond there is an added risk that the corporation may not be able to pay back the principal borrowed in 25 years time ("default risk"). With its powers to tax and create money the federal government will be able to pay your principal back.

BUSINESS SECTION

The total net assets or net worth = (220 978 150 +4 567 230) –790 120 = 224 755 260
NAV/unit = 224 755 260/15 065 221 = $14.92 per unit as of December 31, 2004

CHAPTER 13

MONEY CREATION AND DEPOSIT INSURANCE

PUTTING THIS CHAPTER INTO PERSPECTIVE

Stabilization policy is one of the important roles of the government. In Chapter 11, fiscal policy was analyzed, and Chapter 12 explored the structure of the banking system, the essence and the functions of money, and how money is measured. Before we can analyze the other major stabilization tool, monetary policy, we must study how banks create money (to be more specific, chequable deposits). That is precisely the main objective of Chapter 13: to explain how the Bank of Canada and the commercial banks, together, determine and change the money supply.

To explain how depository institutions (commercial banks) operate and how the money expansion process works, we employ a convenient tool—the balance sheet. (If you have taken a course in accounting, you will recognize our balance sheet as a simplified balance sheet; it is a stock concept.) Be sure to note the distinction between balance sheets that show the overall position of a bank and those that deal with *changes* in individual items in the balance sheet; also be sure to concentrate on the chequable deposit entry and reserves (especially excess reserves).

The essence of deposit creation is that when total bank reserves rise, individual banks will acquire excess reserves and will have an incentive to make loans—because excess reserves earn no interest for banks. Banks lend by creating chequing accounts for borrowers, and chequing accounts, as was pointed out in Chapter 12, are a part of the money supply. The maximum amount of new deposits that can be created by a *single bank* will equal the amount of its excess reserves.

A second major objective in Chapter 13 is to analyze the process of the money multiplier A single bank is constrained in lending out excess reserves because cheques drawn on a chequable account may be deposited in another bank. However, these new deposits in the other bank create new excess reserves, and the potential for new loans and creating new money. The money supply *in the banking system* will change by a multiple. The reciprocal of the desired reserve ratio defines the *maximum* money multiplier. The *actual* money multiplier depends on the extent to which banks are prepared to hold excess reserves and the extent to which the public wishes to hold currency instead of transactions accounts. In the optimal case that banks hold zero excess reserves and there are no currency drains during the money creation process, the actual money multiplier will be equal to the maximum money multiplier.

A third objective is to show the need for the Canadian deposit insurance system that insures depository institutions. Deposit insurance can be flawed and that system could contribute to risky investments made by depository institutions. The concepts of asymmetric information, adverse selection, and moral hazard are employed to help understand the flaws and risks in the financial system.

LEARNING OBJECTIVES

After you have studied this chapter you should be able to:

13.1 Define the links between changes in the money supply and other economic variables.

13.2 Describe the origins of fractional reserve banking.

13.3 Define reserves.

13.4 Explain the relationship between reserves and total deposits.

13.5 Describe the money multiplier.

13.6 Describe deposit insurance and flawed bank regulation.

CHAPTER OUTLINE

13.1 - Define the links between changes in the money supply and other economic variables.
1. Changes in money supply growth are linked to changes in economic growth, to the inflation rate, and to the business cycle.

13.2 - Describe the origins of fractional reserve banking.
2. Commercial banks determine the total money supply in the Canada, which has a **fractional reserve banking** system.

13.3 - Define reserves.
3. Commercial banks desire to maintain a specified percentage of their customer deposits as **reserves**.
   a. Total reserves constitute what banks are allowed by law to claim as reserves; today that consists of deposits held at the Bank of Canada and vault cash.
   b. **Desired reserves** are the minimum amount of reserves that a depository institution wishes to hold to back its chequable deposits; they are expressed as a ratio of desired reserves to total chequable deposits.
   c. **Excess reserves** are the difference between actual reserves and desired reserves.

13.4 - Explain the relationship between reserves and total deposits.
4. A **balance sheet** indicates the relationship between reserves and total deposits in a depository institution (bank).

a. When a bank receives a currency deposit, its total reserves rise by the amount of the deposit; and its excess reserves rise also; the bank can lend an amount equal to its excess reserves by creating a chequable account.

b. The total money supply is unaffected, however, because currency outside the banks has become a chequable deposit and therefore the total money supply is not altered.

13.5 - Describe the money multiplier.

5. When total banking system reserves change, the money supply will change by a multiple of the reserve change.

a. If the reserves of Bank A go up by $100,000, total banking system reserves rise and the money supply will rise by a multiple of $100,000.

b. Continuing this example, if the desired reserve ratio is 20 percent, then the maximum new deposits that can be created by the system (i.e., money supply) will equal $500,000.

c. A financial transaction must increase (decrease) total banking system reserves in order for a multiple expansion (contraction) to occur.

6. The maximum **money multiplier** equals the reciprocal of the desired reserve ratio; the actual change in the money supply equals the *actual* money multiplier times the change in total reserves.

a. There are two major forces that reduce the *money multiplier*.
   i.   Currency drains reduce the money multiplier.
   ii. If depository institutions hold excess reserves, the actual money multiplier will be less than the maximum.

b. The M1 multiplier has varied from about 1.5 to about 2.5. Since 1960, the M2 multiplier has increased steadily over that period, from about 2.25 to over 12 in the 1990s.

13.6 - Describe deposit insurance and flawed bank regulation.

7. The **Canadian deposit insurance corporation** was created in 1967 in order to protect small investors who do not have the resources to accurately assess the soundness of depository institutions.

a. There have been three major flaws in the deposit insurance system: the insurance price has been too low, the rate charged had been the same for all institutions (now changed) regardless of how risky an institution's portfolio was, and the system insures deposits, not depositors.

b. Those flaws have encouraged managers of depository institutions to assume greater risk than they would otherwise; a **moral hazard** exists for such managers.

c. The **adverse selection** problem also exists; knowing that depositors have little or no incentive to monitor bank manager decisions, people willing to engage in fraudulent and risky behaviour are attracted to this industry.

d. Both the moral hazard problem and the adverse selection problem result from **asymmetric information**.

e. Increased risk-taking, in conjunction with adverse economic circumstances, has led to significant numbers of depository institution failures, particularly in the U.S.

KEY TERMS AND KEY CONCEPTS

Reserves	Desired reserves	Moral hazard
Excess reserves	Adverse selection	Net worth
Desired reserves	Balance sheet	Bank run
Asymmetric information	Fractional reserve banking	Money multiplier
Money multiplier process	Canadian Deposit Insurance Corporation (CDIC)	

COMPLETION QUESTIONS
Fill in the blank or circle the correct term.

(LO 13.1)

1. There is a strong link between growth in the _____ and economic growth, the inflation rate, and the business cycle.

(LO 13.2)

2. Predecessors to modern-day banks were _____ and money lenders who had secure vaults and who eventually realized that at any given time only a small _____ of total deposits left with them were withdrawn; this was the beginning of _____ banking.

(LO 13.3)

3. Total demand deposits are determined by the commercial or chartered _____.

4. Total reserves constitute anything that chartered banks are permitted by law to claim as such; today reserves include _____ and _____.

(LO 13.4)

5. Desired reserves are the (minimum, maximum) amount of desired reserves that a chartered bank wishes to hold; the desired reserve ratio is the ratio of desired reserves to _____; excess reserves equal _____ minus _____.

(LO 13.5)

6. When an individual bank has zero excess reserves it (can, cannot) extend more loans; when an individual bank receives a new deposit, its total reserves (fall, rise) by the amount of the deposit and its excess reserves (fall, rise). That bank can now increase its lending by the size of its _____.

7. If Bank A receives a currency deposit, then Bank A's excess reserves will (rise, fall); overall banking system excess reserves will (rise, fall, remain unaltered); the total money supply will _____.

8. If the desired reserve ratio is 10 percent, then the maximum money multiplier equals _____; the actual money multiplier will be less than the maximum due to _____ and _____.

9. If Mr. Calvo deposits a $200 cheque in Bank A, the $200 increase in Mr. Calvo's chequing account is a(n) (asset, liability) of Bank A; Bank A's (assets, liabilities) will also rise by $200 because Bank A's reserves rise by that amount.

(LO 13.6)

10. The Canadian deposit insurance system was created in _____; it was instituted to prevent bank _____.

11. The Canadian deposit insurance system had three flaws: the rate charged to depository institutions has been too (low, high), each depository institution had been charged (the same, a different) rate, and the system insures (deposits, depositors).

12. Individual depository institutions now pay rates that reflect how risky their portfolios are. Canadian deposit insurance now (encourages, discourages) risk-taking by depository institutions.

13. Both the moral hazard problem and the adverse selection problem stem from a(n) _____ of information. The moral hazard problem results because one party to the transaction has superior information (before, after) the transaction, while the adverse selection problem results because one party has superior information (before, after) the transaction.

14. Our deposit insurance system encourages depositors to (ignore, monitor closely) the loan portfolio of depository institutions, hence bank managers have an incentive to take on (less, more) risk and the _____ problem results.

15. Our deposit insurance system encourages depositors to (ignore, monitor closely) the behaviour of bank owners and bank managers. Hence people who are willing to take excessive risk or people who are willing to engage in fraudulent behaviour are (discouraged from, encouraged to) enter(ing) the banking industry, and the _____ problem results.

TRUE-FALSE QUESTIONS

Circle the **T** if the statement is true, the **F** if it is false. Explain to yourself why a statement is false.

(LO 13.1)

T F   1. Commercial banks determine the total money supply.

(LO 13.2)

T F   2. Early goldsmiths discovered that at any given time only a small percentage of people who left gold with them for safekeeping asked for their gold.

(LO 13.3)

T   F   3.   Total reserves equal desired reserves plus excess reserves.

T   F   4.   Today reserves include only vault cash for banks.

(LO 13.4)

T   F   5.   Total deposits multiplied by the desired reserve ratio equals excess reserves.

(LO 13.5)

T   F   6.   If an individual bank has excess reserves, it can make loans.

T   F   7.   When a depository institution makes a loan, it creates chequable deposits.

T   F   8.   When Mr. Plick deposits a $1000 cheque in his chequable account in Bank A, Bank A's assets and liabilities each rise by $1000.

T   F   9.   Depository institutions have an incentive to minimize their excess reserves.

T   F   10.   If a financial transaction increases total reserves in the banking system, the money supply will rise.

T   F   11.   The actual money multiplier will equal the maximum money multiplier, if banks hold excess reserves.

T   F   12.   When people receive cheques they deposit the whole cheque; they never withdraw part in currency.

T   F   13.   The commercial banks can cause an increase in the money supply by lowering the desired reserve ratio.

T   F   14.   A money multiplier exists due to a fractional reserve system.

T   F   15.   The maximum money multiplier equals the reciprocal of the marginal propensity to save.

(LO 13.6)

T   F   16.   Canadian deposit insurance rates vary with how risky a depository institution's portfolio is.

T   F   17.   If the government subsidizes failing banks, bank managers have less incentive to avoid risk or to be efficient.

T   F   18.   The adverse selection problem implies that if depositors have little or no incentive to monitor bank behaviour, so some unscrupulous people will attempt to perform banking services.

T F 19. The adverse selection problem, but not the moral hazard problem, stems from an asymmetric information situation.

T F 20. The moral hazard problem results from asymmetric information that exists before a transaction.

MULTIPLE CHOICE QUESTIONS

Circle the letter that corresponds to the best answer.

(LO 13.2)

1. Early goldsmiths and money-lenders
    a. charged a fee for providing safekeeping for valuables deposited with them.
    b. were the original bankers.
    c. discovered that they could lend out depositors' gold at interest, because only a fraction of gold deposits were requested at any given time.
    d. All of the above

(LO 13.3)

2. Under a fractional reserve system, depository institutions
    a. cannot keep 100 percent of their deposits on reserve.
    b. must keep 100 percent of their deposits on reserve.
    c. desire to keep a certain percentage of their total deposits on reserve.
    d. cannot hold excess reserves.

(LO 13.4)

3. When banks maintain a predictable desired reserve ratio this means
    a. that they will likely increase the chances of a bank run.
    b. the Bank of Canada would have more control over the money supply.
    c. monetary control would be more difficult for the Bank of Canada.
    d. they would hold 100 percent of their deposits on reserve.

4. Today in Canada, chartered bank reserves include
    a. vault cash and deposits at the Bank of Canada.
    b. U.S. government securities.
    c. gold.
    d. All of the above

(LO 13.5)

5. *Analogy*: the desired reserve ratio is to the money multiplier as the _____ is to the national income multiplier.
    a. balance sheet
    b. excess reserve
    c. bond dealer
    d. marginal propensity to save

6. If the Bank of Canada raises the desired reserve ratio from 10 percent to 20 percent, then the maximum money multiplier
   a. will rise from 5 to 10.
   b. will fall from 10 to 5.
   c. is unaffected.
   d. cannot be calculated, due to leakages.

7. In Canada, excess reserves
   a. earn interest.
   b. always equal zero.
   c. must be positive before new lending can occur.
   d. All of the above

8. Actual reserves minus desired reserves equal
   a. the desired reserve ratio.
   b. actual reserves.
   c. vault cash plus deposits at Fed District Banks.
   d. excess reserves.

9. When Mr. McKay deposits a $1000 cheque in Bank A,
   a. Bank A's reserves (assets) rise by $1000.
   b. Mr. McKay's deposit is an additional liability for Bank A.
   c. Bank A's excess reserves rise and it can increase its lending.
   d. All of the above

10. If Bank B has negative excess reserves, then it
    a. is meeting its reserve requirements.
    b. will call in loans and not re-lend as old loans are paid off.
    c. must increase its lending.
    d. must shut down.

11. If the desired reserve ratio is 10 percent, then
    a. the actual money multiplier is 10.
    b. the maximum money multiplier is 10.
    c. the national income multiplier is 10.
    d. excess reserves equal 0.

12. The actual change in the money supply equals the actual money multiplier
    a. times the change in reserves.
    b. plus the change in reserves.
    c. times the change in excess reserves.
    d. plus the change in excess reserves.

(LO 13.6)

13. Deposit insurance…
    a. is unnecessary in a fractional reserve system.
    b. helps to prevent bank runs.
    c. means that investors are fully protected when buying bank stocks.
    d. decreases depository institution risk-taking under the current system.

14. As it now operates, the Canadian deposit insurance system does not
    a. subsidize depository institutions.
    b. charge the same insurance rate to all banks.
    c. encourage depository institutions to assume more risk.
    d. All of the above

15. Asymmetry of information that occurs
    a. before a transaction could lead to a moral hazard problem.
    b. after a transaction could lead to an adverse selection problem.
    c. before a transaction could lead to an adverse selection problem.
    d. presents no economic problem.

16. The moral hazard problem implies that
    a. asymmetry of information exists.
    b. unscrupulous people have an incentive to own and operate banks.
    c. asymmetry of information existed before a transaction.
    d. All of the above

17. Which of the following is an example of adverse selection?
    a. Unhealthy people wish to obtain group health insurance.
    b. Unscrupulous people wish to occupy jobs that are difficult to monitor.
    c. People with cancer wish to buy insurance from companies that don't require a health examination.
    d. All of the above

MATCHING

Choose an item in Column (2) that best matches an item in Column (1).

(1)	(2)
a. money multiplier	1. Excess reserves
b. asymmetry of information	2. 10 maximum money multiplier
c. desired reserve ratio	3. reciprocal of desired reserve ratio
d. 10 percent desired reserve ratio	4. ratio of desired reserves to total deposits
	5. moral hazard
	6. vault cash

PROBLEMS

(LO 13.5)

1. The following table contains several different desired reserve ratios that might apply to chartered banks. In column 2, calculate the maximum money multiplier for each of the figures given in column 1. In column 3, calculate the maximum amount by which a single depository institution can increase its loans for each dollar's worth of excess reserves on deposit. In column 4, calculate the amount by which the entire banking system can increase deposits for each dollar of excess reserves in the system.

1	2	3	4
12 1/2%	_____	_____	_____
16 2/3%	_____	_____	_____
20%	_____	_____	_____
30%	_____	_____	_____
33 1/3%	_____	_____	_____

2. Below you are given a series of bank balance sheets. Assume that each case presented is independent. Use the information given to post the changes that would result from the specified action in each case. Show reductions using a minus sign and additions with a plus sign.

	Assets	Liabilities
A. A small business writes a cheque to pay back a $2000 loan from the same bank.	Reserves: Loans & Securities:	Demand Deposits:
B. The bank makes a $500 loan to you and credits your chequing account.	Reserves Loans & Securities:	Demand Deposits:
C. The bank sells $500 in Treasury Bills to the Bank of Canada to make up a reserve deficiency.	Reserves: Loans & Securities:	Demand Deposits:

D. You withdraw $25   Reserves: Demand Deposits:
    (from your bank) for date
    money.   Loans &
                                        Securities:

3. Suppose you have the balance sheets for three banks, as given in the table below.
    Assume that the desired reserve ratio is 20 percent. Then:
    a. Compute the desired reserves and place these in row A.
    b. Compute the excess reserves and place these in row B.
    c. Compute the amount of new loans a single bank can extend in a multi-bank
        system and place these in row C.
    d. Compute the amount of new loans each bank could extend if each were a
        monopoly bank and place these in row D (Note: This is equivalent to viewing
        each of the balance sheets below as the balance sheet for the entire banking
        system.)

Assets	1	2	3
Reserves	$ 5 000	$ 6 000	$ 6 000
Loans	10 000	10 000	10 000
Securities	5 000	6 000	7 000
Liabilities			
Demand deposits	17 500	20 000	18 000
Net worth	2 500	2 000	5 000
A. Desired Reserves	_____	_____	_____
B. Excess Reserves	_____	_____	_____
C. New Loans (single bank)	_____	_____	_____
D. New Loans (bank system, i.e., monopoly bank)	_____	_____	_____

4. The Bank of Canada purchases a $1 million Government of Canada Treasury Bill
    from Mr. Mondrone, who deposits it in Bank 1. Show the immediate balance sheet
    effects of this transaction on the Bank 1.

Bank 1 (Chartered Bank)

Assets	Liabilities

5. Continuing the example from problem 4, assume the desired reserve ratio equals 5%:
    a. By how much can Bank 1 increase its loans and chequing deposits by?

    b. Suppose Bank 1 creates a new loan, equal to the amount determined in problem 5a, to Rasko Corporation. Rasko Corporation immediately writes a cheque for the full amount of the loan payable to Jensen Enterprises, which banks at Bank 2. After the cheque clears, show the appropriate changes to Bank 1's balance sheet below:

        Bank 1 (Chartered Bank)

Assets	Liabilities

    c. Based on your balance sheet result in problem 5 b. above, can Bank 1 create any more new loans? Explain. Can the banking system continue to create new loans?

6. Based on the Bank of Canada T-bill purchase described in problem 4 above, and assuming a desired reserve ratio of 5%:
    a. What maximum amount of new deposits can result in the chartered banking system?

    b. Show the appropriate changes to the consolidated balance sheet of the private banking system below, after the maximum deposits calculated in problem 6a. have resulted.

        Consolidated Balance Sheet: Chartered Bank System

Assets	Liabilities

BUSINESS SECTION

Finance: Why Do Interest Rates Differ?

At any point in time, different loans and different investments will exhibit different rates of interest. Some of the factors explaining the difference in rates include:

- *Maturity*   This refers to the time left before the loan or investment matures. In general, longer term loans and investments will command a higher interest rate as the lender sacrifices alternate uses of his/her funds over a longer period of time.

- *Liquidity*   Lenders will often accept lower interest rates on investments, which can be sold at any time before maturity without incurring a significant capital loss. These are called liquid or marketable investments.

- *Risk*   The lender will charge a higher rate of interest to borrowers who represent a greater risk in terms of paying back the interest and principal amount borrowed.

- *Administrative Costs* Assuming the same maturity, liquidity and risk, a smaller loan amount will command a higher rate of interest (vs. a larger loan amount) as the administrative cost per dollar borrowed is greater.

Application Problem 1

Loans	*Rate*
Prime rate (rate charged by banks to best corporate borrowers)	4.25%
Consumer demand loan (unsecured, minimum $5,000, negotiable, prime + 6%)	10.25%
One year fixed residential mortgage (secured by home)	5.0%
Visa Gold Card	18.5%

Investments	
Guaranteed investment certificate (2 year fixed term, minimum $1,000)	2.00%
Cashable guaranteed investment certificate (2year, cashable any time, minimum $1,000)	1.75%
Canada government 90 day treasury bill (matures in 90 days)	2.65%
Canada government bond (matures 2023)	4.88%
Ontario government bond (matures in 2010)	4.30%
Great West Life corporate bond (matures in 2010)	4.60%

The figure above describes the rates of interest for different investments and loans in 2004. Sources:
1. Weekly Financial Statistics, Bank of Canada. Internet November 15, 2004. Available http://www.bankofcanada.ca
2. Daily Quotes, Bonds – National Post FP Investing or The Globe and Mail Report on Business.
3. Rates, RBC Royal Bank. Internet November 15, 2004. Available http://www.rbcroyalbank.com

Explain why the figure above displays different interest rates for each of the following pairs of loans or investments. Make sure that you use at least one of the four factors, listed above, in each explanation.

1. a.   Prime rate versus consumer demand loan.

    b.   Consumer demand loan versus one year fixed residential mortgage.

    c.   Prime rate versus Visa Gold Card rate.

    d.   Guaranteed investment certificate – fixed term versus guaranteed investment certificate – cashable anytime.

    e.   Canada government 90-day treasury bill versus Canada government bond maturing in 2023.

    f.   Ontario government bond (2007) versus Great West Life corporate bond (2007).

ANSWERS TO CHAPTER 13

COMPLETION QUESTIONS

1. money supply
2. goldsmiths; fraction; fractional reserve
3. banks
4. vault cash; deposits at the Bank of Canada
5. minimum; total deposits; actual reserves; desired reserves
6. cannot; rise; rise; excess reserves
7. rise; rise; remain constant
8. 10; cash drains; excess reserves
9. liability; assets
10. 1967; runs
11. low, the same, deposits
12. discourages
13. asymmetry; after; before
14. ignore, more; moral hazard
15. ignore; encouraged to; adverse selection

TRUE-FALSE QUESTIONS

1. T
2. T
3. T
4. F   Deposits held in the Bank of Canada also count as reserves.
5. F   That product equals desired reserves.
6. T

7.   T
8.   T
9.   T
10.   T
11.   F   Excess reserves lower the actual money multiplier.
12.   F   They often withdraw cash.
13.   T
14.   T
15.   F   It equals the reciprocal of the desired reserve ratio.
16.   T
17.   T
18.   T
19.   F   Both result from asymmetric information.
20.   F   For the moral hazard problem, the asymmetric information exists *after* the transaction.

MULTIPLE CHOICE QUESTIONS

1.d;   As this question illustrates, the early goldsmiths were the original bankers who charged a fee for providing safekeeping for valuables deposited with them. Moreover, because only a fraction of gold was requested at any given time, these goldsmiths could lend out depositors gold and charge interest.

2.c;   Under a fractional reserve system, depository institution desire to keep a certain percentage of the total deposits on reserve. This is because, on any one day, only a small fraction of reserves is typically "withdrawn" from a depository institution.

3.b;   When banks maintain a predictable desired reserve ratio, this means the Bank of Canada could have more control over the money supply. As an example, the Bank of Canada knows that if they use one of the monetary tools to increase the chartered banks excess reserves by $E, the chartered bank system will increase new chequing deposits by a maximum of $E x (1/Desired Reserve Ratio)

4.a;   Today in Canada, chartered bank reserves include vault cash and deposits at the Bank of Canada. The deposits at the Bank of Canada are frequently used to settle inter-bank transactions. The vault cash is used to cover daily customer withdrawals.
    TIP: Since we have a fractional reserve system in Canada, the chartered bank reserves will only be a small fraction of the chartered bank deposits which appear on the liabilities side of the chartered bank balance sheets.

5.d;   The desired reserve ratio is to the money multiplier as the marginal propensity to save is to the national income multiplier. In other words, the size of the desired reserve ratio will determine the size of the money multiplier.
    TIP: The larger the desired reserve ratio, the smaller will be the money multiplier.

6.b;   If the desired reserve ratio is raised from 10 percent to 20 percent, the money multiplier will fall from (1/.10) or 10 to (1/.20) or 5.

7.c;   In Canada, excess reserves must be positive before new lending can take place.
    TIP: The maximum amount of new loans, typically in the form of new deposits, that any one bank can create is equal to its excess reserves. The new money created would be equivalent to the new deposits created.

8.d;   Actual reserves minus desired reserves equal excess reserves. It is the existence of excess reserves which serves as the source of new lending and deposit creation.

9.d;   When Mr McKay deposits $1,000 cheque in Bank A, this transaction is recorded as both an asset, reserves, and a liability, deposits, in the bank's balance sheet. To the extent that the addition to reserves results in excess reserves for Bank A, it can increase its lending in the form of new chequing deposits.

10.b;   If Bank A has negative excess reserves, then it will call loans and not re-lend as old loans are paid off. In this way, Bank A can increase its (reserves/deposits) ratio to the point of meeting its desired reserve ratio.

11.b;   If the desired reserve ratio is 10 percent, then the *maximum* money multiplier is (1/.10) = 10. The actual money multiplier will be less due the fact that some borrowers will take out part of their new loans as cash. As well, chartered banks may not lend out all of their excess reserves.

12.a;   The actual change in the money supply equals the actual money multiplier times the change in reserves.

13.b;   Deposit insurance helps to prevent bank runs. Bank runs refer to the simultaneous rush of depositors to convert their demand and notice deposits into currency.

TIP: Currently the Canadian Deposit Insurance Corporation (CDIC) will reimburse each depositor up to a maximum of $60,000 per guaranteed account, in case of a bank failure.

14.b;   The Canadian deposit insurance system since May 1, 1999 charges differential premiums. Member institutions are classified into four premium categories based on a system that scores a member institution according to a number of quantitative and qualitative measures. Premium rates vary with each premium category.

15.c;   Asymmetry of information that occurs before a transaction could lead to an adverse selection problem. In other words, before loans take place, the borrowers typically know more than the lenders about the true returns and risks associated with each proposed investment project. Often, the borrowers who are poorer credit risks than they appear to be, are the ones most eager to negotiate a loan. This eagerness to borrow often results in the lenders adversely selecting these borrowers despite the fact that these debtors have an inferior ability to re-pay the loan.

16.a;   Moral hazard arises as the result of asymmetry of information after a transaction has taken place. In financial markets, lenders face the hazard that borrowers may actually engage in activities that are riskier than initially proposed at the time of negotiating the loan. This is because the borrowers have an incentive to invest in high-risk ,high-return projects as they will be able to keep all the extra profits, should the project succeed.

17.d   Each answer option is an example of adverse selection. In general, adverse selection arises when there is asymmetric information *before* a transaction takes place.

MATCHING

a and 3;   b and 5;   c and 4;   d and 2

PROBLEMS

1.   column 2: $8, 6, 5, 3 1/3, 3;   column 3: $1, 1, 1, 1, 1
     column 4: $8, 6, 5, 3 1/3, 3

2.

Assets	Liabilities
Reserves: 0 Loans & Securities: -$2000	Demand Deposits: -$2000
Reserves: 0 Loans & Securities: +$500	Demand Deposits: +$500
Reserves: +$500 Loans & Securities: -$500	Demand Deposits: 0
Reserves: -$25 Loans & Securities: 0	Demand Deposits: -$25

3.   a.   Desired reserves: $3500, $4000, $3600
     b.   Excess reserves: $1500, $2000, $2400
     c.   New Loans: $1500, $2000, $2400
     d.   New Loans: $7500, $10,000, $12,000

4.   **Bank 1 (Chartered Bank)**

Assets	Liabilities
+$1 000 000 reserves	+$1 000 000 demand deposits owned by Mr. Mondrone

5. a. $950 000
    b.   **Bank 1**

Assets		Liabilities	
Total reserves +$50 000		Demand deposits +$1 000 000	
Loans +$950 000		(Mr. Mondrones deposit)	
Total +$1 000 000		Total +$1 000 000	

c. No, as Bank 1 is just meeting its 5% desired reserve ratio. Since Bank 2 will now have excess reserves the bank system can continue to create new loans.

6. a. Maximum new deposits = $1 000 000 x (1/.05) = $20 000 000, illustrated as follows (including the initial depositor's deposit and the borrowers deposits)
    b.
                   Consolidated Balance Sheet: Chartered Banks

Assets		Liabilities	
		Demand Deposits	
Reserves $+1 000 0000		Depositors $+1 000 000	
Loans $+19 000 000		Borrowers $+19 000 000	
Total $+ 20 000 000		Total $+20 000 000	

BUSINESS SECTION

1. a. The risk and administrative costs is typically greater when lending to consumers than when lending to the bank's preferred large corporate customers.
    b. Mortgage loans are less risky than consumer loans as the former is backed by property (home).
    c. The Visa Gold Card rate is higher due to the increased risk and administrative costs in lending to consumers through a credit card system.
    d. The cashable GIC can be cashed in at any time without penalty and loss of interest. Therefore it is more liquid and therefore offers a lower rate of interest.
    e. The length to maturity explains why the 2023 government bond offers a higher rate of interest.
    f. The Ontario government bond is less risky than the Great West Life corporate bond. The government, with its taxing powers, is more able to pay back interest and principal to investors.

CHAPTER 14

THE BANK OF CANADA AND MONETARY POLICY

PUTTING THIS CHAPTER INTO PERSPECTIVE

Chapter 14 explores monetary policy, which is the changing of the money supply and interest rates by the Bank of Canada in order to attain such national economic goals as price-level stability, economic growth, high employment, and an equilibrium in the international balance of payments. To add to this perspective, you may further recall that an important function of government is to stabilize the economy, and monetary policy and fiscal policy are the two major stabilization tools.

The chapter begins with a brief overview of the history of central banks and the creation and operation of Canada's central bank, the Bank of Canada. The organization of the Bank of Canada, its functions, and its Balance sheet are reviewed.

This chapter then explains how the main tools of monetary policy—open market operations (OMO's), deposit switches, and the target for the overnight rate—can affect the money supply and monetary policy.

When the Bank of Canada buys or sells government securities (i.e. T-bills) on the open market, via open-market operations, the money supply *in the banking system* will change by a multiple of the value of the securities. The reciprocal of the desired reserve ratio defines the *maximum* money multiplier. The Bank of Canada can also influence the money supply through drawdowns and redeposits, and by signalling its policy intentions in its setting of the target for the overnight rate. The money supply at a point in time is a vertical curve whatever the interest rate.

To use money, people must hold money and have a demand for money balances. The determinants of the demand for money balances are the transaction demand, the precautionary demand and the asset demand for money balances. Relative to interest rates, the demand for money is a downward sloping curve. In order to conduct monetary policy, the first step is to have a model, or theory, of how changes in the money supply actually affect such macroeconomic variables as the interest rate, national income, and national output. Chapter 14 first shows how money "fits" in the macroeconomy by analyzing three models: the Keynesian model, the crude quantity theory of money and prices, and the monetarist model. You should try to explain to yourself how, starting from equilibrium, a change in the money supply affects changes in the economy in each model.

According to Keynesians, money fits in as follows: (a) the supply of money and the demand for money determine the interest rate; (b) given profit expectations, the interest rate determines the rate of net investment spending (and helps to determine spending on consumer durables); and (c) given the consumption function and G and X, we add investment spending to determine the total planned expenditures curve, or the location of the AD curve.

How does monetary policy work? According to Keynesians, the transmission mechanism, or chain of causality, is as follows: (a) a change in the money supply, given the demand for money, changes the interest rate; (b) given profit expectations, a change in the interest rate changes autonomous investment spending; (c) a change in autonomous investment spending, other things being constant, shifts the aggregate demand curve and leads to a change in the equilibrium level of real national income; (d) a change in real national income leads to a change in employment, in the short run.

In the crude quantity theory of money and prices, an increase in the money supply leads to increased spending (velocity is constant); because full employment is assumed (predicted), this increased spending leads to an increase in the price level; in turn this induces people to hold more money to fulfil the transactions and the precautionary motives. The price level continues to rise until the community wants to hold the, now larger, money supply. Given the economy's tendency toward full employment anyway, monetary policy is rather unnecessary.

According to the monetarists, households arrange their wealth portfolio, of which money is one component, according to desired liquidity, desired risk, comparable rates of return, and so on. When the money supply is increased via monetary policy, people are induced to exchange bonds for money because the Bank of Canada offers higher prices for bonds; this in turn reduces interest rates and increases the degree of liquidity in the community's portfolio. In turn, people may respond to each of these changes by purchasing durable consumer goods.

Finally, after you have the big picture of how money fits in and how monetary policy works, then you can concentrate on some of the ins and outs of monetary policy and its effectiveness. Canada's open economy must be taken into account when setting monetary policy, as well as the state of the overall economy. Should the Bank of Canada target interest rates or the monetary stock (M1 or M2)? Should the Bank of Canada follow a monetary rule or use its discretion? These are interesting and important questions.

This is a very important chapter, one that is full of information and theory. If you allocate more time to mastering it, you will be in a good position to master macroeconomics. After all, much of what you have learned to this point is also in this chapter—or lurking in the background.

LEARNING OBJECTIVES

After you have studied this chapter you should be able to:

14.1   Describe the structure of the Bank of Canada and its major functions.

14.2   Discuss how the Bank of Canada conducts monetary policy.

14.3   Identify the factors that influence the people's demand for money.

14.4   Explain two views of how monetary policy works.

14.5   Assess the effectiveness of monetary policy.

CHAPTER OUTLINE

LO 14.1 Describe the structure of the Bank of Canada and its major functions.
1.   The Bank of Canada, the *central bank* of Canada, was established in 1934 to counter the severe swings in the business cycle and promote stability in the Canadian banking system.
   a.   The Bank of Canada is governed by a Board of Directors consisting of the Governor of the Bank of Canada, the Senior Deputy Governor, twelve directors from non-banking occupations and the Deputy Minister of Finance, who is a non-voting member of the board.
   b.   The Governor is appointed by the Board of Directors, with Cabinet approval, for a term of seven years. Directors are appointed for three-year terms. Regional representation is a priority when appointing directors.

2.   There are four major functions performed by the Bank of Canada.
   a.   It implements the nation's monetary policy, this is the most important function.
   b.   It issues the nation's currrency.
   c.   It is the "lender of the last resort."
   d.   It acts as the fiscal agent and financial advisor for the federal government.

LO 14.2 Discuss how the Bank of Canada conducts monetary policy.
3.   Monetary policy is the Bank of Canada's changing of the money supply (or the rate at which it grows) in order to achieve national economic goals.

4.   The Bank of Canada has three tools at its disposal when it conducts monetary policy.
   a.   **Open market operations** (OMO) occur when the Bank of Canada buys (sells) bonds in order to increase (decrease) the money supply.
      i.   If the Bank of Canada purchases a $100,000 Canadian government security from a bond dealer, it pays for the security by writing a cheque on itself; when the bond dealer deposits the cheque, this becomes a bank liability *and*

a bank asset/reserve; the bank's excess reserves rise and no other bank's reserves fall; banking system total reserves rise.

    ii.   If the Bank of Canada sells a $100,000 U.S. government security to a bond dealer on the open market, the bond dealer pays for it by cheque, and the Bank of Canada reduces the reserves of the dealer's commercial bank, while no other bank's reserves have increased; the net effect is a reduction in the banking system's total reserves.

  b. The Bank of Canada can switch Government of Canada deposits between the chartered banks and the Bank of Canada as described below.

    i.   The Bank of Canada can employ a **redeposit** by moving Government of Canada deposits from the Bank of Canada to the chartered banks. This will increase the reserves in the chartered banks, which in turn will generate new loans and increase the money supply.

    ii.   The Bank of Canada can employ a **drawdown** by moving Government of Canada deposits from the chartered banks to the Bank of Canada. This will decrease the reserves in the chartered banks, which in turn will contract loans and decrease the money supply.

  c. The Bank of Canada can signal changes in monetary policy by changes in the target for the overnight rate.

LO 14.3 Identify the factors that influence the people's demand for money.

5. People want to hold money (hence we analyse the demand for money) in order to make foreseen transactions (the **transactions demand** for money), to make unforeseen expenditures and meet emergencies (**precautionary demand** for money), and to have a store of value (**asset demand** for money).

  a. The opportunity cost of holding money is foregone interest earnings.

  b. The demand curve for money is negatively sloped because there is a trade-off between the benefits to holding money and the costs of holding money; in short, as the (opportunity) cost of holding money rises at higher interest rates, people want to hold less money.

LO 14.4 Explain two views of how monetary policy works.

6. When the money supply is increased there is a direct and an indirect effect on the economy.

  a. Money supply increases (decreases) directly lead people to spend more (less) because they now have an excess (a shortage) of money balances.

  b. Not all of the excess balances will be spent on goods and services; some excess balances will be used to purchase interest-earning assets, which will cause the interest rate to fall; thus, indirectly, spending will increase on business investment and on consumer durables.

  c. In the real world, the money supply usually rises regularly; hence, policy deals with changes in the rate of growth of the money supply.

7. In the long run the higher price level that results from a rightward shift in the AD curve (due to an increase in the money supply) will generate an upward shift in the SRAS curve; ultimately the economy will operate on the LRAS curve, at a higher price level.

8. An abundance of empirical evidence, and economic theory, suggests that if the supply of money is consistently increased relative to the demand for money, the relative price of money will fall continuously—inflation will ensue.

9. Monetarism is the modern quantity theory of money.
    a. The tenets of monetarism are: significant money supply changes lead to significant price level changes in the same direction; money supply changes affect national output and employment only in the short run, but affect only the price level in the long run; fiscal policy is ineffective; the monetary time lags are long and variable, which makes monetary policy difficult to conduct; policymakers should follow a **monetary rule** instead of using their own discretion.
    b. In this model, money supply changes upset the community's equilibrium regarding its wealth portfolio; people substitute among bonds, money, equities, and durable goods as the Bank of Canada changes the money supply.

10. An expansionary monetary policy, if it reduces interest rates, will cause net exports to rise—an effect that is the opposite of an expansionary fiscal policy (which may cause interest rates to rise).

11. Some policymakers wish to conduct monetary policy by selecting and meeting interest rate targets, while others wish to attain money stock growth targets.
    a. The Bank of Canada cannot target interest rates and the money supply at the same time.
    b. In general, if the demand for money is relatively stable, the Bank of Canada should target the money supply; if the demand for money is less stable than private and public expenditures, then the Bank of Canada should target interest rates.

LO 14.5 Assess the effectiveness of monetary policy.
12. Two advantages of monetary policy are its speed and flexibility and its relative isolation from political pressures.

KEY TERMS AND CONCEPTS

Open market operations

Target for the overnight rate

Asset demand

Monetary rule

Crude quantity theory of
  money and prices

Drawdown

Bank Rate

Precautionary demand

Monetarists

Canadian Payments
  Association (CPA)

Redeposit

Transactions demand

Equation of exchange

Keynesian theory

Income velocity of
  money

COMPLETION QUESTIONS
Fill in the blank or circle the correct term.

(LO 14.1)

1.   The Canadian central bank is the _____; it was established in 1934 to counter the financial (instability, stability) that occurred periodically.

2.   The Bank of Canada has four major functions: it _____, _____, _____, and _____; the Bank of Canada's most important function is _____.

(LO 14.2)

3.   The three main tools the Bank of Canada employs to conduct monetary policy are _____, _____, and _____.

4.   When the Bank of Canada buys bonds on the open market the price of bonds tends to (fall, rise) and the interest rate (falls, rises); also bank reserves (fall, rise) which leads to a(n) (decrease, increase) in bank lending; ultimately the money supply (falls, rises).

5.   When the interest rate rises, bond prices (rise, fall); when bond prices rise, the interest rate _____; the opportunity cost of holding money is foregone _____.

6.   If the Bank of Canada transfers Government of Canada deposits from the chartered banks to the Bank of Canada, this will (increase, decrease) chartered bank reserves and will result in a(n) (decrease, increase) in bank loans. The money supply will (fall, rise) and interest rates will probably (fall, rise) in the short run. This policy is called (drawdowns, redeposits).

7.   The important role of the target for the overnight rate is to _____ _____.

(LO 14.3)

8.   People hold money for three motives: _____,
     _____ and _____.

9.   The transactions demand for money varies (directly, inversely) with nominal
     national income; the asset demand for money varies (directly, inversely) with the
     interest rate.

(LO 14.4)

10. The Bank of Canada (can, cannot) control the supply of money, but it (can,
     cannot) control the demand for money.

11. In the Keynesian model, a fall in the interest rate causes autonomous net
     investment to (rise, fall), which in turn causes the aggregate demand curve to shift
     (rightward, leftward); then _____ and employment will rise.

12. If the current interest rate is below the equilibrium rate, an excess
     _____ exists and the community will attempt to (buy, sell) bonds,
     thereby forcing the price of bonds _____ and the interest rate _____.

13. The _____ theory of money and price predicts that changes in the price
     level are determined by changes in the quantity of money in circulation.

14. If the supply of money rises relative to its demand, the price level will (rise, fall)
     and the value of a unit of money will (rise, fall).

15. The number of times, on average, that each monetary unit is spent on final goods
     and services is called the _____.

16. In the crude quantity theory of money model, in the long run national output (will,
     will not) be at full employment, and velocity (is, is not) constant; hence if the
     money supply doubles, the price level will _____.

17. Monetarists maintain that full employment is normal in the long run. They believe
     the following: that the income velocity of money (is, is not) stable; that changes
     in the money supply lead to changes in the price level in the (same, opposite)
     direction; that money supply changes affect _____ and
     _____ in the short run; but that in the long run only the
     _____ is affected by money supply changes.

18. Monetarist critics of the Bank of Canada (do, do not) want the Bank of Canada to
     pursue discretionary monetary policy; they want the Bank of Canada to follow a
     _____.

19. An expansionary monetary policy will tend to cause the interest rate to fall, which
     may lead to a(n) (decrease, increase) in net exports; an expansionary fiscal policy
     financed by deficits may cause the interest rate to (fall, rise), which may lead to a
     (decrease, increase) in net exports.

(LO 14.5)

20.   Two advantages of monetary policy are its _____, and its _____.

TRUE-FALSE QUESTIONS

Circle the T if the statement is true, the F if it is false. Explain to yourself why a statement is false.

(LO 14.1)

T F   1. The Bank of Canada's most important function is to supply the economy with fiduciary currency.

T F   2. The Bank of Canada is prohibited from being a lender of last resort.

(LO 14.2)

T F   3. The Bank of Canada requires chartered banks to hold a certain percentage of their deposits on reserve

T F   4. If the Bank of Canada buys bonds on the open market, bank reserves will rise, and so will bank lending.

T F   5. If the Bank of Canada wants to increase the money supply, it will sell government securities, and employ drawdowns.

T F   6. Treasury Bills of Canada are classed as an asset in the Bank of Canada's consolidated balance sheet.

T F   7. An important objective of monetary policy is to assist the economy in maintaining high employment without undue inflation.

(LO 14.3)

T F   8. The asset-demand-for-money motive stresses money's role as a medium of exchange.

T F   9. The asset-demand-for-money motive stresses money's role as a liquid store of value.

T F   10. The opportunity cost of holding money is loss of liquidity.

T F   11. When interest rates rise, the price of existing bonds falls.

(LO 14.4)

T F   12. In the Keynesian model, the supply of, and the demand for money, directly determine net investment spending

T F   13. The crude quantity theory of money maintains that if the money supply is doubled, the price level is halved.

T F 14. The Bank of Canada cannot target both the interest rate and the money supply.

T F 15. Monetarists believe that discretionary monetary policy is effective, but that fiscal policy is not.

T F 16. An expansionary monetary policy tends to increase a nation's net exports, while an expansionary fiscal policy tends to decrease its net exports.

T F 17. Keynesians prefer a monetary rule to discretionary fiscal policy because they believe that the demand for money is unstable.

MULTIPLE CHOICE QUESTIONS
Circle the letter that corresponds to the best answer.

(LO 14.1)
1. Which of the following is the most important function of the Bank of Canada?
    a. It implements monetary policy.
    b. It is the lender of the last resort.
    c. It supplies the economy with fiduciary currency.
    d. It is the fiscal agent for the federal government.

2. Which of the following is classified as a liability in the Bank of Canada's balance sheet?
    a. Treasury Bills of Canada.
    b. Government of Canada securities.
    c. Foreign currency.
    d. Chartered bank deposits

(LO 14.2)
3. If the Bank of Canada purchases $1 million worth of T-bills on the open market, and the desired reserve ratio is 10 percent, then
    a. the money supply will increase by $10 million, at a minimum.
    b. the money supply will decrease by $10 million.
    c. the money supply will increase by $10 million, at a maximum.
    d. the money supply will increase by $5 million, at a maximum.

4. Which of the following will increase total reserves in the banking system?
    a. Mr. Patullo deposits a cheque in Bank A, drawn on Bank B.
    b. The Bank of Canada sells a security to Mrs. Damson.
    c. Mr. Farano sells a security to the Bank of Canada and deposits the cheque he receives in Bank C.
    d. Mr. Capano withdraws $100 from his chequing account

5. If the desired reserve ratio is 10 percent and the Bank of Canada sells a $10 000 security on the open market, the money supply will
   a. rise by $10 000 at a minimum.
   b. rise by $100 000 at a maximum
   c. fall by $100 000 at a maximum.
   d. fall by $10 000

(LO 14.3)
6. Which of the following stresses money's role as a medium of exchange?
   a. transactions demand
   b. precautionary demand
   c. asset demand
   d. miserly demand

7. Which of the following stresses money's role as a liquid store of value?
   a. transactions demand
   b. precautionary demand
   c. asset demand
   d. miserly demand

8. The opportunity cost of holding money is
   a. foregone liquidity.
   b. foregone interest income.
   c. convenience.
   d. security.

9. The demand for money curve
   a. is upward sloping.
   b. is flat.
   c. is downward sloping.
   d. denies a link between the money supply and the price level.

10. The demand for money curve
   a. reflects a preference for money over bonds.
   b. shows a negative relationship between the quantity demanded for money and the interest rate.
   c. shows that people want to substitute money for bonds at low interest rates.
   d. All of the above.

11. When interest rates rise,
   a. bond prices rise.
   b. bond holders experience capital losses.
   c. bond prices are unaffected.
   d. bond holders experience capital gains.

12. An excess quantity supplied of money
    a. exists at all interest rates above equilibrium.
    b. causes interest rates to rise.
    c. induces people to want to sell bonds.
    d. All of the above

13. The intersection of the supply of and the demand for money determines the
    a. aggregate demand curve.
    b. planned expenditures curve.
    c. price level.
    d. interest rate.

(LO 14.4)
14. According to Keynesians, an increase in the money supply will
    a. reduce the interest rate.
    b. reduce net investment spending.
    c. reduce total planned expenditures.
    d. All of the above

15. An expansionary monetary policy is beneficial if
    a. the unemployment rate is relatively high.
    b. a recession exists.
    c. the price level is falling.
    d. All of the above

16. Which of the following clearly is NOT a result of an expansionary monetary policy?
    a. higher price level
    b. lower inflation rate
    c. increase in nominal national income
    d. increased total expenditures

17. A contractionary monetary policy
    a. shifts the AD curve rightward.
    b. shifts the AD curve leftward.
    c. shifts the LRAS curve, but not the AD curve.
    d. None of the above

18. In the equation $M_S V = PQ$, according to the crude quantity theory,
    a. M_S is independent of the price level.
    b. V is the number of times each dollar is spent, on average, per year.
    c. Q is the real price level.
    d. P rises as V falls, other things constant.

19. In the crude quantity theory, as the money supply rises (other things constant),
    a. the quantity demanded for money rises.
    b. velocity rises.
    c. velocity falls.
    d. the price level rises proportionately.

20. The equation of exchange states that
    a. expenditures equal receipts.
    b. spending equals saving.
    c. saving equals investment.
    d. aggregate demand exceeds aggregate supply.

21. If the velocity of money is less stable than private expenditures, then the Bank of Canada
    a. should target the interest rate.
    b. should pursue fiscal policy.
    c. should target a monetary aggregate.
    d. cannot target the interest rate.

22. According to the crude quantity theory (assuming V and Q are constant), if the money supply is tripled, the price level will
    a. rise.
    b. fall.
    c. triple.
    d. more than triple,

23. Traditional Keynesians maintain that
    a. investment is a function of the interest rate.
    b. monetary policy works through changes in the interest rate.
    c. the Bank of Canada should target interest rates, not the money supply.
    d. All of the above

24. Which of the following is NOT a tenet of monetarism?
    a. Monetary policy is destabilizing.
    b. The Bank of Canada should follow a monetary rule, and not use its discretion.
    c. Changes in the money supply affect only the price level, in the long run.
    d. Keynesian multipliers are sufficiently reliable to conduct stabilization policies.

25. Globalized money capital markets
    a. affect fiscal policy results but not monetary policy results.
    b. make monetary policy more difficult.
    c. facilitate monetary policy.
    d. do not affect the conduct of monetary policy.

MATCHING

Choose the item in Column (2) that best matches an item in Column (1).

(1)	(2)

<table>
<tr><td>a.</td><td>equation of exchange</td><td>1.</td><td>non-discretionary monetary policy</td></tr>
<tr><td>b.</td><td>monetarism</td><td>2.</td><td>preference for liquidity</td></tr>
<tr><td>c.</td><td>Keynesian view</td><td>3.</td><td>monetary aggregate</td></tr>
<tr><td>d.</td><td>transactions motive</td><td>4.</td><td>crude quantity theory of money</td></tr>
<tr><td>e.</td><td>monetary target</td><td>5.</td><td>transmission mechanism</td></tr>
<tr><td>f.</td><td>monetary rule</td><td>6.</td><td>inflation as a monetary phenomenon</td></tr>
<tr><td>g.</td><td>asset motive</td><td>7.</td><td>money as a medium of exchange</td></tr>
<tr><td></td><td></td><td>8.</td><td>net export effect</td></tr>
<tr><td></td><td></td><td>9.</td><td>moral suasion</td></tr>
</table>

WORKING WITH GRAPHS

(LO 14.2)

1. On the next page in part (a) is the investment demand function for the economy. Part (b) represents the supply and demand functions for money. The interest rate in the economy is currently 12 percent. The money supply is $200 billion. Part (c) is the Keynesian model of the economy, which is currently at an equilibrium level of output and income of $800 billion. Full employment output and income is $1000 billion. Further assume that the desired reserve ratio is 20 percent and there are no excess reserves in the banking system. Also assume that the economy's MPC is 0.6. Autonomous investment is currently $180 billion. Fill in the paragraph that follows the graphs.

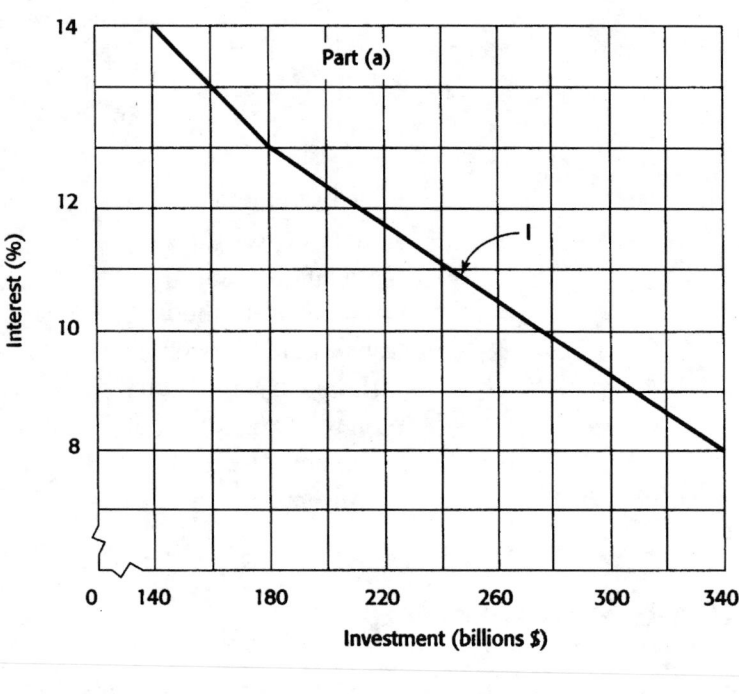

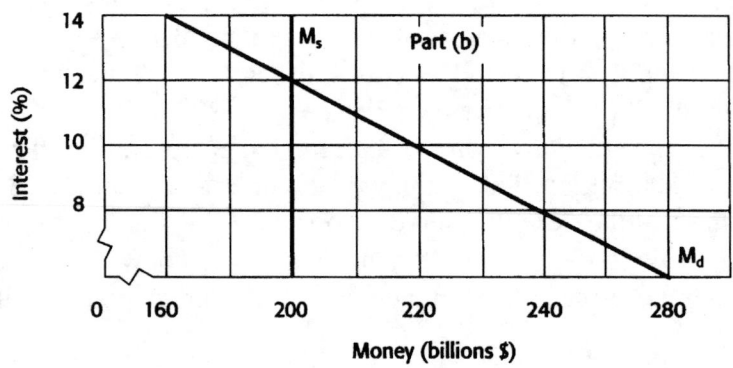

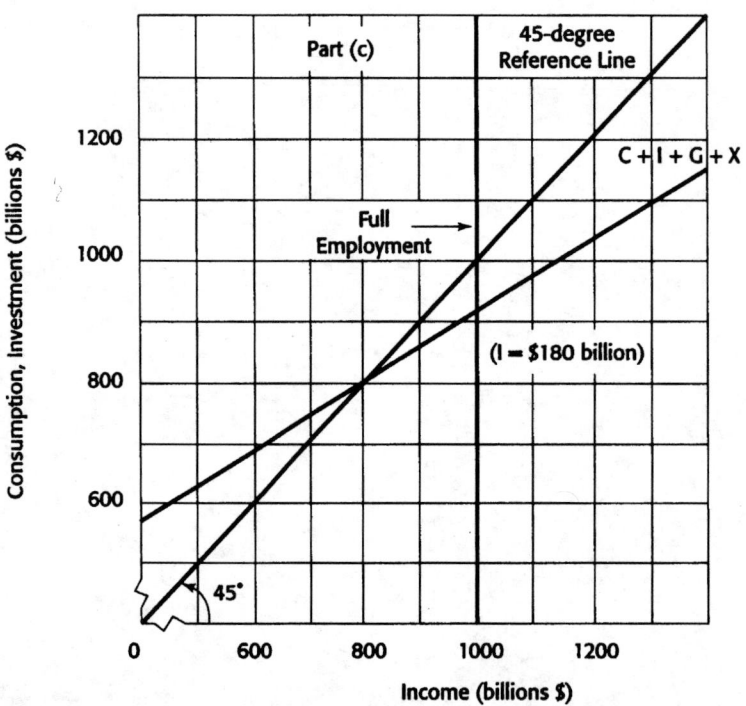

If the goal of the monetary authorities is to reach full employment, the Bank of Canada would want to (increase, decrease) the money supply by $_____, which would (raise, lower) interest rates to _____ percent. This would (increase, decrease) the level of autonomous investment by $ _____ to $_____. This (increase, decrease) in investment would be subject to a multiplier effect of _____ and therefore increase equilibrium level of income and output by $_____ to $_____. Assuming the Bank of Canada chose buying securities on the open market to (increase, decrease) the money supply, how many dollars of securities must the Bank of Canada purchase from the nonbank public to (increase, decrease) the money supply that would be consistent with full-employment equilibrium? $_____.

2.   Analyze the graphs below, then answer the questions that follow.

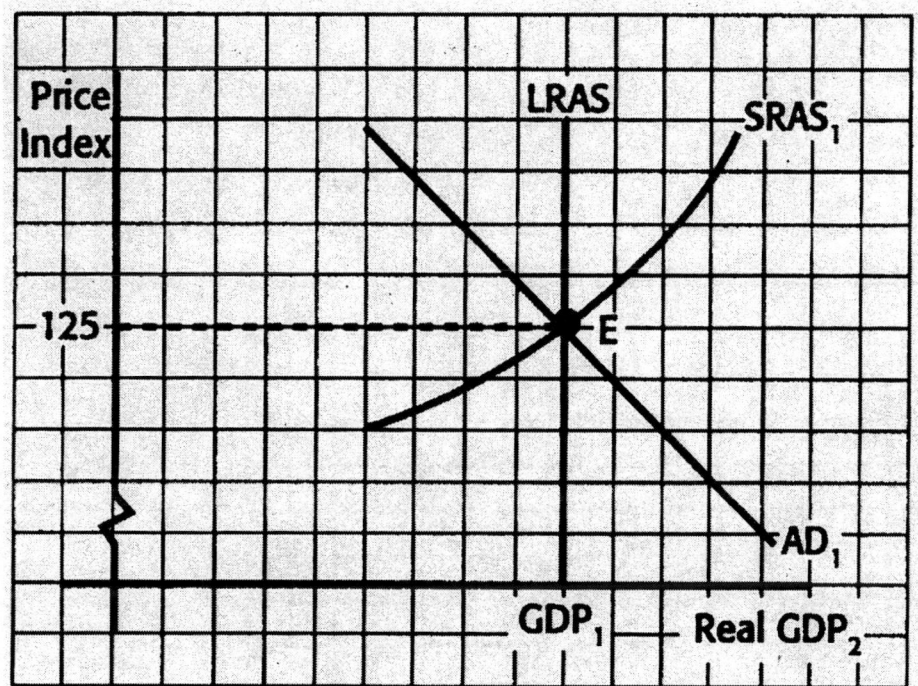

Assume that the economy is operating at point **E**, and that the Bank of Canada wants to reduce the price level.

a.   Should it reduce or increase the money supply?

b.   Should it buy or sell bonds on the open market?

c.   Should it employ drawdowns or redeposits?

d.   If the Bank of Canada follows your advice what will happen to the AD curve? (Draw it on your book or on a piece of paper).

e. What will happen to real GDP and the price level? Label the new short run equilibrium point as **A**.

f. After resource supplies adjust to the new price level, what happens to the SRAS curve? (Draw it.)

g. Indicate the new position in which both long run and short run equilibrium exist by labelling it **B**.

h. Compare the price level and real GDP level at points **E** and **B**.

3. Analyze the graph below and answer the questions that follow.

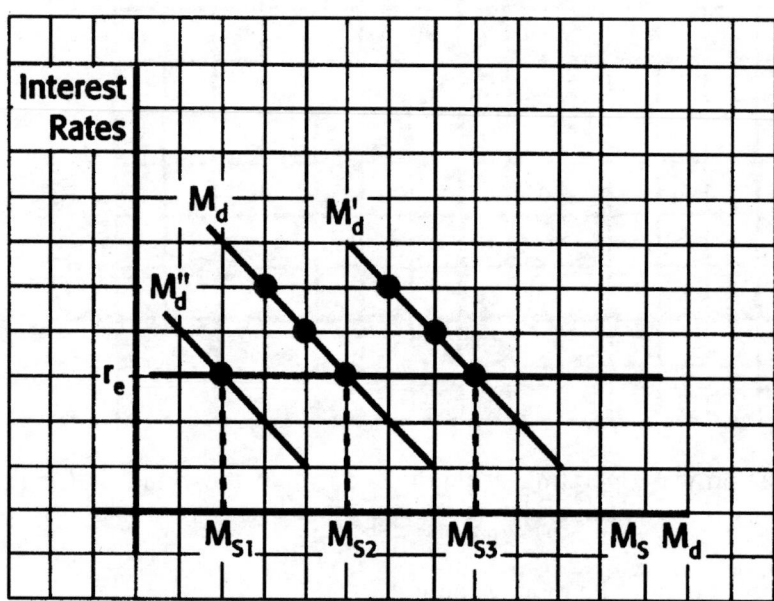

a. If the Bank of Canada targets the interest rate at r_e, and if the demand for money shifts leftward (falls) from M_d to M''_d, what happens to the money supply? Is this a stabilizing change in the money supply? Why?

b. If the Bank of Canada targets the interest rate at r_e, and if the demand for money shifts rightward (increases) from M_d to M'_d, what happens to the money supply? Is this a stabilizing money supply change? Why?

PROBLEMS

(LO 14.2) and **(LO 14.4)**

1. Suppose the economic advisors to the Prime Minister feel it is necessary to raise our national income. These advisors and the Prime Minister are traditional Keynesians. The governor of the Bank of Canada is summoned to the Cabinet and told to stimulate the economy. Although the chairman does not have to obey, he decides to accept the directive.

   Below you will find a series of interrelated questions concerning the execution of this directive. Be careful! An early mistake can affect your remaining answers. Circle the correct answer for each question.

   1. The Bank of Canada will do which of the following?
      a. sell securities
      b. employ drawdowns
      c. buy securities
      d. encourage the banks to raise the desired reserve ratio

   2. This action will
      a. raise the desired reserve ratio.
      b. raise the excess reserves of chartered banks.
      c. cause banks to increase their participation in the IMF.
      d. lower the amount of reserves required that are on deposit with the Bank of Canada.

   3. We know banks are profit maximizers. They will therefore
      a. lend out excess reserves, which create more demand deposits.
      b. lend out excess reserves, which decrease demand deposits.
      c. call in outstanding loans.
      d. a and b

   4. After the results of question 3,
      a. the money supply will decrease.
      b. the money supply will increase.
      c. the money supply will increase initially but then will return to its previous level.
      d. there will be no effect on the money supply.

5. If you have answered question 4 correctly, what will happen next?
   a. The interest rate will decrease, and investment will decrease.
   b. The interest rate will go up, with no effect on investment.
   c. The interest rate will remain unaffected.
   d. The interest rate will decrease, and investment will increase.

6. With the correct answer to question 5, we know that
   a. national income will increase by the amount of investment.
   b. national income will decrease by the amount of investment.
   c. national income will change by more than the amount by which investment will change.
   d. national income will change by less than the amount by which investment will change.

7. The change in national income will be
   a. change in I times $1 / (1 - MPS)$.
   b. change in I times $1 / (1 - MPC)$.
   c. change in I times $1 / (1 - MPC - MPS)$.
   d. change in I times change in the interest rate.

(LO 14.4)

2. Given the equation of exchange $MV = PQ$ and $M = \$50$, $V = 4$, and $Q = \$100$ then
   a. What does P equal?

   b. If M doubles, to $100, what happens to P?

   c. If M is reduced to $25, what happens to P?

3. Given the equation of exchange $MV = PQ$ and $M = \$100$, $V = 5$, and PQ = nominal national income then
   a. What is the value of nominal national income?

   b. If price level equals 1, what is the value of real national income?

   c. If the money supply triples, other things constant, what is the value of nominal national income? of real national income?

Chapter 14   The Bank of Canada and Monetary Policy   259

4.   The Bank of Canada purchases $10 million worth of T-bills directly from Prudence Bank, a chartered bank. Show the immediate balance sheet effects of this transaction on the Bank of Canada and Prudence Bank. Display the immediate effects (changes) in terms of dollar amounts and pluses and/or minuses, on each of the balance sheets below. At this point the chartered banks have not yet begun the money multiplier process. Not all balance sheet items shown below will be changed.

The Bank of Canada

Assets		Liabilities	
Government Securities	_____	Chartered Bank Deposits	_____
		Government of Canada Deposits	_____
		Notes in Circulation	_____

Prudence Bank

Assets		Liabilities	
Reserves	_____	Deposits (Demand)	_____
Loans	_____	Capital Stock	_____
Securities	_____		

5.   Refer to the previous question, and assume that the desired reserve ratio equals 4%. The chartered bank system can change the money supply by what maximum amount and in what direction?

6.   Assume that the chartered bank system changes the money supply by the maximum amount (calculated in the previous question). Show the appropriate balance sheet changes in terms of dollar amounts and pluses and/or minuses on the chartered banks consolidated balance sheet below. Note that you may not have to change all the balance sheet items below.

Chartered Banks System - Consolidated Balance Sheet

Assets		Liabilities	
Reserves	_____	Deposits (Demand)	_____
Loans	_____	Capital Stock	_____
Securities	_____		

(LO 14.4)

7.   Based on the Keynesian transmission mechanism, explain how the Bank of Canada bond purchase described in question 4 above will affect the direction of interest rates, investment expenditures, the money supply, and equilibrium GDP. Is this situation best described as contractionary or expansionary monetary policy?

BUSINESS SECTION

Finance: Monetary Policy and Asset Allocation Decisions

The asset allocation refers to the specific mix of different financial assets that an investor owns at any one time. Due to the fact that the economy experiences fluctuations in real GDP and inflation, an investor may enhance his or her rate of return by periodically changing the asset allocation between investments such as short and long term bonds, preferred dividends, and common stocks.

It is instructive at this point to outline and review a few relevant points.

- Fixed income investments include financial assets such as bonds and preferred stocks. Bonds promise to pay a fixed periodic interest payment to the investor. As well, preferred stocks undertake to pay investors a specified dividend each year (subject to discretion of the firm's board of directors).

- Bond prices tend to vary inversely with interest rates in the economy. As an example, consider a $1000 bond purchased in 1998, which promises an annual interest payment (coupon rate) of 5% per year. If interest rates subsequently rise to 8%, the value or price of the bond promising a coupon rate of 5% will decrease. If the investor has to sell this bond, he/she will have to sell the bond at a price below $1000, therefore experiencing a capital loss.

- In response to interest rate fluctuations, short-term bond prices fluctuate less than long-term bond prices.

Application Problem 1

(LO 14.2) and (LO 14.4)

Suppose, after experiencing a recession, economists believe that the Canadian economy is in the late stages of the trough phase of the current business cycle. The Bank of Canada has just announced that it will be conducting expansionary monetary policy.

1.   a.   According to the theory in Chapter 14, explain in what direction Canadian interest rates are likely to move. Also explain what is likely to happen to real GDP.

         b.   In the early stages of economic expansion, do you think that Canadian investors are more likely to increase or decrease their holdings of short-term bonds vs. long-term bonds, in determining their overall financial asset mix? Explain.

         c.   In the early stages of economic expansion, do you think that Canadian investors are more likely to increase or decrease their holdings of preferred stocks relative to common stocks? Explain.

d. Do you think that Canadian investors are more likely to increase or decrease their holdings of cyclical common stocks vs. defensive common stocks? Explain.

e. Will the expansionary monetary policy likely have any affect on export lead stocks? Explain.

f. In the early stages of the expansion phase, which types of cyclical stocks will most likely exhibit the greatest increase in prices – consumer durable products vs. stocks of firms engaged in industrial and commercial construction? Explain.

g. As the economy actually starts to pick up steam and inflation starts to increase, which direction will interest rates likely move? Provide two reasons for your answer. In the mid stage of economic expansion, do you think that Canadian investors are more likely increase or decrease their holdings of long term bonds vs. common stocks, in determining their overall financial asset mix. Explain.

ANSWERS TO CHAPTER 14

COMPLETION QUESTIONS
1   Bank of Canada; instability
2.   issues currency, acts as the government's fiscal agent, lender of last resort; implements monetary policy, monetary policy
3.   open-market operations, deposit switches, setting the target for the overnight rate
4.   rise; falls; rise; increase; rises
5.   fall; falls; interest earnings
6.   decrease; decrease; fall; rise, drawdowns
7.   communicate changes in monetary poicy
8.   transactions; precautionary; asset
9.   directly; inversely
10.   can; cannot
11.   rise; rightward; real national income
12.   quantity demanded for money; sell; downward; upward
13.   crude quantity
14.   rise; fall
15.   income velocity of money
16.   will; is; double
17.   is; same; national output; employment; price level
18.   do not; monetary rule

19.   increase; rise; decrease
20.   speed and flexibility, relative isolation from political pressures

TRUE-FALSE QUESTIONS

1.   F   Its most important function is to implement monetary policy.
2.   F   That is a function of the Bank of Canada.
3.   F   The Bank Act of 1992 eliminated this requirement.
4.   T
5.   F   No, the Bank of Canada would buy securities and employ redeposits.
6.   T
7.   T
8.   F   It stresses money's role as a store of value.
9.   T
10.   F   The opportunity cost is foregone interest earnings.
11.   T
12.   F   They determine the interest rate; hence investment is indirectly determined.
13.   F   The price level will also double.
14.   T
15.   F   They believe that neither is effective.
16.   T
17.   F   Monetarists prefer a monetary rule; Keynesians prefer an activist fiscal policy.

MULTIPLE CHOICE QUESTIONS

1.a;   The most important function of the Bank of Canada is implementing monetary policy. In this function, the Bank of Canada is charged with keeping inflation under control in order to maintain the stability of the financial system and promote economic growth.

2.d;   Chartered bank deposits are classed as a liability in the Bank of Canada balance sheet. One way of understanding this is to think of the Bank of Canada as owing the chartered banks currency, on demand.

3. c;   If the Bank of Canada purchases $1 million worth of T-bills on the open market, and the desired reserve ratio is 10 percent, the maximum increase in the money supply will be ($1 million) x (1/.10) = $10 million

4. c;   If Mr. Farano sells a security to the Bank of Canada and deposits the cheque he receives in his chartered bank C, this will create new reserves in the banking system.

5. c;   If the desired reserve ratio is 10 percent and the Bank of Canada sells a $10 000 security on the open market, the money supply will fall by a maximum of ($10 000) x (1/.10) = $100 000. This means that both loans and deposits will decrease by $100 000.
    TIP: When the Bank of Canada sell securities to the public, those who purchase the bonds will be writing cheques drawn on their chartered bank accounts. This will reduce the reserves in the chartered banking system and reduce the overall money supply by a multiplied amount.

6. a;   The transactions demand for money stresses money's role as a medium of exchange. Consistent with the transactions demand for money, as national income rises, the community will want to hold more money as a medium of exchange.

7. c;   The asset demand for money stresses money's role as a store of value due to its liquidity and lack of risk. According to the asset demand for money, there is an inverse relation between the interest rate and the money balances that people want to hold.
    TIP: As the interest rate on financial assets like bonds rises, the opportunity cost of holding money balances increases, leading the community to demand less money.

8.b;   The opportunity cost of holding money is the foregone interest income that can be earned on other financial assets such as bonds.

9. c;   The demand for money curve, which describes the relation between the interest rate and the demand to hold money, is downward sloping. In other words, as the interest rate increases, the demand to hold money decreases.

10. d;   The demand for money curve suggests that the community's preference to hold money balances, as opposed to interest bearing financial assets like bonds, will increase when the

interest rate level decreases. This negative relationship, is due to the fact that the opportunity cost of holding money balances will decrease when the interest rate decreases.

11. b;   When interest rates rise, those investors who hold bonds that offer lower rates of interest will see their bond prices fall resulting in potential capital losses.

12. a;   An excess quantity supplied of money will result in a decrease in the price of money (the interest rate). This situation would occur at any rate of interest above the equilibrium rate.

13. d;   The intersection of the supply of and demand for money determines the interest rate which is the price of holding money.

14. a;   According to the Keynesians, an increase in the money supply will reduce the interest rate, increase net investment, and therefore increase total planned expenditures.

15. d;   If the economy is in a recession situation with a high degree of under-utilised resources (i.e., high unemployment rate) expansionary monetary policy can generate increases in real GDP that would be beneficial to society.
TIP: Both the direct and indirect effects of expansionary monetary policy will result in an increase in aggregate demand.

16. b;   Since an expansionary monetary policy will increase planned spending and aggregate demand, a higher, not lower, inflation rate is likely to result.

17. b;   A contractionary monetary policy will decrease aggregate demand. Graphically, this means that the aggregate demand curve will shift leftward.

18. b;   The velocity of money, V, is the number of times per year each dollar is spent, on average. The crude quantity of money assumes that V is stable resulting in a direct proportionate relation between the money supply and the price level.

19. d;   In the crude quantity theory, as the money supply rises, the price level will rise proportionately.
TIP: According to the crude quantity theory of money $M_SV = PQ$ where V and Q are assumed to be constant.

20. a;   The equation of exchange refers to the equation: $M_SV = PQ$. In other words, the total amount of money spent on final output is equal to the total amount of money received for the final output.

21. a;   If the velocity of money is unstable, then there will not be a direct, predictable relation between the money supply and nominal GDP. In this case the Bank of Canada should target the interest rate and not the money supply.

22. c;   According to the crude quantity theory of money (where V and Q are assumed constant) there is a direct proportionate relation between the money supply and the price level. In other words, if the money supply were to triple, this would cause the price level to triple.

23. d;   Traditional Keynesians believe that monetary policy works in an indirect fashion, in affecting the national income level. Specifically, a change in the money supply will change the interest rate level, which will change planned investment spending, which will then result in a change in nominal GDP.
TIP: The Keynesian transmission mechanism refers to the indirect process whereby a change in the money supply must first affect the interest rate level, in order to then affect planned investment expenditures, in order to finally affect the level of national income.

24. d;   Because monetarists believe that Keynesian multipliers involve time lags and unpredictable effects on national income, they are not in favour of conducting fine tuning stabilization policies.
TIP: Monetarists urge policy makers to follow a simple monetary rule where the money supply should be increased smoothly at a rate consistent with the long run average growth rate in real national income.

25. b   Globalized money capital markets make domestic monetary policy control more difficult. In the world dollar market, an increasing number of dollars can be obtained from private institutions around the world (and not just from the actions of the domestic central bank).

MATCHING

a and 4;   b and 6;   c and 5;   d and 7;   e and 3;   f and 1;   g and 2

WORKING WITH GRAPHS

1.   increase, $40 billion, lower, 10; increase, $80 billion; $260 billion; increase; 2 1/2; $200 billion, $1000 billion; increase, increase; $8 billion in securities from the nonbank public. Note: This problem actually requires you to work backward in order to obtain the necessary increase in the money supply. That is, you must first find how much of an increase in autonomous investment is required to increase the equilibrium level of income by $200 billion (change in I x multiplier = change in income). Substitute 2 1/2 for the multiplier and $200 billion for the change in investment (I). Now go to panel (a) and find how much the interest rate must fall to increase investment by $80 billion. Then find how much the money supply must increase to lower the interest rate to 10 percent. The answer is obviously $40 billion. If the Bank of Canada purchased $8 billion of securities from, for example, businesses and security dealers, they would deposit this in their checking accounts, which would increase demand deposits in the banking system by $8 billion. Finally, the money multiplier of 5 would increase the money supply by the necessary $40 billion.

2.   a. reduce; b. sell; c. drawdowns; d. It will shift leftward, to AD_2 on the graph below; e. both fall; f. It shifts downward, to $SRAS_2$. g. See the graph below. h. Real GDP is the same; the price level is lower.

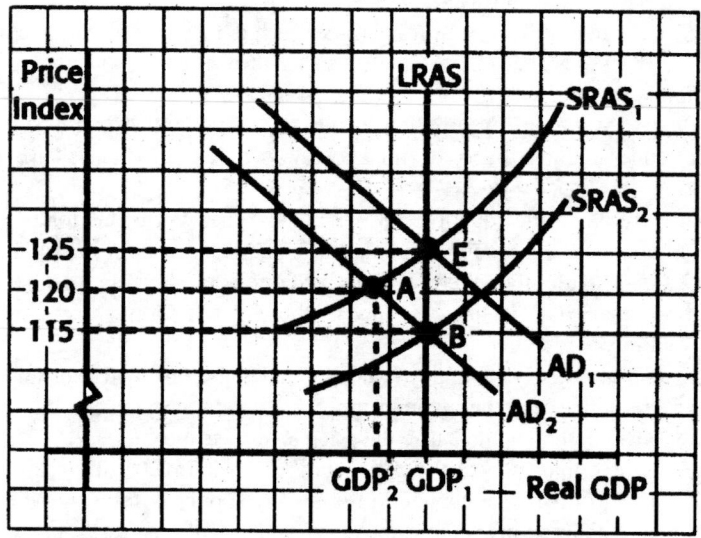

3.   a.   Decreases to M_{s1}. Yes, because if the demand for money falls and the supply of money falls, then the interest rate will be unaffected and private spending won't change due to a change in the money supply.

      b.   Increases to M_s3. Yes, because if the demand for money rises and the supply of money rises, then the interest rate will be unaffected; hence private spending won't change due to an unstable demand for money.

PROBLEMS

1.   1.c   2.b   3.a   4.b   5.d   6.c   7.b
2.   a. P = 2   b. it doubles; P = 4   c .it is halved, P = 1
3.   a. $500   b. $500   c. $1500; $500
4.   Bank of Canada: Government Securities +10, Chartered Bank Deposits +10
      Prudence Bank: Reserves +10, Securities -10
5.   Money supply will increase by 250
6.   Chartered Banks: Loans +250   Deposits (Demand) +250
7.   Interest rates decrease, investment increases, money supply increases, GDP increases. Expansionary policy.

BUSINESS SECTION

1. a. Expansionary policy will reduce interest rates and increase real GDP.

   b. Since the interest rates on short-term bonds will be reduced before existing long-term bonds, investors are likely to sell off short-term bonds. Since interest rates are still likely to fall, investors can still achieve capital gains by holding on to long-term bonds.

   c. Investors are more likely to prefer common stocks. The prices of common stocks vary more in response to changes in real GDP compared to preferred stock prices. Since real GDP is projected to increase the potential for capital gain on common stocks is higher than for preferred stocks.

   d. Investors are likely to prefer cyclical stocks as they tend to increase in price more than the defensive stocks.

   e. Yes. Export led stocks are likely to increase in price. As interest rates fall, the Canadian exchange rate should depreciate. In turn, demand for exports will increase.

   f. Consumer durables. Since there still exists significant excess capacity in the economy, business construction firms will not exhibit strong price increases until later in the cycle.

   g. Interest rates will likely increase as inflation increases and the demand for money increases. As interest rates are expected to increase, investors will likely start to sell off long-term bonds in order to avoid capital losses. Instead investors will purchase stocks of companies that do better later in the business cycle such as commercial and industrial construction and heavy industrial equipment.

CHAPTER 15

ISSUES IN STABILIZATION POLICY

PUTTING THIS CHAPTER INTO PERSPECTIVE

Economists are no strangers to controversy. In every generation one economic theory has claimed the minds and souls of a majority, but significant minority points of view have also existed. And at times these minority views have become the majority conventional wisdom. Interestingly enough, economists (and their intellectual heirs) have carried on some debates for centuries. In Chapter 15 we introduce other theories—rational expectations, or new classical, real business cycles, and new Keynesian. You should not be concerned with deciding which theory is "correct," nor should you worry about memorizing every little detail of each theory. Instead try to concentrate on only the main issues, which are summarized for you in Table 15-1.

The single most important issue in macroeconomics—and one that has been debated hotly by economists since the eighteenth century—is whether or not capitalism is stable. Such an economy is often shocked by random forces (gold and silver discoveries in the past, changes in taste, technology, and profit expectations always). If a shocked economy eventually returns to the original, near-full-employment equilibrium position, then it is stable; if not, it is unstable.

If capitalism is stable, then stabilization policy is not necessary unless it takes *too long* to return to equilibrium and can use some help. If capitalism is unstable, it *should* be stabilized by the government (through monetary policy and fiscal policy), *if it is possible to stabilize it.*

In recent years, several exciting advances in macroeconomic theory have emerged, and such advances have caused the age-old "is capitalism stable" debate to evolve. Monetarists maintain that monetary policy only works in the short run by fooling workers and employers into underestimating the actual rate of inflation. If economic agents expect the inflation rate to be less than it actually is, then more inflation can "buy" less unemployment and the Phillips curve is negatively sloped. But because in the long run, the true rate of inflation will be known by economic agents, the trade-off between inflation and unemployment will disappear. Eventually, the actual unemployment rate will equal the natural unemployment rate; short-run Phillips curves are negatively sloped, but long-run Phillips curves are vertical at the natural unemployment rate (reflecting the vertical long-run aggregate supply curve, which is *now* conceived of as the real GDP level consistent with the natural rate of unemployment.

The rational expectations hypothesis (REH) model, however, rejects even this conception of how monetary policy works. The REH maintains that because economic agents are rational, they will use all the information available to them when they make decisions—including the probability that specific monetary and fiscal policies will be enacted. The REH proponents contend that policy-makers cannot cause economic agents to make *systematic* expectational (forecasting) errors. They conclude that economic agents are just as likely to overestimate the true inflation rate as they are likely to underestimate it. Unannounced monetary policy can affect real national income (output) and employment, but it is just as likely to reduce them as to increase them! Furthermore, *announced* stabilization policies will have little or no effect on real national income and employment.

While the REH model is not widely accepted, it nevertheless presents a challenge to modern macroeconomists, and it certainly will cause the economics discipline to evolve toward more rigorous and more robust models. In addition, it provides more controversy for a contentious group of social scientists.

In this chapter also note that economists have also long debated the issue of the extent of competition and price wage flexibility/rigidity, an issue closely related to the "is capitalism stable" controversy. New Keynesian theories—small-menu cost theory and efficiency wage theory are modern, more subtle, versions of the Keynesian wage rate rigidity theory. Not to be outdone, the new classical economists have developed new theories that incorporate price wage flexibility rational expectations and real business cycle theories.

Supply-side theorists maintain that creating incentives for individuals and firms will increase productivity, will cause the aggregate supply curve to shift outward, and will increase tax revenues. Such an aggregate supply curve shift to the right, without any other effects, would mean greater GDP output without upward pressure on prices.

New growth theorists maintain that stabilization policies to eliminate business cycles are largely irrelevant. Instead, they claim, we should be concerned with encouraging innovation, which contributes to growth—and business cycles.

LEARNING OBJECTIVES

After you have studied this chapter you should be able to:

15.1   Explain why the actual unemployment rate might depart from the natural rate of unemployment.

15.2   Describe why there may be an inverse relationship between the inflation rate and the unemployment rate, reflected by the Phillips curve.

15.3   Evaluate how expectations affect the relationship between the actual inflation rate and the unemployment rate.

15.4   Describe the rational expectations hypothesis and the new classical model and their implications for economic policy making.

15.5   Identify the central features of the real-business-cycle challenge to policy making.

15.6   Identify the central features of supply-side economics to policy making.

15.7   Distinguish among alternative modern approaches to strengthening the case for active policy making.

CHAPTER OUTLINE

LO 15.1 Explain why the actual unemployment rate might depart from the natural rate of unemployment.
1. The **natural rate of unemployment** is determined by
   a. frictional unemployment and
   b. unemployment due to price and wage rigidities in the economic system.

LO 15.2 Describe why there may be an inverse relationship between the inflation rate and the unemployment rate, reflected by the Phillips curve.
2. Some economists have argued that a trade-off exists between the rate of unemployment and the rate of inflation.
   a. If such a relationship (called a **Phillips curve**) existed, policy-makers could simply try to balance the problems associated with inflation with those associated with unemployment; they could then select the "optimal" mix of unemployment and inflation consistent with societal values.
   b. In reality no such policy option exists; the Phillips curve relationship has proved to be unstable.

3. A consistent short-run trade-off between inflation and unemployment seems to have existed in the past, when the actual inflation rate was relatively low for long periods.
   a. In recent years the inflation rate has been much more variable.
   b. If workers underestimate the true inflation rate, they will be fooled into accepting a lower wage rate than they bargained for, and the actual unemployment rate will fall.

4. **NAIRU** is that rate of unemployment below which the rate of inflation tends to rise and below which it tends to fall.

LO 15.3 Evaluate how expectations affect the relationship between the actual inflation rate and the unemployment rate.
5. The Friedman-Phelps model indicates how monetary policy can account for the Phillips curve trade-off between inflation and unemployment in the short run, but not in the long run.
   a. If the Bank of Canada secretly increases the rate at which the money supply is growing, then economic agents will underestimate the actual inflation rate.
   b. Job searchers, therefore, are fooled into accepting jobs sooner than they otherwise would have.

    c. The shorter duration of unemployment caused by unanticipated inflation causes the unemployment rate to fall; hence higher inflation rates have "bought" a lower unemployment rate in the short run, and the short-run Phillips curve is negatively sloped.

    d. In the long run the actual inflation rate will be correctly anticipated, the duration of unemployment will return to its prior level, and the unemployment rate will return to the natural rate of unemployment and the economy will be operating on its LRAS curve.

    e. The long-run Phillips curve, therefore, is vertical; in the long run monetary policy affects only the price level; real GDP and employment are unchanged.

6. An unanticipated expansionary monetary policy causes the AD curve to shift rightward and the short-run AS curve to remain constant; hence real national income (output) and employment will rise with the price level.

7. In the long run the AS curve is vertical; hence expansionary monetary policy will increase only the price level.

LO 15.4 Describe the rational expectations hypothesis and the new classical model and their implications for economic policy making.

8. The rational expectations hypothesis (REH) contends that economic agents will try to anticipate future stabilization policy and its effects.

    a. Economic agents will allocate resources to predict stabilization policy and its effect on the value of future economic variables—especially the future inflation rate.

    b. The REH predicts that policymakers cannot cause economic agents to make consistent forecasting errors; workers will not consistently and systematically underestimate the inflation rate; sometimes they will overestimate the inflation rate.

    c. Eventually, once economic agents know that policymakers are trying to fool them, not even a *short-run* (systematic) trade-off between inflation and unemployment exists.

        i.   The REH predicts that an anticipated (announced) stabilization policy will have little impact on the employment rate and on real national income.

        ii. Expansionary demand policies in the past may have worked because economic agents had not been fooled by *previous* government stabilization policies.

        iii. In recent years stabilization policy has been more difficult to conduct because economic agents have found it rational to allocate resources to economic forecasting.

9. The **new classical model** incorporates the assumptions of the rational expectations model, and adds the assumptions that (a) all markets are highly competitive and (b) all prices and wages are perfectly competitive.

10. The **policy irrelevance proposition**, an implication of the new classical model, is that policy actions have no real effects in the short run if the policy actions were anticipated, and not in the long run even if the policy actions were unanticipated.

11. The new classical model seems to imply that fluctuations in real variables are a result of *mistakes*, either on the part of policymakers, or economic agents.

LO 15.5 Identify the central features of the real-business-cycle challenge to policy making.

12. Various theories have been developed to explain fluctuations in real variables (business cycles) that are *not* due to mistakes.
    a. **Small-menu cost theory** hypothesizes that it is costly for firms to change prices in response to demand changes, hence some price rigidity is rational.
    b. The **efficiency wage theory** maintains that high wages tend to increase labour productivity and worker loyalty, hence wage reductions might interfere with both; employers are therefore reluctant to lower wages in recessions and wage rates are inflexible downward.
    c. **Real business cycle theory** maintains the assumption of price and wage flexibility, but suggests that the source of business cycles is changes in supply.
        i.   Supply shocks such as the oil supply disruption or the sudden increase in the price of oil in the 1970s, or any significant change in the price of a crucial resource shift the SRAS curve (and maybe the LRAS curve) and change real economic variables.
        ii. Technological changes and changes in the composition of the labour force are additional (nonmonetary) supply shocks that have short run and long run effects on real economic variables.

LO 15.6 Identify the central features of supply-side economics to policy making.

13. **Supply-side economists** maintain that too much attention has been focused on aggregate demand and that increasing levels of taxation and regulation were reducing incentives to work, save, and invest. They maintain that the real problems of the economy could be more gainfully addressed by focusing on incentives to increase aggregate supply.

LO 15.7 Distinguish among alternative modern approaches to strengthening the case for active policy making.

14. New growth theorists believe that encouraging innovations which contribute to economic growth (and contribute to business cycles) is more important than stabilizing the economy in the short run.

KEY TERMS AND KEY CONCEPTS

Phillips curve
New Keynesian economics
Real business cycle theory
Active (discretionary) policymaking
Passive (nondiscretionary) policymaking
Policy irrelevance proposition
Non-accelerating inflation rate of
  unemployment (NAIRU)

Natural rate of unemployment
New classical model
Supply-side economics
Small-menu cost theory
Rational expectations hypothesis
Efficiency wage theory

COMPLETION QUESTIONS
Fill in the blank or circle the correct term.

(LO 15.1)

1. The natural rate of unemployment prevails in the (short, long) run when the economy is in (equilibrium, disequilibrium); when the natural rate of unemployment is reached, the actual inflation rate (is less than, is greater than, equals) the expected inflation rate, and there (is, is not) a tendency for the inflation rate to accelerate.

2. In order to keep the actual unemployment rate below the natural unemployment rate, the actual inflation rate must be (greater than, less than, equal to) the expected inflation rate; thus the inflation rate must always be (constant, accelerating, decelerating).

(LO 15.2)

3. The Phillips curve posits a trade-off between the _____ rate and the _____ rate.

4. In recent years in Canada, the Phillips curve relationship (is, is not) supported by empirical evidence.

(LO 15.3)

5. The rational expectations hypothesis contends that policymakers (can, cannot) induce economic agents to make systematic forecasting errors. According to this model, if a government stabilization policy is announced it will have (much, little) effect on output and unemployment; if a stabilization policy is not announced and is unanticipated by economic agents, it (will, will not) have a short-run impact on the economy, and the impact (will, will not) be systematic on output and employment.

6. If inflationary expectations are high and the Bank of Canada pursues an unanticipated contractionary policy, the unemployment rate will (fall, rise), because economic agents will (underestimate, overestimate) the future inflation rate. If the Bank of Canada announces a contractionary policy and such a policy is believed by economic agents, the rational expectations hypothesis predicts that the unemployment rate (will, will not) rise significantly.

(LO 15.4)

7. The new classical model accepts the assumptions of the rational expectations hypothesis, and adds the assumptions of _____ and _____; that model implies that fluctuations in real variables are a result of mistakes on the part of _____ and _____.

8. The policy irrelevance proposition states that if policy actions are anticipated, such actions will have (no, a great) effect on real variables in the short run; if policy actions are unanticipated then they (will, will not) have an effect on real

variables in the short run, but that effect (is, is not) predictable; in the long run unanticipated policy (will, will not) have real effects.

9.   Small-menu cost theory maintains that if the cost of frequent changes in prices exceeds the costs of not changing such prices, it is (rational, irrational) to leave prices unchanged in the face of changes in demand; this theory suggests that prices and wages (are, are not) perfectly flexible.

10. The efficiency wage hypothesis maintains that (high wages lead to high productivity, high productivity leads to high wages), and therefore producers may be reluctant to reduce wages in recessions; hence this theory suggests that wage rates are (inflexible, flexible) in the downward direction.

(LO 15.5)
11. Real business cycle theory assumes that prices and wages are (inflexible, flexible) and that changes in real economic variables result from (supply, demand) shocks; this theory suggests that changes in _____, _____, and _____ could affect real economic variables.

(LO 15.6)
12. Supply-side economists believe that business costs have been increased because governments have raised taxes and these taxes have increased business _____ and reduced business _____. High marginal tax rates reduce _____ to work, save, and invest. These economists argue that governments should substantially (increase, decrease) _____ taxes.

(LO 15.7)
13. New growth theorists believe that short-run stabilization policy (is, is not) a worthwhile pursuit.

TRUE-FALSE QUESTIONS
Circle the **T** if the statement is true and the **F** if it is false. Explain to yourself why a statement is false.

(LO 15.1)
T F   1. In macroeconomic equilibrium, the actual unemployment rate exceeds the natural unemployment rate.

(LO 15.2)
T F   2. The Phillips curve relates inflation rates to growth rates.

T F   3. If workers underestimate the true inflation rate, the Phillips curve will be negatively sloped.

T F   4. If workers overestimate the true inflation rate, the unemployment rate could rise as inflation rises.

T   F   5.   The Friedman-Phelps model predicts that no trade-off exists between inflation and unemployment in the short run.

T   F   6.   In recent years in Canada, there seems to be no systematic, negative relationship between the inflation rate and the unemployment rate.

(LO 15.3)

T   F   7.   Monetary policy works by fooling people only in the long run.

(LO 15.4)

T   F   8.   The new classical model predicts that if the government announces its stabilization policy, the unemployment rate will be affected greatly.

T   F   9.   Both the Friedman-Phelps model and the rational expectations model predict that in the long run the actual unemployment rate equals the natural rate.

T   F   10.   The Friedman-Phelps model contends that high inflation does not keep unemployment down; only not fully anticipated rising inflation does.

T   F   11.   If the inflation rate falls unexpectedly, the unemployment rate will fall, according to the Friedman-Phelps model.

T   F   12.   The rational expectations hypothesis argues that policymakers cannot systematically change the unemployment rate in the short run.

T   F   13.   The rational expectations/new classical model argues that policymakers simply cannot affect the unemployment rate in the short run.

T   F   14.   Keynesians and classical economists all believe that the demand for money is sensitive to the interest rate.

(LO 15.5)

T   F   15.   In the short run, the aggregate supply curve is upward sloping because nominal wages rise as prices rise.

T   F   16.   In the long run, the aggregate supply curve is vertical at the GDP level of output consistent with the natural rate of unemployment.

(LO 15.6)

T   F   17.   Supply-side economists believe that increasing incentives for individuals and businesses will cause the aggregate supply curve to shift outward and GDP to increase.

(LO 15.7)

T   F   18.   Traditional Keynesians believe that capitalism is stable, and that stabilization policy is too difficult to conduct.

T   F   19. New growth theorists think that we should be more concerned with growth rates, and less concerned with short-run stabilization.

MULTIPLE CHOICE QUESTIONS
Circle the letter that corresponds to the best answer.

(LO 15.1)
1. If the actual unemployment rate equals the natural unemployment rate, then
    a. no inflation is possible.
    b. macroeconomic equilibrium exists.
    c. no unemployment exists.
    d. All of the above

2. The natural rate of unemployment equals the actual unemployment rate
    a. in the long run.
    b. only when the actual inflation rate is zero.
    c. only when the natural inflation rate is zero.
    d. only in the short run.

(LO 15.2)
3. The Phillips curve relates
    a. inflation rates and productivity rates.
    b. inflation rates and unemployment rates.
    c. unemployment rates and growth rates.
    d. the natural unemployment rate and the actual unemployment rate.

4. A trade-off between inflation and unemployment
    a. exists only in the long run.
    b. can exist if workers underestimate the true inflation rate.
    c. can exist if workers underestimate the natural inflation rate.
    d. is depicted by the production possibilities curve.

5. If workers underestimate the true inflation rate, then
    a. more inflation can "buy" less unemployment.
    b. the Phillips curve will be vertical in the short run.
    c. the Phillips curve will be positively sloped.
    d. the unemployment rate will rise.

6. If workers anticipate a 10 percent inflation rate, they will
    a. add 10 percent to their wage requests.
    b. subtract 10 percent from their wage requests.
    c. quit work.
    d. work longer hours.

7. In the Friedman-Phelps model, if the inflation rate falls unexpectedly, then
   a. workers will overestimate the true inflation rate.
   b. the unemployment rate will rise.
   c. the short-run Phillips curve will be negatively sloped.
   d. All of the above

LO15.3
8. Under the Friedman-Phelps model
   a. the short-run Phillips curve is vertical.
   b. a short-run Phillips curve exists for each actual inflation rate.
   c. a short-run Phillips curve exists for each expected inflation rate.
   d. only one Phillips curve exists, and it is negatively sloped at the natural unemployment rate.

9. The natural rate of unemployment
   a. occurs when the inflation rate is correctly anticipated.
   b. is always above the actual rate of unemployment.
   c. is always below the actual rate of unemployment.
   d. occurs usually in the short run.

10. The only way to keep the actual unemployment rate below the natural unemployment rate is to
   a. have the actual inflation rate be less than the expected inflation rate.
   b. have the actual inflation rate be higher than the expected inflation rate.
   c. constantly reduce the inflation rate.
   d. provide job security.

(LO 15.4)
11. The rational expectations hypothesis
   a. rejects the Friedman-Phelps model.
   b. maintains that policymakers cannot get economic agents to make systematic forecasting errors.
   c. maintains that economic agents will use all information, including expected stabilization policies, when they estimate the future inflation rate.
   d. All of the above

12. The irrelevancy proposition maintains that
   a. anticipated government stabilization policies cannot reduce unemployment below the natural rate.
   b. unanticipated stabilization policies cannot reduce unemployment below the natural rate.
   c. anticipated stabilization policies cannot reduce the increase in actual unemployment resulting from a decrease in the inflation rate.
   d. unanticipated stabilization policies are very effective in reducing actual unemployment below natural unemployment.

13. The new classical model
    a. rejects the rational expectations approach.
    b. assumes that price and wages are flexible.
    c. maintains that monetary policy cannot affect real variables in the short run.
    d. was developed by Keynes.

14. When expansionary monetary policy is unanticipated, in the short run
    a. the unemployment rate will fall.
    b. actual inflation will exceed anticipated inflation.
    c. workers are fooled into accepting jobs sooner.
    d. All of the above

(LO 15.5)

15. Which of the following is most unlike the others
    a. Theories that assume fixed prices in the short run
    b. Efficiency wage theory
    c. Real business-cycle theory
    d. Small-menu cost theory

16. Real business cycle theory
    a. assumes that prices and wages are flexible.
    b. maintains that real economic variables can change even if mistakes are not made.
    c. suggests that supply creates its own demand.
    d. All of the above

(LO 15.6)

17. Supply-side economists view economic underperformance as the result of:
    a. government deregulation
    b. excessive taxation
    c. unanticipated inflation
    d. a shifting Phillips curve

18. Supply-side economists believe that high levels of taxation:
    a. increase govenment tax revenues
    b. reduce incentives to work, save, and invest
    c. reduce unemployment but increase inflation
    d. reduce transfer payments to the poor

19. The Laffer curve diagrams the relationship between
    a. the tax rate and tax revenues
    b. the tax rate and budget deficits
    c. the rate of inflation and the rate of employment
    d. the rate of inflation and the rate of unemplotment

(LO 15.7)

20. Which of the following models predicts that capitalism is not inherently stable?
    a. traditional classical
    b. traditional Keynesian
    c. new classical
    d. new Keynesian

21. Which of the following economic schools of thought is most unlike the others?
    a. traditional classical
    b. new Classical
    c. traditional Keynesian
    d. new Keynesian

22. New growth theorists maintain that
    a. short-run stabilization policy is overrated.
    b. economic growth is overrated.
    c. innovations are harmful.
    d. None of the above.

MATCHING
Choose the item in column (2) that best matches an item in column (1).

(1)	(2)
a. Phillips curve	1. unanticipated inflation
b. new growth theory	2. efficiency wage hypothesis
c. NAIRU	3. non-inflationary unemployment
d. price-wage rigidity	4. innovations
e. long-run Phillips curve	5. supply creates its own demand
f. policy irrelevancy proposition	6. rational expectations hypothesis
g. real business cycle theory	7. relationship between inflation and unemployment
	8. vertical LRAS curve
	9. supply-side theory

WORKING WITH GRAPHS

(LO 15.2)

1. Suppose you are given the Phillips curve in the graph on the next page.

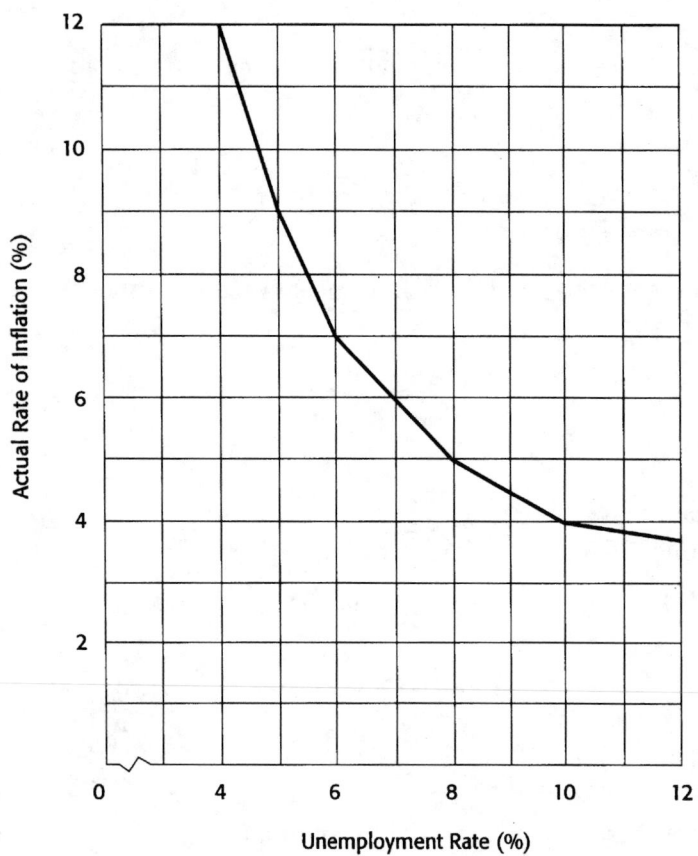

a.   If the rate of 7 percent unemployment constitutes "full" employment, what rate of inflation should the economy expect at full employment?

b.   Suppose the government were to set a goal of lowering inflation to 4 percent. If the Phillips curve above is accurate and stable, what level of unemployment will have to be tolerated if the goal for inflation is to be achieved?

c.   Suppose the Phillips curve above describes the inflation-unemployment trade-off with individuals anticipating inflation of 6 percent. If individuals suddenly begin to expect inflation of 8 percent, and this raises the level of unemployment for each level of actual inflation by 1.5 percent, draw in the new Phillips curve.

d.   What will be the level of unemployment if the actual rate of inflation is the anticipated rate, 8 percent?

e.   If the actual rate of inflation turns out to be 6 percent rather than 8 percent, what will the level of unemployment be?

f.   What conclusion can be drawn from answers to parts c through e?

(LO 15.2) and 15.3

2.   Analyze the graph below, then answer the questions that follow.

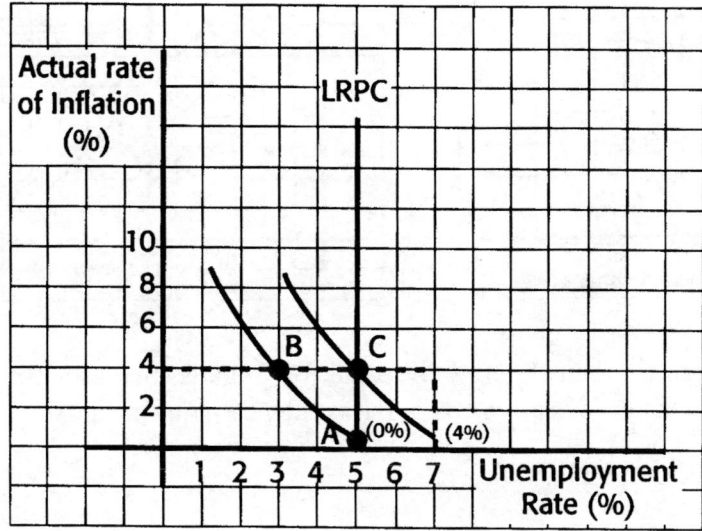

a.   What is the natural rate of unemployment for the economy depicted in the graph above?

b.   Starting from point A and assuming that economic agents anticipated 0 percent inflation, what will be the actual unemployment rate if the actual inflation rate is 4 percent? 6 percent?

c.   If the anticipated inflation rate is 4 percent, and the actual inflation rate is 4 percent, what will be the actual unemployment rate? The natural unemployment rate?

d.   When does the short-run Phillips curve shift?

3.   Consider the graphs on the next page and then answer the questions that follow.

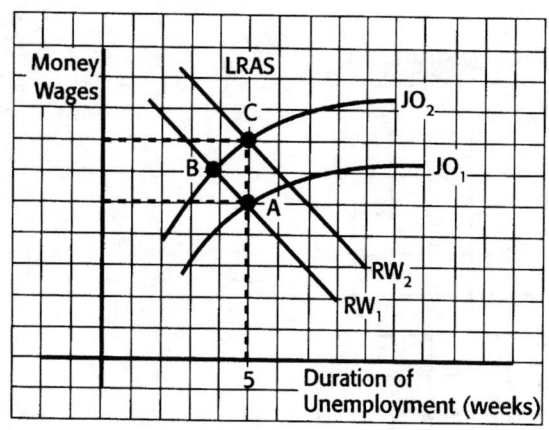
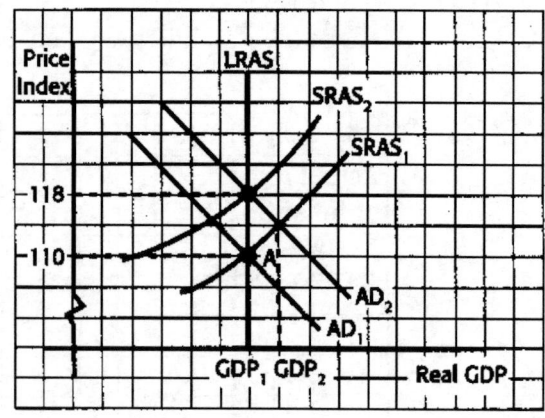

a.   Assume that we begin at point A. Now the Bank of Canada increases the money supply in secret. Which curve is affected? What is the new equilibrium?

b.   Continuing (a) above, what has happened, at this point in our analysis, to employment, unemployment, and real GDP?

c.   In the long run economic agents will now fully anticipate the higher price level, consequently which curve will now be affected? What is the new equilibrium point?

d.   What is the new equilibrium real GDP level? The new equilibrium price level?

PROBLEMS

(LO 15.2)

1.   In the table below are three short-run Phillips curves. Columns 1 and 2 show the relationship between the unemployment rate (U) and the actual rate of inflation (R) when the anticipated rate of inflation in the economy is 0 percent; columns 3 and 4 when the anticipated R is 6 percent; and columns 5 and 6 when the anticipated R is 12 percent.

Phillips Curve 1		Phillips Curve 2		Phillips Curve 3	
(1)	(2)	(3)	(4)	(5)	(6)
U	$R_{0\%}$	U	$R_{6\%}$	U	$R_{12\%}$
10	0	10	6	10	12
9	1	9	7	9	13
8	3	8	9	8	15
7	6	7	12	7	18
6	10	6	16	6	22
5	15	5	21	5	27
4	21	4	27	4	33

a. Suppose the anticipated rate of inflation and the actual rate of inflation are 0. The unemployment rate U is _____ percent.

b. If expansionary monetary or fiscal policies are used to increase aggregate demand and to reduce U to 7 percent, the actual R will (increase/decrease) to _____ percent.

c. When the economy comes to anticipate this R, U will be _____ percent; and if expansionary stabilization policies are again used to reduce U to 7 percent, the actual R will _____ to _____ percent.

d. And when the economy comes to anticipate this R, U will be _____ percent; if stabilization policies are once more used to reduce U to 7 percent, the actual R will _____ to _____ percent; and when the economy comes to anticipate this R, U will again _____ to _____ percent.

e. Use your answers to parts (a), (b), (c), and (d) above to show U in the long run at each of the actual R's in the table.

R	U
0	_____
6	_____
12	_____

BUSINESS SECTION

Finance: Nominal vs. Real Interest Rates?

(LO 15.4)

Economist Phillip Cagan analyzed the post-World War I German hyperinflation period, during which that economy experienced high and variable money supply growth and inflation rates. Over the period from 1921 to 1923 the inflation rate ranged from about 0 percent to 500 percent *per month*. Cagan found that during that period relatively small changes occurred in the levels of real national output and total employment.

It became extremely difficult for economic agents to predict the inflation rate—and therefore to determine the "best" nominal interest rate at which to lend or borrow.

1.   Does this historical experience lend some support to the rational expectations hypothesis? Why?

2.   What would you predict happened to the number of loans made at nominal interest rates, during that period?

3.   Would you guess that important redistribution of income effects occurred during that period? Why?

ANSWERS TO CHAPTER 15

COMPLETION QUESTIONS

1. long; equilibrium; equals; is not
2. greater than; accelerating
3. inflation, unemployment
4. is not
5. cannot; little; will; will not
6. rise; overestimate; will not
7. pure competition; price/wage flexibility; policymakers; economic agents
8. no; will; is not; will not
9. rational; are not
10. high wages lead to high productivity; inflexible
11. flexible; supply; oil prices; technology; composition of the labour force
12. costs, profits; incentives; decrease.
13. is not

TRUE-FALSE QUESTIONS

1. F   In equilibrium they are equal.
2. F   It relates inflation rates to unemployment rates.
3. T
4. T
5. F   It predicts no trade-off in the long run.
6. T
7. F   It fools people only in the short run.
8. F   Unemployment will not be affected very much, if policy is announced.
9. T
10. T
11. F   It will rise as workers prolong their job search.
12. T
13. F   They can change unemployment, but the direction is uncertain.
14. F   Classical economists believed the demand for money was insensitive to the interest rate.
15. F   The short run AS curve is upward sloping because higher prices = higher profits = increased output
16. T
17. T
18. F   They believe it is unstable, and that stabilization policy is possible.
19. T

MULTIPLE CHOICE QUESTIONS

1.b;   If the actual rate of unemployment equals the natural rate of unemployment, macroeconomic equilibrium exists. This is because the natural rate of unemployment is defined as the rate of unemployment that would exist in the long run after everyone in the economy has fully adjusted to any changes that have occurred.
       TIP: When the economy is at the natural unemployment rate it is producing the level of output implied by the long-run aggregate supply curve.

2.a;   The natural rate of unemployment equals the actual unemployment rate in the ***long run. See the TIP immediately below.
       TIP: Recall that the natural rate of unemployment is defined as the rate of unemployment that would exist in the long run after everyone in the economy has fully adjusted to any changes that have occurred.

3.b;   The Phillips curve relates inflation and unemployment rates. More specifically, this curve suggests that a negative relationship exists between inflation and unemployment rates.

TIP: It was originally believed that the Phillips curve represented a policy trade-off between inflation and unemployment.

4.b;   A trade-off between inflation and unemployment can exist if workers understate the true inflation rate. As an example, if employers offer higher nominal wages in response to unanticipated inflation, workers perceive an increase in real wages if they understate the true new rate of inflation. As a result, unemployed workers will accept job offers, resulting in a lower unemployment rate at the higher inflation rate.

5.a;   If workers underestimate the true increase in inflation resulting from an increase in aggregate demand the previous question suggests that a negative relation can exist between inflation and unemployment rates. In other words, more inflation can "buy" less unemployment.

6a;   If workers anticipate a 10 percent inflation rate, they will add 10 percent to their wage requests in order to maintain real wage rates.

7.d;   In the Friedman-Phelps model, if, as a result of a decrease in aggregate demand, the inflation rate falls unexpectedly, in the short run the Phillips curve will be negatively sloped. Since workers overestimate the inflation rate, they are not ready to accept lower nominal wages, and so firms will experience decreasing profit levels. As a result, the lower inflation rate is accompanied by layoffs and a higher unemployment rate.

TIP: According to the Friedman-Phelps model, in the long run, no predictable or stable trade-off will exist between the unemployment rate and the inflation rate. In other words, for a given level of unemployment any inflation rate is possible depending on the actions of policymakers.

8.c;   Under the Friedman-Phelps model a short-run Phillips curve exists for each expected inflation rate. As an example, if the expected rate of inflation is 4% but aggregate demand increases at a higher level than expected, unemployed workers will accept job offers under the belief that the higher nominal wage offers will translate into higher real wage rates. Therefore, in the short run, while inflation is increasing, unemployment is decreasing.

TIP: Recall that a Phillips curve implies that a negative relationship exists between the inflation rate and unemployment rate.

9.a;   The natural rate of unemployment occurs when the inflation rate is correctly anticipated. Refer to the TIP described immediately above.

10.b;   The only way to keep the actual unemployment rate below the natural unemployment rate is to have the actual rate be higher than the expected rate. If policymakers were to attempt to maintain this situation they would have to create an accelerated rate of inflation.

11.d;   The rational expectations hypothesis assumes that individuals base their forecasts (expectations) on all available past and current information as well as their understanding of how policies affect the economy.

TIP: The rational expectations hypothesis assumes that the following old saying is correct: "It is true that you may fool all of the people some of the time, but you can't fool all of the people all of the time."

12.a;   The irrelevancy proposition maintains that anticipated stabilization policies cannot reduce unemployment below the natural rate. Under the assumptions of rational expectations on the part of decision makers in the economy, the irrelevancy proposition states that anticipated monetary policy cannot alter either the rate of unemployment or the level of real GDP.

13.b;   The new classical model assumes that prices and wages are flexible. Consistent with the policy irrelevance proposition, fully anticipated stabilization policies will only affect wage and price levels and will have no effect in determining the levels of real variables.

14.d;   In the short run, when expansionary monetary policy is unanticipated, actual inflation will exceed expected inflation, workers will be fooled into accepting jobs sooner which will cause the unemployment rate to fall.

15.c;   Real business cycle theory holds that even if all prices and wages are perfectly flexible, real shocks to the economy, such as technological change, can cause national business fluctuations. All of the other answer options to this question assume fixed prices in the short run.

16.d;   Real business-cycle theory holds that even if prices and wages are perfectly flexible, real shocks to the economy such as a significant change in the supply of resources (e.g. oil) can cause national business fluctuations.

17.b;   Supply-side economists believe that excessive levels of taxation and too much government regulation reduce incentives to work, save, and invest and contribute to an economy that underperforms..

18.b;   Supply-side economists believe that high levels of taxation reduce incentives to work, save, and invest.

19.a;   The Laffer curve indicates that tax revenues initially increase with a higher tax rate; however, eventually high tax rates become a disincentive and tax revenues decline.

20.b;   The traditional Keynesian model predicts that capitalism is not inherently stable. Due to this prediction, traditional Keynesians are in favour of active, discretionary policymaking.

21.c;   Traditional Keynesian is the school of thought most unlike the others. It is the only school of thought that predicts that capitalism is not inherently stable. Moreover this school of thought views fiscal policy as a necessary means to promote economic stability. Monetary policy is considered ineffective, particularly in deep recessions.

22.a;   New growth theorists maintain that short run stabilization policy is overrated. The federal government should focus its policy efforts on fostering a climate that will generate higher economic growth rates.

MATCHING

a and 7;   b and 4;   c and 3;   d and 2;   e and 8;   f and 6;   g and 5

WORKING WITH GRAPHS

1.   a. 6 percent
     b. 10 percent
     c. see graph below
     d. 7 percent
     e. between 8 and 8.5%
     f. When actual inflation is less than anticipated inflation, unemployment rises.

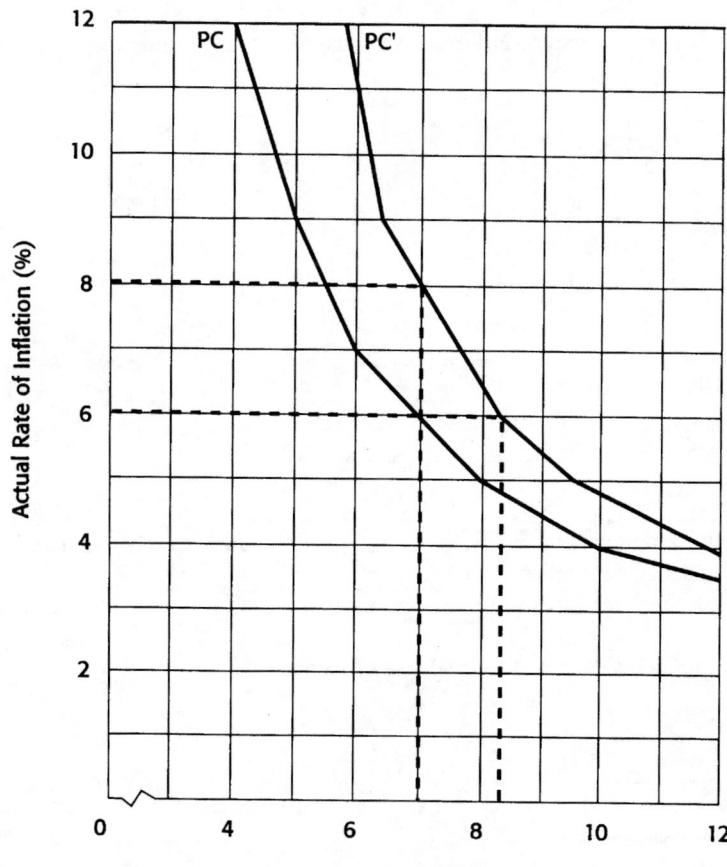

2. a. 5 percent
    b. 3 percent; 2 percent
    c. 5 percent; 5 percent
    d. Every time the anticipated inflation rate changes.

3. Your new graph should be labelled as indicated below.

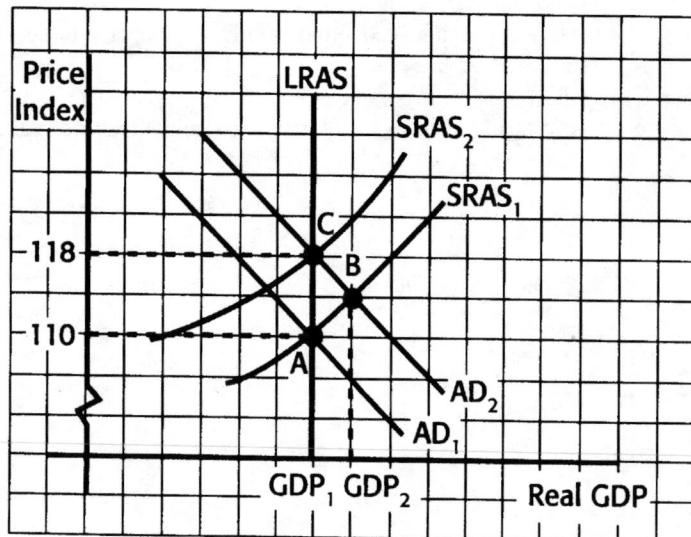

    a. The AD curve shifts to AD₂, point B; See graph above.
    b. employment increases because the duration of unemployment falls, unemployment falls, real GDP
         rises to GDP₂.
    c. The short run aggregate supply curve shifts upward to SRAS₂, the new equilibrium point is point C;
         See graph above.
    d. GDP₁, 118.

PROBLEMS

1. a.   10
    b.   increase, 6
    c.   10, increase, 12
    d.   10, increase, 18; increase, 10
    e.   10 percent, 10 percent, 10 percent

BUSINESS SECTION

1. Yes, some support. Apparently economic agents tried to anticipate money supply changes and,
    therefore, real variables did not change very much.
2. Decreased, because people would be forced to speculate on the inflation rate if they borrowed or lent
    at nominal interest rates.
3. Yes; borrowers who owed *nominal* debts gained at the expense of lenders.

CHAPTER 16

COMPARATIVE ADVANTAGE AND THE OPEN ECONOMY

PUTTING THIS CHAPTER INTO PERSPECTIVE

Chapter 16 is the first chapter in Part Five – Global Economics, and the first of two chapters dealing with international trade. International trade and finance have always been important topics in economics, and they have become increasingly important over the past ten years. The percentage of GDP due to exports has increased significantly since the inauguration of the Canada-U.S. Free Trade Agreement (FTA) and the North American Free trade Agreement (NAFTA). Our nation and many of our trading partners seem to be moving toward "protection from foreign competition," and monetary policy and fiscal policy have become increasingly difficult as recent technological innovations in communications and computers have made the countries of the world more interdependent. For these and other reasons, it is important for you to understand the principles that underlie international trade and finance.

The most important goal of Chapter 16 is to demonstrate how voluntary trade between nations is based on comparative advantage. Each nation specializes in the production of those goods for which it has a comparative advantage, which means that it produces those goods with the lowest opportunity costs. As a result, world economic growth is fostered and world living standards, with minor short-run exceptions, rise.

Another objective of Chapter 16 is to expose some myths concerning international trade. Many people are induced to favour import restrictions because they believe that imports take jobs away from domestic workers. The truth is that import restrictions merely help save some workers' jobs at the expense of others, and as a by-product consumers must pay higher prices. This chapter analyzes and compares graphically the effects of tariffs and import quotas.

Chapter 16 also analyzes several methods by which nations restrict foreign trade. It is a source of wonderment that the one issue on which virtually all economists agree—that free trade is advantageous—is the same issue on which nearly all non-economists seem to disagree. We don't insist that others agree with us; we merely ask that you try to understand our reasoning. We hope that your text and this *Study Guide* will help you do so.

LEARNING OBJECTIVES

After you have studied this chapter you should be able to:

16.1   Discuss the worldwide importance of trade and the importance of trade to Canada.

16.2   Distinguish between comparative advantage and absolute advantage.

16.3   Explain why nations can gain from specializing in production and engaging in international trade.

16.4   Outline common arguments against free trade.

16.5   Describe two ways that nations restrict foreign trade.

16.6   Identify Canada's most significant international agreement and name the primary organization that adjudicates trade disputes among nations.

CHAPTER OUTLINE

LO 16.1   Discuss the worldwide importance of trade and the importance of trade to Canada.

1.   The proportion of GDP accounted for by trade for individual nations varies greatly, but if trade were curtailed, trading nations such as Canada would be affected significantly.
   a.   A nation ultimately pays for its imports by exports; thus restrictions on imports ultimately reduce exports.
   b.   If trade is voluntary, then both nations participating in a trading-exchange benefit.
   c.   International trade increases the international transmission of ideas.

LO 16.2   Distinguish between comparative advantage and absolute advantage.

2.   A nation has an **absolute advantage** in the production of good A if it can produce more units of good A than other nations can, from a given quantity of inputs; a nation has a **comparative advantage** in producing good A if out of all the goods it can produce, good A has the lowest opportunity cost.

3.   Opportunity costs, and hence comparative advantages, differ among nations.

LO 16.4 Outline common arguments against free trade.

4. There are numerous arguments that have been presented as being anti-free trade. Such arguments include the **infant industry argument**, protecting a way of life, stability, protecting domestic jobs, and countering foreign subsidies and **dumping**. Some of these arguments are simply wrong, and others emphasize costs (losses) and neglect benefits (gains).

LO 16.5 Describe two ways that nations restrict foreign trade.

5. There are two basic methods that nations have used to restrict foreign trade.
   a. Some nations place *import quotas* on foreign goods.
   b. Some nations place taxes or *tariffs* on foreign goods.
   c. Both quotas and tariffs raise prices to domestic consumers and reduce the quantity of goods traded; a tariff, however, generates revenues to the government, while a quota does not.

KEY TERMS AND KEY CONCEPTS

General Agreement on Tariffs and Trade (GATT)
World Trade Organization (WTO)
Voluntary export restraint agreement (VER)
Comparative advantage
North American Free Trade Agreement (NAFTA)

Quota system
Dumping
Absolute advantage
Infant industry argument
Free Trade Agreement (FTA)

COMPLETION QUESTIONS
Fill in the blank or circle the correct term.

(LO 16.1)

1. Worldwide trade is expanding (less, more) _____ rapidly than worldwide GDP.

2. Canadian exports and imports of goods and services each amount to about _____% of GDP.

3. If world trade ceased to exist, all trade-related jobs (would, would not) be lost in the long run; instead nations would simply _____. Nevertheless, worldwide living standards would (fall, rise) significantly.

(LO 16.2)

4. International trade permits each nation to specialize in the production of those goods for which it has a(n) _____ advantage; each nation specializes in the production of goods for which its opportunity costs are the (lowest, highest).

(LO 16.3)

5.   Nations have an incentive to specialize and trade because they have different collective tastes and because different nations will always have different _____ costs to producing goods.

6.   A nation ultimately pays for imports by _____.

(LO 16.4)

7.   There are numerous arguments against free trade; they include the _____ industry argument, and the argument that trade leads to (increased, decreased) stability as comparative advantage changes with technological changes and changes in taste.

(LO 16.5)

8.   Two ways to restrict foreign trade analyzed in the text are _____ on imports and _____ on imported goods.

9.   Most restrictions on international trade have one major element in common: they interfere with nations' ability to specialize in the production of goods for which they have a _____ advantage. Therefore they are economically (inefficient, efficient).

10.   Sometimes when a foreign firm undersells Canadian firms in the Canadian economy, they are accused of _____, a practice of selling in foreign markets at less than the _____.

11.   Because a nation ultimately pays for imports with its _____, restricting imports to save jobs destroys jobs in the _____ sector of the economy; hence, on net, import restrictions (do, do not) save jobs.

TRUE-FALSE QUESTIONS
Circle the **T** if the statement is true, the **F** if it is false. Explain to yourself why a statement is false.

(LO 16.1)

T   F   1.   If all world trade ceased, import sector jobs and export sector jobs would be permanently destroyed.

T   F   2.   Because international trade is voluntary in the private sector, both nations benefit from trade that is continued.

T   F   3.   Imports are paid for by exports.

(LO 16.2)

T   F   4.   In a two-country world, it is possible for both countries to have a comparative advantage in the production of a specific good.

T   F   5. If Canada has a comparative advantage in producing wheat, it must be true that the opportunity cost for producing wheat in Canada is below that opportunity cost in other nations.

(LO 16.3)

T   F   6. Because in the real world nations have different resource endowments and different collective tastes, trade will always be advantageous.

T   F   7. Free trade may increase a nation's instability in the short run, because over time a nation's comparative advantage can change.

(LO 16.4)

T   F   8. It is easy to determine the industries to which the infant industry argument applies.

T   F   9. When a nation restricts imports to protect jobs it, in effect, preserves less productive employment at the expense of more productive employment.

(LO 16.5)

T   F   10. In effect, a tariff makes the supply of the good in question a vertical line at a level below the original equilibrium quantity.

T   F   11. A Canadian tariff on Japanese-made goods will lead to an increase in the demand for Canadian goods that are substitutes for those Japanese-made goods.

T   F   12. Import quotas harm domestic consumers but help domestic producers of those goods on which quotas are placed.

T   F   13. Tariffs harm domestic consumers and harm domestic producers of goods that compete with the goods on which tariffs are placed.

T   F   14. A tariff on good X will cause a leftward shift of the supply of good X in the foreign country, and a rightward shift of the demand for good X in the country that imposed the tariff.

T   F   15. If a nation imposes anti-dumping laws, its consumers will pay lower prices for goods.

T   F   16. One difference between the economic effects of quotas versus tariffs is that tariffs lead to a higher price to consumers but quotas do not.

T   F   17. Tariffs increase government revenues, but import quotas do not.

MULTIPLE CHOICE QUESTIONS
Circle the letter that corresponds to the best answer.

(LO 16.1)
1. The Canadian ratio of imports to GDP is about _____ percent.
    a. 13
    b. 24
    c. 40
    d. 32

(LO 16.2)
2. Country A can produce both wheat and oranges using fewer resources than country B. Which of the following statements is true?
    a. Country A has a comparative advantage in producing both goods.
    b. Country A has an absolute advantage in producing both goods.
    c. Country B has no comparative advantage.
    d. Country B must have an absolute advantage in producing one of the goods.

3. If Country C has a comparative advantage in producing wheat, then its opportunity cost of producing wheat
    a. is maximized.
    b. equals the opportunity cost of producing other goods.
    c. cannot be determined.
    d. is lowest among its trading partners.

4. Nations find it advantageous to trade because they
    a. have different resource endowments.
    b. have different collective tastes.
    c. have different comparative advantages.
    d. All of the above

(LO 16.3)
5. A nation pays for its imports by
    a. exporting.
    b. creating money.
    c. extending credit to the exporting nation.
    d. All of the above

6. If trade between two nations is voluntary and continued, then
    a. both nations benefit.
    b. one nation could benefit more than the other.
    c. living standards are higher in both nations than if trade were not permitted.
    d. All of the above

(LO 16.4)

7. Which of the following is **NOT** an argument used against free trade?
   a. Free trade makes nations more interdependent.
   b. Free trade causes instability in a nation because a nation's comparative advantage changes over time.
   c. Free trade increases average and total worldwide incomes.
   d. Imports may destroy some domestic jobs.

8. Which statement is **NOT** true, concerning the use of import restrictions to save jobs?
   a. The cost to consumers often exceeds the value of the jobs saved.
   b. Some jobs are destroyed in the export sector.
   c. In the long run they do not save jobs in those industries in which a nation has lost its comparative advantage.
   d. They are the most efficient way to help domestic workers threatened by foreign competition.

(LO 16.5)

9. Which of the following is most unlike the others?
   a. import quota
   b. tariff
   c. free trade
   d. anti-dumping laws

10. Concerning import quotas and tariffs, which of the following statements is true?
    a. Both lead to lower prices for consumers.
    b. Both lead to more imports.
    c. Tariffs lead to higher prices, but quotas do not.
    d. Tariffs generate government revenues, but import quotas do not.

MATCHING

Choose an item in Column (2) that best matches an item in Column (1).

(1)	(2)
a. anti-dumping law	1. minimum opportunity cost of production
b. tariff	2. trade restriction
c. comparative advantage	3. tax on foreign-produced goods
d. absolute advantage	4. producing at a lower cost
	5. voluntary quota
	6. WTO

WORKING WITH GRAPHS

(LO 16.5)

1. Analyze the graph below, then answer the questions that follow. They deal with an import quota set on foreign-made sugar. Start at point A.

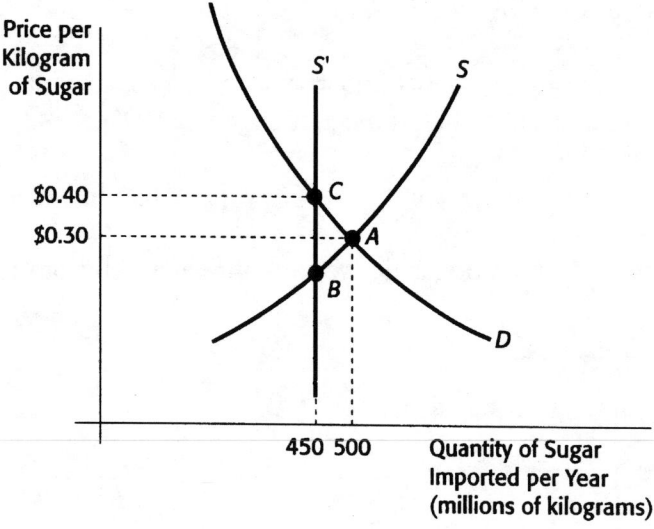

a. What is the price of sugar in this country, without the import quota?

b. What is the maximum amount of imported sugar given the quota?

c. What is the price of sugar, given the import quota?

d. What is the effective import supply curve, given the quota?

2.   Analyze the graphs below, which deal with a Canadian tariff placed on Japanese-made autos, then answer the questions that follow. Start with point A.

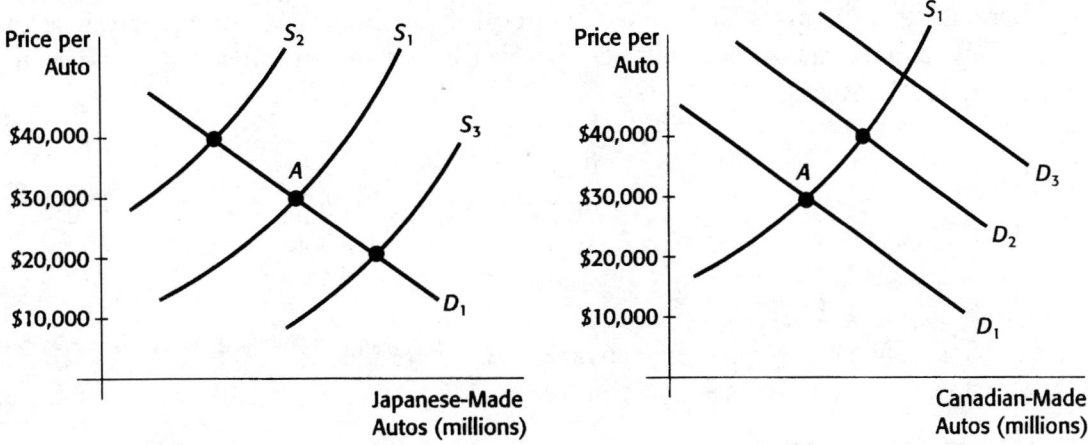

a.   What is the price of Canadian and Japanese-made autos in Canada., without the tariff?

b.   Which curve represents the supply of Japanese-made autos into Canada, after the tariff?

c.   Which curve shows the demand for Canadian-made autos in Canada, after the tariff?

d.   What is the price of autos in Canada, after the tariff is imposed?

PROBLEMS

(LO 16.3)

1.   Suppose that Germany and Canada are both fully employed and can produce the following amounts of wine and beer per week. Use this information to answer the following questions.

	Wine (litres)	Beer (litres)
Germany	600	1200
Canada	400	1600

a.   Germany has a comparative advantage in the production of _____, whereas Canada has a comparative advantage in the production of _____.

b.   What is the cost of wine in terms of beer in Germany? What is the cost of wine in terms of beer in Canada?

2.   Let us assume we are again in a two-country world, with the countries being Germany and Canada. Again, to simplify, let us assume that there are only two goods produced, coal and steel. In the table that follows, you will find the production possibilities of both countries. Assume that each country is currently operating at combination B on its production possibilities schedule. Use this information to answer the following questions. (Hint: Remember that movements along production possibilities curves involve opportunity costs and that comparative advantage and trade depend on opportunity costs.) Entries are in thousands of tonnes per week.

		A	B	C	D
Germany:	Coal	0	24	48	72
	Steel	18	12	6	0
Canada:	Coal	0	36	72	108
	Steel	36	24	12	0

a.   Which country has an *absolute* advantage in the production of coal? _____ steel? _____

b.   Which country has a *comparative* advantage in the production of coal? _____ steel? _____

c.   What is the cost of steel in terms of coal in Germany? _____
What is the cost of steel in terms of coal in Canada? _____

(Remember that these are opportunity costs as determined by production possibilities.)

d. What is the current world production of coal and steel? _____

e. If both countries specialize in the production of goods in which they have a comparative advantage, Germany will produce _____ thousand tonnes of _____, Canada will produce _____ thousand tonnes of _____, and the world output of coal will increase by _____ thousand tonnes.

Assume that at this point in the question, both Germany and Canada specialize completely in their areas of comparative advantage (as in part e. above).

The *terms of trade* equals the real rate at which one product trades for another product between nations. For both countries – Germany and Canada – to share the gain in total world output (due to specialization and trade), the terms of trade must be somewhere between each country's opportunity cost for that product. Each country's opportunity cost becomes the *"limits of the terms of trade."*

f. Find the *limits of the terms of trade* for one tonne of steel. That is, for each country – Germany and Canada - to gain from trade, one tonne of steel will have to trade at a rate somewhere between _____ tonnes of coal and _____ tonnes of coal.

g. Suppose that Germany and Canada agree to terms of trade where 1 tonne of steel trades for 3.5 tonnes of coal and that 12 tonnes of steel are traded for 42 tonnes of coal. Calculate each country's gain from specialization and trade in this transaction.

TIP: To answer this question you may find it useful to complete the following table:

Country	Outputs before Specialization	Outputs after specialization	Trade	Outputs after trade	Gains
Germany Coal Steel					
Canada Coal Steel					

After completing the table answer the following questions:

Germany's gain from this trade transaction = _____ coal and _____ steel.

Canada's gain from this trade transaction = _____ coal and _____ steel.

BUSINESS SECTION

Management and Small Business: Predicting the Effects of International Trade at the Industry Level

In Chapter 16, the text examines international trade at the world and national level. If one were in a general management position concerned with strategic planning, one would like to determine the potential effects of international trade at the industry level. If one were to extend the analysis of the theory of comparative advantage to predict the effect that trade will have on domestic industry prices, the following principles would be formulated, assuming constant costs:

- *If the domestic industry experiences an increase in imports, the industry price will decrease.*
- *If the domestic industry experiences an increase in exports, the industry price will increase.*

Business Application Problem

(LO 16.3)
The following graphs describe the hypothetical product possibility curves for Canada and the U.S. for the two products—dimension lumber (2"x4") and Concord grapes used in table wines.

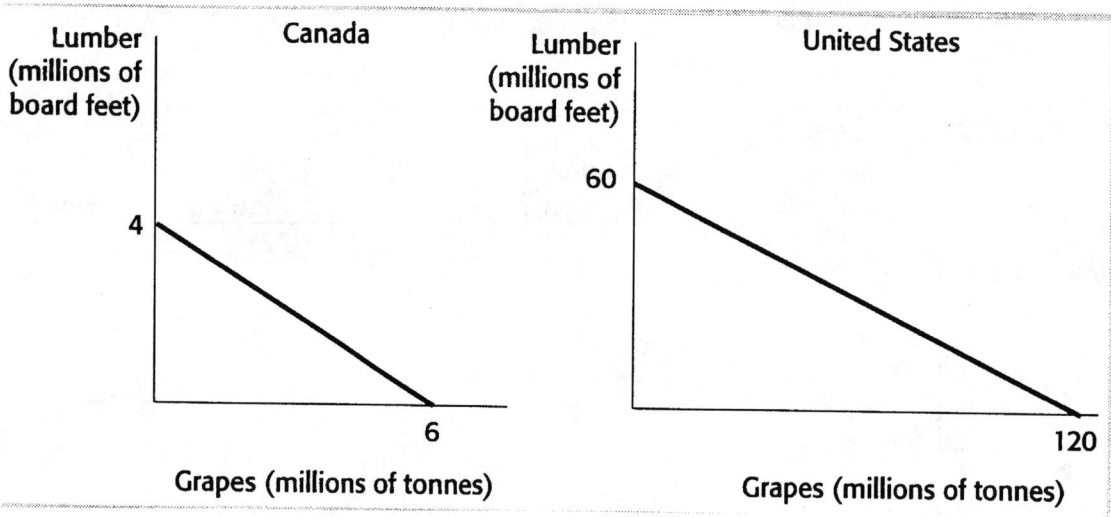

1. a. According to the theory of comparative advantage, which country should specialize and export which product?

b. After trade takes place between Canada and U.S., in which direction will the price of lumber change in the Canadian lumber market? *TIP*: base your answer on a. and the two principles outlined above.

c. In the Canadian lumber market, will international trade be beneficial to the buyers or sellers of lumber? Base your answer on the predicted price change in b.

d. After trade takes place between Canada and U.S., in which direction will the price of Concord grapes change in the Canadian grape industry? *TIP*: base your answer on a. and the two principles outlined above.

e. In the Canadian grape industry, will international trade be beneficial to the buyers or sellers of grape? Base your answer on the predicted price change in b.

f. Based on your answers above, would management in the Canadian lumber industry likely lobby for or against international trade?

g. If you were part of the upper management team in a Canadian lumber firm, what U.S. industries might you contact in order to assist you in your lobby efforts?

h. Suppose the Canadian and U.S. governments have just signed a free trade agreement involving lumber and grapes. Assuming the production possibilities described above, would it be appropriate for a small Canadian winery to proceed to expand its Canadian operations? Explain.

ANSWERS TO CHAPTER 16

COMPLETION QUESTIONS

1.   more
2.   40%
3.   would not; produce the goods themselves; fall
4.   comparative; lowest
5.   opportunity
6.   exporting
7.   infant; decreased
8.   quotas; tariffs
9.   comparative; inefficient
10.   dumping, cost of production
11.   exports; export; do not

TRUE-FALSE QUESTIONS

1.   F   Eventually each nation will produce its own goods—but at a higher cost and (perhaps) lower quality.
2.   T
3.   T
4.   F   Not for a *specific* good.
5.   T
6.   T
7.   T
8.   F   In practice it is difficult to predict which industries will eventually be successful without aid.
9.   T
10.   F   That describes the effect of an import quota.
11.   T
12.   T
13.   F   They help domestic producers of such goods.
14.   T
15.   F   Consumers will pay higher prices.
16.   F   Both lead to higher prices for consumers.
17.   T

MULTIPLE CHOICE QUESTIONS

1.c;   Canada's level of imports as a percentage of GDP is considerably higher than many of her trading partners such as the United States, Japan, Britain, France, and Germany. Since trade plays such a prominent role in Canada, it is extremely important that we are able to stay competitive on a worldwide basis.

2.b;   When one country can produce both wheat and oranges using fewer resources, this country is said to have the absolute advantage in producing both goods.
    TIP: As this chapter will illustrate, it is comparative advantage and not absolute advantage, which forms the basis of trade.
    TIP: Economists generally are in favour of international trade as it is not a zero sum game (where with goods, one country's gain is the result of another country's loss). Instead, trade can be a "win-win" situation from a national viewpoint.

3.d;   If Country C has a comparative advantage in producing wheat this means that its opportunity cost of producing wheat is lower than its trading partner. In turn, world production can be increased if Country C specializes and exports wheat.

4.d;   To the extent that resource endowments differ between nations, these nations will have different opportunity costs of production for different goods. Different collective tastes reinforce the need to produce a variety of goods with differing opportunity costs. All of these factors help explain the rapid increase in world trade witnessed in the 20th century.

5.a; The reason imports are ultimately paid for by exports is that foreigners want something in exchange for the goods that are shipped to Canada.

TIP: A country could pay for its imports by selling off some of its own assets or by going further into debt. However, these methods of financing imports are short term in nature. The only viable long-term way of ensuring a consistent flow of imports is by continually being able to export goods and services.

6.d; From a rational view point, if two countries engage in trade voluntarily on a continued basis, then this activity must be mutually beneficial.

7.c; This option is clearly a strong argument in favour of trade.

8.d; From a long-run viewpoint, the most efficient way to promote employment in the domestic economy threatened by global competition is to encourage employees to work in industries in which Canada has a comparative advantage. Protectionist tactics such as import restrictions may serve as an obstacle to international competitiveness.

9.c; All of the other answer options relate to trade barriers, in some way. Import quotas directly restrict the physical quantity of imports. Tariffs indirectly serve as a trade barrier, by taxing imports. Anti-dumping laws restrict a country from exporting goods at a price below its cost of production.

10.d; Both quotas and tariffs lead to higher consumer prices. However, since tariffs are taxes on imports, they will increase government revenues. Import quotas will not increase government tax revenues.

MATCHING

a and 2;   b and 3;   c and 1;   d and 4.

WORKING WITH GRAPHS

1. a.   30 cents per kilogram
    b.   450 million kilogram
    c.   40 cents per kilogram
    d.   The same as the regular supply curve up to 450 million kilograms; vertical from that point on.
2. a. $30 000 per auto.
    b.   S2
    c.   D2
    d. $40 000 per auto.

PROBLEMS

1. a.   Germany = wine, Canada = beer
    b.   1 litre wine = 2 litres beer; 1 litre wine = 4 litres beer
2. a.   Canada, Canada
    b.   Germany, Canada
    c.   Germany: 1 tonnes steel = 4 tonnes coal; Canada: 1 tonnes steel = 3 tonnes coal
    d.   60 000 tonnes coal; 36 000 tonnes steel
    e.   Germany = 72, coal; Canada = 36, steel, 12
    f.   Between 3 tonnes and 4 tonnes of coal
    g.   Germany gains 6 tonnes coal and no gain in steel
         Canada gains 6 tonnes coal and no gain in steel

BUSINESS SECTION

1. a.   Based on opportunity cost calculations, Canada has the comparative advantage in lumber, so Canada should export lumber and import wine. The U.S. has the comparative advantage in wine and therefore should export wine and import lumber.
    b.   Since lumber will be a Canadian export, the price of lumber will increase in Canada after trade takes place.

c.   The Canadian sellers of lumber (lumber companies) will benefit as the price of Canadian lumber is predicted to increase.

d.   Since grapes will be a Canadian import, the price of grapes in Canada will decrease after trade takes place.

e.   The Canadian buyers of grapes will benefit as the price of grapes decreases due to trade.

f.   Since trade will increase the price of Canadian lumber in Canada, management in the Canadian lumber industry would lobby in favour of trade.

g.   As part of the management team, I would contact the U.S. homebuilders association who are buyers of the lumber in the U.S. This is because trade would result in lower prices of lumber in the U.S. (lumber being an import in the U.S.)

h.   Yes it would be appropriate. Since, under free trade, grapes would be imported into Canada, this would reduce the price of grapes. In turn, this would reduce the costs of operating a Canadian winery and enhance the profit prospects.

EXCHANGE RATES AND THE BALANCE OF PAYMENTS

PUTTING THIS CHAPTER INTO PERSPECTIVE

Chapter 17 is the second of two chapters on international economics. Chapter 16 discussed why trade arises between nations, the various arguments against free international trade, and the various restrictions on such trade. Chapter 17 is concerned with how trade between nations is financed. The summary that follows below is somewhat long, but well worth the effort to learn. It is, we hope, a rigorous and thorough perspective on this chapter.

For simplicity let's assume a two-country world in which residents of one nation transact with residents of the other nation in three ways. First, they sell (export) to and buy (import) from each other; second, they lend to or borrow from each other; and third, they give gifts to or receive gifts from each other. When a nation exports goods and services to, borrows from, and receives gifts from another country, it (in effect) receives the other country's currency. In contrast, when a nation imports from, lends to, or gives gifts to another country, it (in effect) surrenders its own currency to the other country.

If the value of country A's exports exceeds the value of its imports, then A's balance of trade is a positive number. (Most people would refer to this as a trade surplus.) If the value of its exports is less than the value of its imports, then A's balance of trade is a negative number (also referred to as a trade deficit). In a two-country world, by definition, the other country, B, has a positive balance of trade if A has a negative balance of trade. (B has a trade surplus if A has a trade deficit.)

If the value of the goods and services that A exports plus the value of private and government gifts it receives from B exceed the value of the goods and services that it imports plus the value of private and government gifts it gives to B, then B will have a negative balance on current account and A will have a positive balance on current account.

Countries A and B also transact by direct investments (purchases) of each other's financial assets and by lending to and borrowing from each other. If the value of A's direct investments in B's financial assets plus the value of its loans to B exceed the value of B's investments in A and B's loans to A (A's borrowings from B), then A's balance on capital account will be a negative number and B's balance on capital account, by definition, will be a positive number.

If governments did not enter the picture, then, if A's current account were negative, its capital account would be positive and exactly offsetting. And, by definition, B's current account would be positive and its capital account would be negative and exactly offsetting. In other words, if the residents in A buy more from and give more to B than B buys from and gives to A, then B must "finance" this activity by acquiring A's assets or by lending to A. In the process for each nation the sum of its balance on current account and its balance on capital account is zero.

Once government gets into the act, however, all bets are off. Governments, by mutual agreement, can permit country A to have a negative current account and a negative capital account. (A can be a big spender, a big donor, and a big lender!) This is accomplished through official (government) transactions that, in effect, finance such activities. By definition, if the sum of A's current account balance plus its capital account balance is non-zero, then the value of official transactions will be that number that makes that sum equal to zero.

Note that all of the above is definitional. That does not mean that negative or positive numbers for the current account plus capital account sum can persist indefinitely; eventually an equilibrium in the balance of payments must prevail. If governments do not intervene, forces will be set in motion that see to it that eventually the value of what residents of one nation buy from, give to, and lend to other nations (the other nation in our simple two-country model) will roughly be equal to the value of what those same residents sell to, receive from, and borrow from other nations. Exactly what those forces are depends on what the particular international financial structure is, which is the subject of the second major section of Chapter 17.

Assume, for simplicity, that no government transactions exist. When residents of country A sell (export) goods and services to, receive gifts from, and borrow from residents in country B, then country A receives B's currency, which it supplies on the foreign exchange market because residents of country A ultimately demand their own currency. Thus such activities lead, simultaneously, to a supply of B's currency and a demand for A's currency.

When residents of country A buy (import) goods and services, give gifts to, and lend to residents in country B, then B's residents take A's currency and supply it to foreign exchange markets, because B's residents demand their own currency. Thus, when A's residents import, give gifts, and lend to foreigners (in B), these actions lead, simultaneously, to a demand for B's currency and a supply of A's currency.

In short, when residents of A and B interact economically, a supply of and a demand for each country's currency automatically arises. And foreign exchange markets reflect such supply and demand conditions.

Assume that the sum of A's current account plus its capital account is a negative number and that, therefore, the sum of B's current account plus its capital account is a positive number. This means that there will be an excess demand for (shortage of) B's currency and (by definition) a surplus of A's currency. Under a flexible exchange rate international payments system in which the forces of supply and demand prevail unhindered in the foreign exchange marketplace, B's currency will appreciate and A's currency will depreciate. In other words, it will take more units of A's currency to equal one unit of B's currency. This change in the exchange rate will induce residents in country A to import less from, give less to, and lend less to residents in B; and it will induce residents in country B to import more from, give more to, and lend more to residents in A. Thus, a change in the exchange rate will occur until residents of each nation voluntarily behave so as to generate a current account plus capital account sum that is roughly equal to zero. Thus exchange rates will adjust until a payments equilibrium exists.

What if the world is on a gold standard and the sum of A's current account plus its capital account is negative? Then A will pay for its "excess spending" with gold; gold flows from A to B. A's price level (and national income level) falls relative to B's, because gold and currencies are exchangeable under such a system. The results are the same as under the other fixed exchange rate system analyzed in the previous paragraph; under a gold standard gold flows occur (if disequilibrium exists) until relative price levels change sufficiently to create a balance of payments equilibrium.

LEARNING OBJECTIVES

After you have studied this chapter you should be able to:

17.1   Distinguish between the balance of trade and the balance of payments.

17.2   Identify the key accounts within the balance of payments.

17.3   Outline how exchange rates are determined in the markets for foreign exchange.

17.4   Discuss factors that can induce changes in equilibrium exchange rates.

17.5   Outline how policy makers can go about attempting to fix exchange rates.

17.6   Explain alternative approaches to limiting exchange rate variability.

CHAPTER OUTLINE

LO 17.1 Distinguish between the balance of trade and the balance of payments.

1. A **balance of trade** reflects the difference between the value of a nation's merchandise exports and its merchandise imports; the **balance of payments** reflects all economic transactions between a nation and the rest of the world.

LO 17.2 Identify the key accounts within the balance of payments.

2. The balance of payments is calculated as follows:
    a. The current account balance equals the sum of (1) the balance of trade, (2) the balance of services, (3) investment income, and (4) transfers (private gifts and government grants). If the current account balance is negative, a current account deficit exists; if it is positive, a current account surplus exists.
    b. Capital account transactions consist of direct investment purchases in financial assets among countries and loans to and from foreigners. If the capital account is a negative number, a capital account deficit exists; if it is positive, a capital account surplus exists.
    c. If the sum of a nation's current account and its capital account is negative, that nation has an international payments disequilibrium (deficit) that must be financed by official (government) reserve account transactions; of course, another nation must have an international payments surplus.
        i.   Official reserve account transactions include sales or purchases of foreign currencies, gold, special drawing rights, the reserve position in the International Monetary Fund, and financial assets held by official government agencies.
        ii. Official transactions must exactly equal (but be of opposite sign to) the balance of payments.

LO 17.3 Outline how exchange rates are determined in the markets for foreign exchange.

3. Under a **flexible exchange rate** system of international payments, exchange rates between nations are determined by the forces of supply and demand.
    a. When Canadian residents import a foreign good or service, this leads to a supply of dollars and a demand for foreign currency on **foreign exchange markets**.
    b. When Canadian residents export goods and services to a foreign country, this leads to a supply of foreign currency and a demand for dollars.
    c. The equilibrium exchange rate is determined in the same way that the equilibrium price for anything is established.
        i.   The Canadian demand curve for (say) French francs is negatively sloped; as the dollar price of the franc falls—it takes fewer dollars to purchase a given quantity of francs—the quantity demanded for francs, by Canadian residents, rises.
        ii. The Canadian demand for francs is a derived demand; we demand French francs because we demand French goods and services.
        iii. The French supply francs because they want (say) Canadian goods and services; as the dollar price of francs rises—it takes fewer francs to purchase

one dollar—the French will increase their quantity supplied of francs in order to purchase more Canadian goods.

iv. The equilibrium dollar price per franc is established at the intersection of the Canadian demand for francs curve and the French supply of francs curve; the equilibrium franc price per dollar is automatically determined thereby.

LO 17.4 Discuss factors that can induce changes in equilibrium exchange rates.

4. Factors that can cause the exchange rate to change are:
   a. If Canadian residents experience a change in tastes in favour of French goods, the demand for francs will increase. The dollar price of francs rises and the franc price of dollars falls; the dollar depreciates and the franc appreciates.
   b. Other determinants of exchange rates include (relative) changes in real interest rates, changes in productivity, changes in tastes, and perceptions of economic stability.

LO 17.5 Outline how policy makers can go about attempting to fix exchange rates.

5. Under a **gold standard**, each nation fixes its exchange rate in terms of gold; therefore all exchange rates are fixed. Under the pure gold standard, each nation would have to abandon an independent monetary policy; each nation's money supply would automatically change whenever a balance of payments disequilibrium occurred.

6. In 1944, representatives of the world's capitalist nations met in Bretton woods to create a new international payments system to replace the gold standard that had collapsed in the 1930's.
   a. The **International Monetary Fund (IMF)** was established in 1944; the IMF established a system of fixed exchange rates and a means to lend foreign exchange to deficit nations.
   b. Member governments were obligated to intervene in foreign exchange markets, to maintain the values of their currencies within 1 percent of the declared **par value**.
   c. In 1967, the IMF created **Special Drawing Rights (SDR's)**, a new type of international money exchange (only) between monetary authorities.
   d. In the early 1970's, Canada, The United States and Europe went off the Bretton Woods system.

LO 17.6 Explain alternative approaches to limiting exchange rate variability.

7. Between a flexible exchange rate system and a fixed exchange rate is a "**dirty float**," or a managed exchange rate system, in which governments (through their central banks) intervene in foreign exchange markets in order to affect the short-term price of currencies. This is common in the current world monetary system.

KEY TERMS AND KEY CONCEPTS

Flexible exchange rates
Foreign exchange market
Foreign exchange rate
Appreciation
Depreciation
Dirty float
Accounting identities
Hedge
Target Zone

International Monetary Fund (IMF)
Gold standard
Balance of trade
Balance of payments
Special drawing rights (SDRs)
Par value
Foreign Exchange Risk
Crawling Peg

COMPLETION QUESTIONS

Fill in the blank or circle the correct term.

(LO 17.1)

1.   If the value of Canadian imports exceeds the value of its exports, the Canadian balance of trade will be a (negative, positive) number, and another country's balance of trade must be a _____ number; then Canada is said to have a trade (deficit, surplus), while the other nation has a trade _____.

(LO 17.2)

2.   If governments do not intervene, by definition the sum of a nation's balance on current account plus its balance on capital account will equal _____; if governments intervene in the balance of payments process, then the sum of a nation's balance on current account plus its balance on capital account must exactly _____, but be of opposite sign to, its official transactions.

3.   Official reserve account transactions involve the following assets of individual countries: _____, _____, _____, _____, and _____.

4.   A nation's balance of payments is affected by, among other things, relative changes in that nation's _____, and _____.

(LO 17.3)

5.   If the value of a nation's exports is less than the value of its imports, it is running a trade _____; its currency will (depreciate, appreciate) under a flexible exchange rate system.

6.   When Canadians wish to import French-made goods, they supply _____ to the foreign exchange market and demand _____ on that market; when the French wish to import Canadian-

made goods, they supply _____ and demand _____ on the foreign exchange market.

7. In a flexible exchange rate system, exchange rates are determined by (governments, supply and demand); if the exchange rate goes from 25 cents per franc to 50 cents per franc, the dollar has (appreciated, depreciated) and the franc has _____ .

8. If the franc depreciates, it takes (fewer, more) francs to purchase a dollar; this leads to a(n) (increase, decrease) in the quantity demanded of francs by Canadians and a(n) (increase, decrease) in the quantity supplied of francs by the French.

(LO 17.4)
9. If Canadian tastes move in favour of French goods, there will be a(n) _____ in the demand for francs; other things being constant, the franc will (appreciate, depreciate) on the foreign exchange market. This eventually will induce Canadians to export (less, more) to the French and import _____ from the French.

(LO 17.5)
10. Under a pure gold standard, exchange rates (float, are fixed).

(LO 17.6)
11. When nations intervene in foreign exchange markets in order to affect exchange rates, a freely floating exchange rate system becomes a _____ float.

TRUE-FALSE QUESTIONS
Circle the **T** if the statement is true, the **F** if it is false. Explain to yourself why a statement is false.

(LO 17.2)
T F   1. In today's world, the sum of a nation's current account balance plus its capital account balance must be zero.

T F   2. If one nation has a current account deficit, another nation must have a current account surplus.

T F   3. A nation can finance a current account deficit with a capital account surplus.

(LO 17.3)
T F   4. If you wish to buy German goods, you ultimately offer dollars and demand German currency.

T F   5. If you wish to send money to your relatives in England, you ultimately offer dollars and demand English currency.

T   F   6.   In a flexible exchange rate system, gold flows lead to international payments equilibrium.

T   F   7.   Under a flexible exchange rate system, if disequilibrium exists in the world's balance of payments, exchange rates will change until payments equilibrium is restored.

T   F   8.   Under a flexible exchange rate system, each nation must give up control over its own monetary policy.

(LO 17.4)

T   F   9.   If French tastes move in favour of Canadian goods, the supply of dollars on the foreign exchange market rises relative to the demand for dollars.

T   F   10.   The Canadian demand for French francs rises if the French inflation rate exceeds the Canadian inflation rate.

T   F   11.   In a flexible exchange rate system, if French tastes move away from Canadian goods (other things being constant), both the dollar and the franc will depreciate.

(LO 17.5)

T   F   12.   The gold standard is one form of fixed exchange rate system.

T   F   13.   Under the gold standard, if disequilibrium exists in the world's balance of payments, gold will flow from one nation to another until payments equilibrium is restored.

T   F   14.   Under a flexible exchange rate system, payments equilibrium is brought about by a change in the exchange rate; under a gold standard, national price levels change to restore payments equilibrium.

(LO 17.6)

T   F   15.   A dirty float results because nations do not want to pay the price of adjusting to a balance of payments disequilibrium.

MULTIPLE CHOICE QUESTIONS
Circle the letter that corresponds to the best answer.

(LO 17.2)

1.   A nation can finance a deficit on its current account with
   a.   a surplus on its capital account.
   b.   a deficit on its capital account.
   c.   official purchases of foreign currencies with its own currency.
   d.   purchases of gold from foreign countries with its own currency.

2. If a nation has a deficit on both its current account and its capital account, then
   a. it is in a balance of payments equilibrium.
   b. the world must be on a flexible exchange rate system.
   c. it must have official transactions that are identical to (but opposite in sign to) the sum of those two deficits.
   d. it will experience gold inflows.

3. A nation's balance of payments is affected by its relative
   a. interest rate.
   b. political stability.
   c. inflation rate.
   d. All of the above

(LO 17.3)
4. If the foreign exchange rate is that $1 is equivalent to 5 francs, then 1 franc is worth
   a. $5.
   b. 50 cents.
   c. 20 cents.
   d. 5 cents.

5. The demand schedule for francs on the foreign exchange market
   a. is derived partially from foreign demand for French goods.
   b. reflects the fact that the French want to import goods and services.
   c. shows the quantity demanded for francs at different income levels.
   d. is unimportant if France is on a fixed exchange rate system.

6. Which of the following does not lead to an increase in the demand for French francs?
   a. A worldwide change in tastes in favour of French goods occurs.
   b. The French inflation rate exceeds the world inflation rate.
   c. France's interest rate rises relative to world rates.
   d. World real income rises.

7. Which of the following leads to an increase in the demand for the Canadian dollar on the foreign exchange market?
   a. an increase in Canadian exports
   b. an increase in foreign investment in Canada
   c. an increase in gifts from foreigners to Canadian residents
   d. All of the above

8. If a nation has an international payments surplus in a flexible exchange rate system, then
   a. its currency will appreciate.
   b. its price level will rise.
   c. gold will flow from it to nations with a payments surplus.
   d. All of the above

9. Which of the following statements is not true?
    a. Under flexible exchange rates, international payments equilibrium is restored through changes in exchange rates.
    b. Under a gold standard, international payments equilibrium is restored through changes in national price levels.
    c. Under a flexible exchange rate system, a nation cannot pursue a monetary policy that is independent of its trading partners.
    d. Under the gold standard, international payments disequilibrium leads to gold flows, which restore equilibrium.

10. If France has a payments deficit, payments equilibrium can be restored if France's
    a. price level rises relative to the world's.
    b. interest rate rises relative to the world's.
    c. real national income rises relative to the world's.
    d. money supply rises relative to the world's.

(LO 17.6)
11. The dirty float
    a. has emerged in recent years because nations want less flexible exchange rates.
    b. makes fixed exchange rates more flexible.
    c. is common under a gold standard.
    d. is favored over a pure float by people who want their nation to have a monetary policy independent of its trading partners.

MATCHING
Choose an item in Column (2) that best matches an item in Column (1).

(1)	(2)
a. appreciation	1. managed float
b. depreciation	2. fall in one currency's value relative to another's
c. fixed exchange rate system	3. balance of payments settlements
d. special drawing right	4. gold standard
e. trade deficit	5. value of exports exceeds value of imports
	6. rise in one currency's value relative to another's
	7. floating exchange rates

WORKING WITH GRAPHS

(LO 17.3)
1. Consider a situation in which exchange rates are flexible. Consumers in Canada wish to import a good from Germany.

a. Calculate the Canadian price of this good, given the German price of the good and the different exchange rates that might prevail as listed in the table below, and place these calculations in the appropriate column. Calculate the quantity of euros demanded by Canadian consumers in order to purchase the import good at different exchange rates. Enter these numbers in the last column.

Exchange rate ($/euro)	German price of the good	Canadian price of the good	Quantity demanded	Total Canadian DM expenditures
1.20/1	1 euro	_____	90	_____
1.40/1	1 euro	_____	80	_____
1.60/1	1 euro	_____	70	_____
1.80/1	1 euro	_____	60	_____
2.00/1	1 euro	_____	50	_____

By looking at the table above, one can conclude that as it takes more dollars to purchase one euro; therefore, the dollar price of the import good will _____.

b. In the table above, you are given the quantity of the import good at different prices. Graph the demand for euros on the grid provided below.

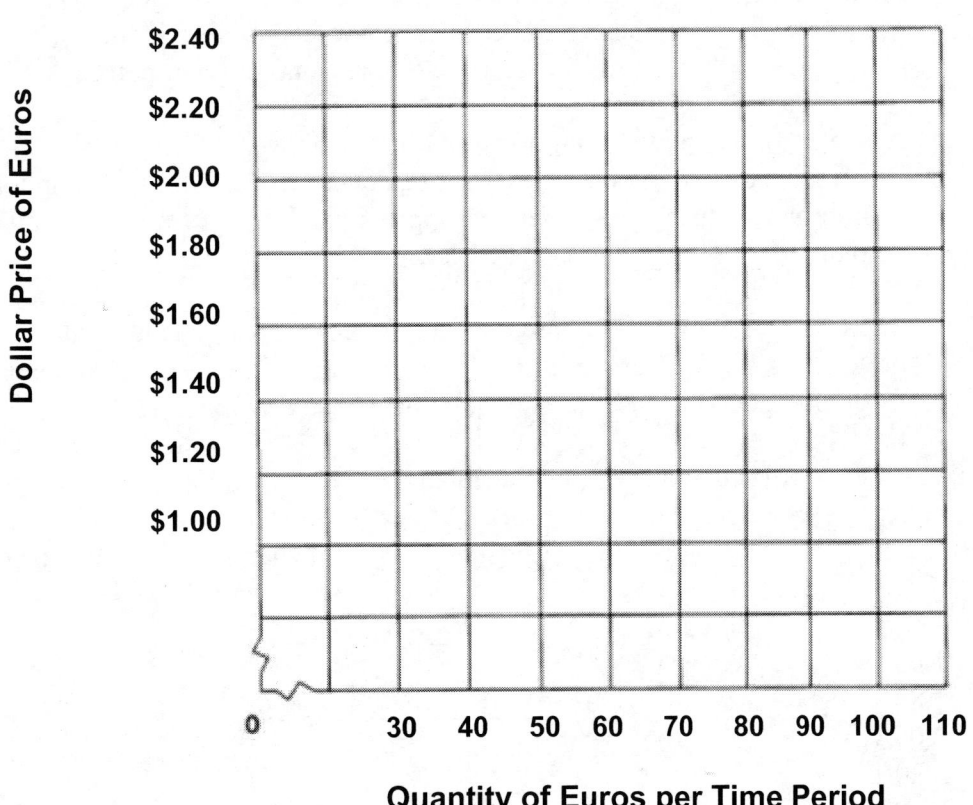

Quantity of Euros per Time Period

c. Let us now assume that people in Germany wish to import from Canada some good that costs $1 per unit. Calculate the German price of the good given the Canadian price and the different exchange rates that might prevail, as listed in the table below, and place these numbers in the appropriate column.

Exchange rate ($/euro)	Canadian price of the good	German price of the good	Quantity demanded	Total German $ expenditures
1.20/1	$1	_____	36.1	_____
1.40/1	$1	_____	70.4	_____
1.60/1	$1	_____	111.1	_____
1.80/1	$1	_____	160.7	_____
2.00/1	$1	_____	220.0	_____

By looking at the above table, one can conclude that as it takes more dollars to purchase 1 euro; therefore, the euro price of the good will _____.

d. In the last table, you are given the quantity of the import good that German consumers wish to purchase at different German prices. Use this information to calculate the quantity of euros that German consumers will be willing to supply at different exchange rates in order to import the Canadian good. (Note: Round off to the nearest whole number.) Enter these numbers in the last column. Graph the supply of euros on the same grid as your graph of part b.

e. Assume for simplicity that the only trade between Canada and Germany involves the two goods discussed above. Under this assumption, the equilibrium exchange rate will be approximately _____ dollars per euro or _____ euros per dollar.

f. Suppose that now Canadian consumers undergo a change in tastes and preferences for the German import good. As a result, the Canadian demand for the import good increases as shown in the table below.

Exchange rate ($/euro)	German price of the good	Canadian price of the good	Quantity demanded	Total Canadian euro expenditures
1.40/1	1 euro	_____	110	_____
1.60/1	1 euro	_____	100	_____
1.80/1	1 euro	_____	90	_____
2.00/1	1 euro	_____	80	_____
2.20/1	1 euro	_____	70	_____
2.40/1	1 euro	_____	60	_____

Enter in the last column the quantity of euros now demanded by Canadian consumers for use in purchasing the German import good. Graph the new demand for euros on the same grid provided for part b.

The new equilibrium exchange rate will be approximately _____ dollars per euro, or _____ euros per dollar. As a result of the increase in the Canadian demand for German imports, with all else constant, the dollar will _____ and the euro will _____ .

g. Now consider the above problem assuming that the exchange rate was fixed at $1.60/euro. When Canadian demand for German goods increased, Canada would have purchased _____ units and paid a total of $_____ for German imports. The Germans would have bought _____ units from Canada and paid a total of $_____ for Canadian exports. As a result, Canada would have lost $_____ , or approximately _____ euros, in foreign exchange.

2.   The figure below shows the supply of, and the demand for, British pounds, as a function of the exchange rate—expressed in Canadian dollars per pound. Assume that Britain and Canada are the only two countries in the world.

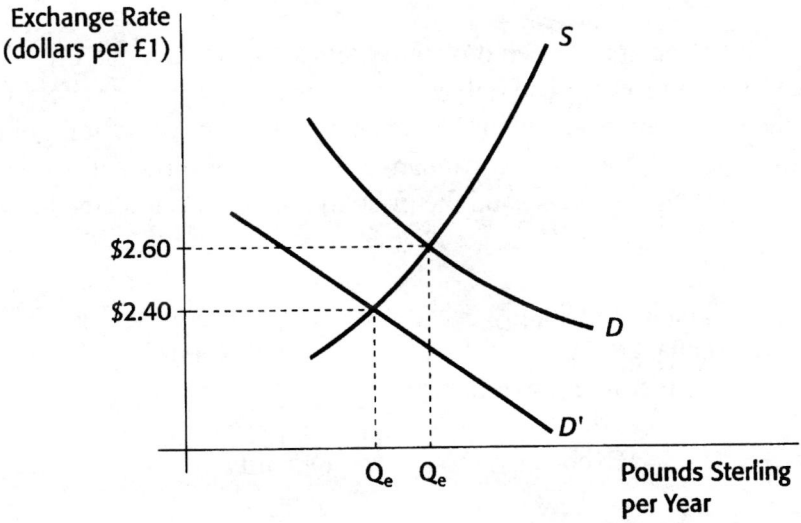

a. How might the shift from D to D' be accounted for?

b. Given the shift from D to D', what exists at $2.60 = #1?

c. Will the pound now appreciate or depreciate?

PROBLEMS

(LO 17.2)

1.   Below are balance-of-payments figures for Pleasureland during 2004. (All figures are in billions of dollars.)

Allocations of special drawing rights	$ 710
Balance on the capital account	-3 507
Foreign official assets	10 475
Errors and omissions	-1 879
Balance on the current account	-5 795
Pleasureland official assets	-4

a.   The official settlement balance was (+/–) _____ $_____.

b.   The official reserve transactions were

   (1) the sum of $_____, _____, and _____

   (2) totalled (+/–) _____ $_____

(LO 17.3)

2.   Suppose both France and Canada had been on a pure gold standard; and the French government had been willing to buy and sell gold at a price of 140 euros for an ounce of gold, and the Canadian government had been willing to buy and sell gold at a price of $35 an ounce. In the foreign exchange markets the price of a euro would have been $_____ and the price of a dollar would have been _____ euros.

3.   Below are hypothetical demand and supply schedules for the euro during a week. (The quantities of euros demanded and supplied are measured in millions and the exchange rate for the euro is measured in dollars.)

Quantity Demanded	Exchanged Rate	Quantity Supplied
100	$1.90	570
200	1.80	520
300	1.70	460
400	1.60	400
500	1.50	330
600	1.40	260
700	1.30	180

a.   The equilibrium exchange rate for the euro is $_____; and at this equilibrium the rate of exchange for the dollar is _____ euros.

b.   At the equilibrium exchange rate:

(1) _____ million euros are demanded and supplied each week.

(2) _____ million dollars are bought and sold each week.

c. If the European central bank wished to peg the exchange rate for the euro at:

(1) $1.70 it would have to (buy/sell) (how many) _____ million euros for dollars each week.

(2) $1.50 it would have to (buy/sell) (how many) _____ million euros for dollars each week.

(LO 17.4)

4. Which of the following will cause the yen to appreciate?

a. Canadian real incomes increase relative to Japanese real incomes.

b. It is expected that in the future the yen will depreciate relative to the dollar.

c. The Canadian inflation rate rises relative to the Japanese inflation rate.

d. The after-tax, risk-adjusted real interest rate in Canada rises relative to that in Japan.

e. Canadian tastes change in favour of Japanese-made goods.

(LO 17.2)

5. If you were to examine a nation's balance of payments in more depth, you would often find two revealing accounts in the Capital Account section. The first, called Foreign Direct Investment, summarizes the degree to which foreign direct control of domestic companies (and domestic control of foreign companies) changed during the year through the purchase and sale of majority shareholdings. The second account, referred to as Portfolio Investment, monitors the annual sale and purchases of bonds (and minority shares) between the domestic economy and other countries.

Consider the following hypothetical data for the nation of Palmania during 2004. Figures are in millions of dollars. Palmania's currency, the "PAL" is currently trading for $2.00.

Service Imports	-40,949
Net Portfolio Investment	18 462
Merchandise Exports	217 854
Net Transfers	979
Service Exports	31 519
Net Official Transactions (Reserves)	???
Other Capital Flows	494

Net Direct Investment	-1 713
Net Investment Income	-28 895
Merchandise Imports	-202 807

a. Calculate Palmania's Current Account balance. Also indicate whether Palmania has a Current Account surplus or deficit during 2004.

b. Calculate Palmania's Capital Account balance. Also indicate whether Palmania has a Capital Account surplus or deficit during 2004.

c. During 2004, does the Capital Account indicate that Palmania attracted capital inflows due to large increases in foreign ownership and control of Palmania's companies or due to large increases in foreign investor purchase of Palmania's bonds?

d. Can you hypothesize a relation between the surplus on the Net Portfolio Investment account and the deficit on the Net Investment Income account? Explain. What is the large deficit on the Net Investment Income account doing to the PAL exchange rate?

e. Overall, during 2004, Palmania incurred a balance of payments (surplus/deficit) equal to _____.

f. Based on your answer to e. above, briefly explain what actions the Palmanian government took, if any, to affect the PAL exchange rate during 2004.

BUSINESS SECTION

Marketing: Exchange Rates and the Marketing Mix

Recall that a firm's marketing mix refers to the 4 P's – product, price, place, and promotion. In an open economy such as Canada, the exchange rate trend may warrant a modification of a firm's marketing mix as the next example illustrates.

Business Application Problem

(LO 17.3 and LO 17.4)

The Devonshire Hotel, a three-star hotel situated in a major Eastern Canadian city, is just completing major renovations on its rooms, restaurants and large pub. This hotel traditionally has promoted and catered to primarily Canadian tourists and Canadian companies. During the past two years the Canadian dollar has depreciated significantly relative to the U.S. dollar. Due to the renovations the marketing director of the Devonshire Hotel is in the process of reviewing the hotel's marketing mix. How might the marketing director modify the marketing mix in response to the weak Canadian dollar? Be specific as possible in making suggestions for:

1.   a. Product policies

       b, Price policies

       c. Promotion policies

       d. Place policies

ANSWERS TO CHAPTER 17

COMPLETION QUESTIONS

1.   negative; positive; deficit; surplus
2.   zero; equal
3.   foreign currencies; gold; SDRs; reserve position in the IMF; any financial asset held by an official government agency
4.   inflation rate; political stability
5.   deficit; depreciate;
6.   dollars; francs; francs; dollars
7.   supply and demand; depreciated; appreciated
8.   more; increase; decrease
9.   increase; appreciate; more; less
10.   are fixed
11.   dirty

TRUE-FALSE QUESTIONS

1.   F   In today's world, nations intervene in exchange markets; hence international settlements among governments are necessary.
2.   T
3.   T
4.   T
5.   T
6.   F   Changes in exchange rates lead to payments equilibrium.
7.   T
8.   F   Floating exchange rate systems permit an independent monetary policy.
9.   F   The demand for dollars rises relative to the supply of dollars, because the French want to buy relatively more Canadian goods.
10. F   Canadians will demand fewer francs because French goods are now relatively higher priced.
11. F   The dollar will depreciate relative to the franc; the franc therefore must appreciate relative to the dollar.
12. T
13. T
14. T
15. T

MULTIPLE CHOICE QUESTIONS

1.a;   A surplus on the capital account will provide the inflow of foreign currency, which will "finance" the current account deficit.
TIP:A surplus on the capital account may be due to an inflow of funds from foreign investor purchases of domestic stocks, bonds, short-term accounts, and so forth.

2.c;   In general, the net balances on all the accounts in the balance of payments must add up to zero. If both the current and the capital accounts are in deficit position, this must be totally offset by a positive entry in the official transaction account.

3.d;   Relative interest rates, political stability, and inflation rates all affect exports and import transactions in the current account or the capital account or both. Therefore, each of these factors will affect the nation's balance of payments.

4.c;   One franc is worth (1/5) = .2 or 20 cents
TIP: Based on this formula, you can see that when the franc appreciates relative to the dollar, this means that the dollar depreciates relative to the franc.

5.a;   In other words, in order for foreigners to buy French goods, they must first purchase French francs in the currency exchange markets (banks) to buy the French goods.
TIP: The derived demand concept helps to explain the downward-sloping demand curve for francs. As the franc depreciates, foreigners find it cheaper to buy French goods, so the quantity of francs demanded increases.

6.b;   If the French inflation rate exceeds the world inflation rate, then French-made goods become more expensive to buy relative to goods produced in other countries. Hence, the demand for French-made goods will decline, resulting in an decrease in demand for francs.

7.d;   Since each transaction listed represents a "receipt" by Canadian residents and corporations, each transaction will result in an increase in the demand for the Canadian dollar.

8.a;   An international payments surplus means that, overall, exports exceeded imports on all accounts. Therefore, the demand for the currency exceeds the supply, resulting in an appreciation of the currency.
TIP: International deficits will have the opposite effect – cause the currency to deprecate.

9.c;   One key advantage of a flexible exchange rate system is that the nation can pursue monetary policy that is independent of its trading partners (different from a fixed exchange rate system).

10.b; If France raises its interest rates above the world rates, foreign investors will increase the demand for the high interest rate French bonds. The resulting capital inflow will tend to lead to a capital account surplus, which will tend to eliminate a balance of payments deficit.

11.a; The dirty float is a policy by which the government "manages" the daily fluctuations in the exchange rate. In other words, the currency is allowed to fluctuate, but the government will intervene to avoid disruptive, large swings in the exchange rate. This implies a system of less flexible exchange rates.

MATCHING

a and 6;   b and 2;   c and 4;   d and 3;   e and 5.

WORKING WITH GRAPHS

1. a. Canadian prices of the good: 1.20, 1.40, 1.60, 1.80, 2.00. Total Canadian euro expenditures: 90, 80, 70, 60, 50; be higher in Canadian dollars

    b.

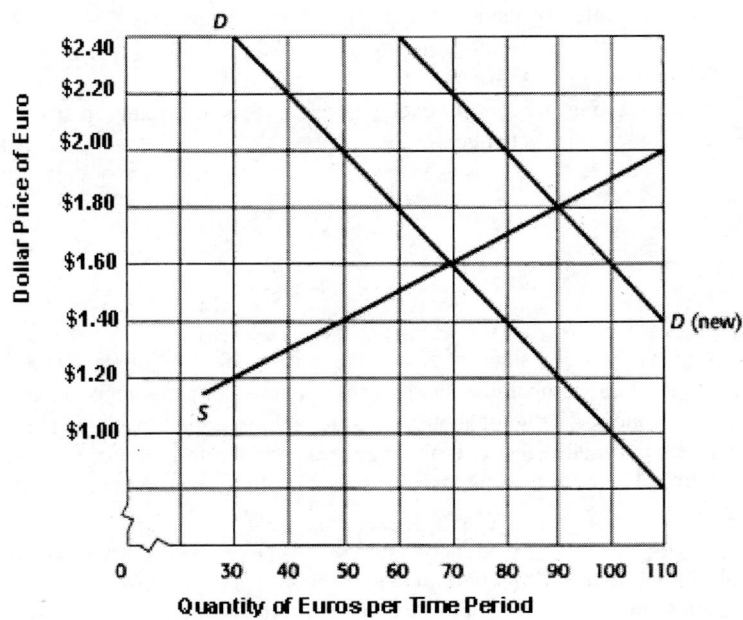

    c. German prices of the good: 0.83, 0.71, 0.63, 0.56, 0.50; be lower in euros
    d. Total German expenditures in euro: 30, 50, 70, 90, 110. See graph.
    e. 1.60, 0.63
    f. Total Canadian euro expenditures: 120, 110, 100, 90, 80. See graph. 1.80, 0.56; depreciate, appreciate
    g. 100 units, $160; 111.1 units, $111.1; 48.9 (or $160 - $111.1), 30.6 (48.9 ÷ $1.60).
2. a. A decrease in the demand for British pounds will occur if world tastes change away from British-made goods, the British price level rises relative to the world's, world income falls relative to British income, and/or British interest rates fall relative to world interest rates, among other reasons.
    b. A surplus of British pounds, a British balance-of-payments deficit.
    c. depreciate

PROBLEMS

1. a. $-, 11181 = -3507 - 5795 - 1879$
   b. (1) 710, 10475, -4 (any order)
      (2) +, 11181
   c. deficit; sold
2. 0.25, 4
3. a. $1.60, 0.625;
   b. (1) 400
      (2) 640;
   c. (1) buy, 160
      (2) sell, 170
4 a,c,e
5. a. Current account deficit = 22 299
   b. Capital account surplus = 17 243
   c. Due to large purchases of bonds due to large surplus on the Net Portfolio Investment account.
   d. Based on the bond purchases noted in c., Palmania is borrowing large amounts and therefore is faced with ever-growing annual interest payments to foreigners as indicated in the Net Investment Income account. This will cause a depreciation in the PAL.
   e. Palmania had a balance of payments deficit = 5056
   f. The Palmanian government was selling off foreign exchange reserves and buying up PALs in order to put upward pressure on the PAL exchange rate.

BUSINESS SECTION

1. a. Product policy: You may suggest that the restaurant design menu items that are known to be popular to American tourists and U.S. companies. The pub should consider stocking popular American beer, wine and hard liquors. The hotel should consider selling a room package that also includes discounted tickets to scheduled entertainment events popular to U.S. visitors, such as baseball, basketball tickets and popular U.S. bands and Broadway plays playing in the Canadian city.
   b. Price policy: Since the renovations have just been made, and the Canadian dollar is a bargain to U.S. visitors, the director may seriously consider significantly increasing nightly room rates. As well, to attract U.S. convention business, the hotel might consider hotel corporate discounts, especially during the week and seasonally slow periods.
   c. Promotion policies: The hotel should target much more of their promotional budget to large cities and companies located in the eastern part of the U.S. The promotions should emphasize the "bargain basement Canadian dollar. As well, the promotions should feature elements of the product mix which have been designed to appeal to those situated in the U.S.
   d. Place policies: To make it more convenient for U.S. visitors to visit the Devonshire Hotel, the hotel should consider offering room packages that include discount rates on air fare and airport shuttles for U.S. visitors in eastern U.S.